BITTER CHICORY TO SWEET ESPRESSO

SURVIVAL AND DELIVERANCE FROM WW II IN THE NAPLES, ITALY, AREA, 1940-49

CARMINE VITTORIA

Purpo, Inc., Key Biscayne

Purpo, Inc.
1111 Crandon Blvd
Key Biscayne, FL 33149

Copyright @ 2017 by Carmine Vittoria
All rights reserved,
Including the right of reproduction
In whole or in part in any form.

Purpo is a registered trademark of Purpo, Inc.

Maps Courtesy of Google.com
Photos Courtesy of Anmarie Vittoria

For information about discounts, please contact Purpo,
Inc. at 305-989-8522.

Library of Congress Cataloging-in-Publication Data
is available.

ISBN 978-0-692-91815-9

Printed in South Korea

To my wife Rie, Reginella mia.
My fellow traveler and explorer to old battlegrounds
with whose encouragement this book was written.

NEAPOLITAN CREDO:
"Ci Arrangiamo"
"We adapt to survive"

ACKNOWLEDGEMENTS

I thank Zio Renato and Zia Sarah Renato for recounting their ordeal under Nazi occupation in Rome, and Professor Antonio Paoletti of the University of Rome who apprised me of the turmoil about the Via Rasella affair and the Via Ardeatina massacre. Also, my gratitude to Giuseppe Primeggia and cousins Carmine and Giannina Primeggia, Francesca Vittoria, Sebastiano Vittoria, brother Sebastiano, Serafina Renato and sister Carmela, Captain Carmine Iaccarino, Don Camillo Zucarelli, Andrea Zucarelli, Vito Pecchia, Paolo Bevibene, Bruno Di Pasquale, Mastro Nicola Ercolani, Zia Tommasina, Suora Felice, Zio Pierino Vittoria, Angelo Pagliuca, and all the soccer teammates who shared their rumors with me in Avella. To Frank Stewart, who was stationed in the Naples American base during the war, Mastro Antonio, Dr. Richard Richter, residents of Via Rasella, and Maestro Nicola heartfelt appreciation for recounting events in Avella and Rome as related to the occupations during WW II and the post-War period from 1945-49. H. Polito contributed to the riddle that stymied me for years. I also thank Luigi Iardina for describing life in Sicily during and after the war. In many ways this is their story as well as mine.

Caterina Vittoria, and Jens Vittoria encouraged me throughout the years to undertake this enormous project culminating in forty years of literature search and hard evidence from publications, and individuals living in that period of time.

It is one thing to collect data and information about events of that period; it is a totally different matter to piece the puzzle together and put all parts on paper that make logical sense in explaining interconnecting events. For transcribing it all on paper in an orderly fashion, I was fortunate and very thankful to have dedicated help like that of Charlotte Frank. She did a professional job of editing, and encouraged me at every point to keep writing. Mr. Aung Si was very helpful in transferring maps to this book. My thanks to Jonas Baker of Yale University Library for tracking down the New York Times report on the air raid on Agedabia, Libya. The maps were courtesy of Google.com. For Anmarie Vittoria's delicate touches and opinions of the book, as well as the inclusion of her many photos, I am forever grateful.

Finally, I thank Gene Hull, Alfonso Caso, Professor Gary Goshgarian of Northeastern University and Ralph Caputo (LLD) for helpful suggestions about the format and marketing of this book.

CONTENTS

PREFACE ... 8

THE WAR PERIOD, 1940-44

ONE	Almost an Orphan	11
TWO	Beginning of the End	29
THREE	German Occupation of Avella	50
FOUR	From Purgatory To Hell on Earth	67
FIVE	Turning Point	92
SIX	Via Ardeatina Massacres	106
SEVEN	Without Warning or Provocation	124
EIGHT	Shades Of Anarchy and Chaos	143
NINE	End Of Fascism in Italy	160

THE TRANSITION PERIOD, 1944-46

| TEN | Few Returned Home | 166 |
| ELEVEN | Anarchy in Fermentation | 180 |

THE RECOVERY PERIOD, 1946-48

TWELVE	The arduous Road to Recovery	193
THIRTEEN	School Years	227
FOURTEEN	Church Recitals and San Gennaro	249
FIFTEEN	Politics Avella Style	270
SIXTEEN	America the Beautiful	283
EPILOGUE		304
FAMILY TREE		310
MAPS		311
CHRONOLOGY		317
BIBLIOGRAPHY		322
INDEX		326

PREFACE

Monte Avella overlooks the order of things in nature from above it all and her strong icy blast of winds reveals her mood and seasons. Fields of red poppies, chicory flowers, lavender violets, white and pink daisies, and wild dandelions adorn the farms and foothills of Avella in the spring, much like Monet's landscape paintings. The flowers remind farmers and shepherds it is time to prepare for the next crop and remove the thick wool coats on sheep. Since ancient Roman times, Hazelnuts and olives from here have been exported to every corner of the world. The mountains have protected the people in the valleys below from invading armies for centuries. They were a source of food and a symbol of inspiration to resist or survive foreign invasions. Ownership of grass fields in the mountains was like wearing a badge of honor and pride in town.

On the day that we emigrated to America my mother somberly mentioned to us boys that grass fields atop Monte Avella were taken from the family during the War (WW II). The news hit me like a thunderbolt. It was like someone ripped the heart and soul from my body. She didn't elaborate as to who and how. I am about to tell you the "who and how" and about the fate of the family as well as the fate of other people in Avella during the War.

Avella sits at a critical junction point on the slopes of the Apennine Mountains near Naples. From the surrounding mountains Via Appia, the old Roman road, Bay of Naples, Vesuvius and the coastline along the Tyrrhenian Sea are visible on a clear day. For over 3000 years invading armies have come and gone in the town of Avella. The town has adapted and survived through all these invasions in the past as well as WW II. More than 50 million casualties resulted from WW II, as the War spread from the far-east to Europe and North Africa, where devastation and atrocities beyond human comprehension occurred. Naples and vicinity were invaded by foreign armies from Germany, Britain, America, France, Algeria, Tunisia, Morocco, Australia, Poland, New Zealand, India, and

Canada. German soldiers came to occupy Italy, and Allied soldiers came to liberate it.

It was Mussolini who made the decision to go to war, not the people, who had no choice in this. However, it was the people who suffered the brunt of the war. Troops from Germany and Allied countries camped in my home town of Avella. To us, it didn't matter which Army camped in town; life was miserable no matter who was there. Depending on what army was in town, different shades of misery came with them. Dante Alighieri's "Divine Comedy" described imaginary atrocities during travels from purgatory to hell; our travels in Avella from purgatory to hell were of this earth and the atrocities were real.

Why write a book that covers the years from 1940 to 1949 in Italy when there are at least a thousand books describing every imaginable aspects of that period of time? I believe that the history of WW II taking place in the Naples area has yet to be told. New and past facts have been assimilated in this book to re-tell part of the story of those events. We owe future generations a full account of past events.

Usually books about WW II are presented from the perspective of an adult, whereby general topics such as war strategies, number of casualties, devastation and territories occupied are written about. These topics in themselves are important in understanding events of WW II and how it impacted society. The point is that the description of this period has always been from a window seen by an adult, but rarely from a child's perspective. Ordinary people in society are usually presented in previous books as being separate entities from strategies of war, with no linkage to war or decision makers. I believe that perspective is much too narrow a view to present, especially when wars are waged on lands where casualties to local adults and children are unavoidable.

Destruction of buildings and harm to innocent people during the war are often referred to today as "collateral damage". Most people are familiar with the direct results of collateral damage, because damage or destruction of buildings can be seen directly as soon as they occur. As such, damage can be assessed immediately where destruction occurred. However, there is another form of collateral damage whereby damage may be assessed only many years later. This type of collateral damage is rarely discussed and understood. This form of hidden collateral damage is usually more devastating than the destruction of buildings per se.

Hidden collateral damage in Southern Italy due to the War included the resurgence of criminality due to the gross mishandling of the

Allied Military Administration in assigning criminals as Mayors to run Southern Italy before and after the War. The expected results were that no fair justice was being applied and favoritism was up for sale. From my point of view, as a child, it meant, for example, no food from the American surplus could be shared equally among the poor, since the poorest of the poor in towns were not connected to the "right" people. There was complete breakdown of law and order in the Naples area. To this day the world is suffering the consequences of the resurgence in criminality in Southern Italy during and after the War.

I was born in 1940 and as early as ~ 1942 I vividly remember scenes in Avella. I will recount every memory and describe to you what my impressions were at the time of the casualties and devastation brought on by war. The descriptions are representative of similar events that took place in many small towns in the Naples area. Many small towns dot the foothills of the Apennine chain of mountains from Avellino to the Naples-Salerno area. Thus, the events that I am about to tell you of Avella apply equally well to other small towns nearby.

After years of research into historical facts, as related to battlefields in the area, I am able to piece together some semblance of realism to those nightmares, or blurred visions, and identify soldiers with Army groups that camped in Avella. For example, the invasion of Salerno by the Allies spilled over to Avella and I recount observations of those events. Memories are inter-mixed or connected to war plans by generals and decision makers only to the extent that the plans affected Avella and other towns in the Naples area.

In trying to assimilate events of the times I came to the startling realization that there was linkage between our family and the Via Ardeatina massacre of civilians by the Nazis in Rome, resulting in an important and new revelation of the massacre. Finally, soldiers of the French Expedition Force, Goumier troops, were identified camping in Avella and involved in atrocities directed against my family and others in town, in violation of the 1907 Hague Convention on rules of war. The Expedition Force was part of the Allied Army to attack Monte Cassino. High ranking Nazis were convicted at the Nuremberg trials for the same violations. The atrocities committed by the Expedition Force in Avella and elsewhere in Southern Italy were glossed over by military tribunal authorities of the Allies after the War.

THE WAR PERIOD, 1940-44

ONE
ALMOST AN ORPHAN

Europe and North Africa were already engulfed in major battles in World War II [34], when I was born. British and Italian armies battled each other in the deserts of Libya while the German army was invading Belgium, Holland and France. My father, Michele, was stationed in Agedabia, Libya, at an Italian Army field hospital. He died in a British bombing raid of the hospital on Dec. 29, 1940. I read about the bombing raid forty years later in a small article in the New York Times (dated December 28, 1941). The following report was filed.

> **WIRELESS TO THE NEW YORK TIMES.**
> **CAIRO, Egypt, Dec. 28**-While operations in Western Cyrenaica paused, apparently awaiting either a battle or the complete retreat _of the Germans into Tripolitania, Royal Air Force and Free French bombers pounded the isolated enemy force at Bardia yesterday, blasting pillboxes, gunnery defense positions, trucks and barracks buildings. Fires broke out amid the wreckage. The only organized German and Italian forces remaining in Cyrenaica are at besieged Bardia and Solum, in the Egyptian- Libyan frontier area.

Interestingly, the report did not mention the bombing of a military hospital, where my father was stationed. His tour of military duty officially ended ten days before the raid. He decided not to leave for Naples at the end of duty, because transport by boat was extremely dangerous. The British Navy controlled the Mediterranean Sea with their powerful fleet equipped with radar. Radar was discovered at the Naval Research Laboratory (NRL), Washington DC in 1926. The American and British fleets were equipped with radar in the late thirties, whereas the Italian fleet was not equipped with radar throughout WW II.

Ironically, my first employment in America was with NRL where radar was discovered by accident. An engineer was assigned to measure the radiation patterns of dipole antennas. In performing the experiments, he was upset that each time a boat sailed on the Potomac River near his experimental setup, it "screwed up" his measurements, or the radiation pattern changed. As it turned out, the "screwing up" of the radiation pattern, or interference, had a useful application forever to be known as RADAR.

My father, Papa, delayed his departure for Naples, since his friend offered him an airplane ride. The delay cost his life. His friend and captain in the Italian Air Force did manage to fly to Naples by plane a day later, after Papa died. Many years later my mother, Francesca, told me that the captain promised to hire Papa in his import, export and real estate Company in Naples. Prior to the war, Papa was a barber, tailor, chef and a man of many trades. In short, he was the "Figaro" figure in the town of Avella. Everybody knew of him, consulted with him, kibitzed with him, and "shot the breeze" with him. His barbershop was his "office". In effect, he could have been the town psychiatrist as everyone in town went to him for personal advice.

The likelihood that Papa and mother got married was rather low given that in the early 30's, in small towns like Avella, most marriages were arranged by respective families. Even today, there is not much admixture between urbanites and shepherd families in Avella and certainly not in the 30's. Papa represented the middle class society from town and mother came from a shepherd's family which roamed the hills or mountains of Avella. Their descendants date back to the early Samnite tribes [88]. In some sense these shepherds were like nomads, as they ranged long ways on the mountains searching for grass fields to feed the sheep. They represented the "lower" class and were invariably poor.

My maternal Grandmother Imalda was the matriarch of the shepherd clan which was a very close knit society. Besides settling disputes among members of the clan, Imalda's main concern was the preservation and fostering of the special ethnicity of the shepherd community. They knew each other and a lot of their marriages were pretty much arranged in those days. Imalda was eager for Francesca to marry a shepherd, since that was a profitable endeavor of the family. Grandfather Carmine owned grazing fields on Monte Avella, the tallest mountain in the area, although he immigrated to the United States in 1914. Obviously, with my grandfather Carmine in America and no skill to get a job, perhaps my grandmother Imalda was entertaining the thought of going back to shepherding with Francesca hopefully marrying someone from a shepherd family. Imalda stayed with Francesca and had a part time job making ricotta and various assortments of cheese.

In the customs and traditions of shepherds there were certain protocols to be followed in order to engage in courtship. Michele (Papa) followed none of those traditions that shepherds held so dear. Grandmother Imalda, being a matriarch, was put in an awkward position, when Francesca (mother) and Michele started their courtship. After all, Imalda was the person to keep traditions alive in the shepherd clan, especially with regards to one of her own.

Michele was not deterred for he kept serenading Francesca often before the marriage proposal. I was told by my mother that Papa would have his friend, Renato, play the mandolin to serenade her on occasion, for a year. Grandmother Imalda would pour buckets of water to stop the singing of the two "canaries". In a way it was like a cat and mouse game between Imalda and the two courtesans. Renato and Michele were classmates in elementary school, and knew each other from childhood. Renato went on to become a medical doctor in Rome.

During the time of my parents' courtship, Renato was studying to become a physician at the University of Naples and did his residency at the University hospital. Despite that, he and Michele remained devoted friends and were inseparable when Renato was home. There was also another connection; when home, Renato lived with his parents and two seamstress sisters, across the street from Francesca. The seamstresses' specialty was making sweaters, while the shepherd ladies, Francesca and Imalda, produced wool, which often melded into a collaboration.

It took some time before our family addressed Renato as Zio di Roma (uncle from Rome), although we were not related to him. I was told by mother that Papa insisted that we treat Renato as Zio by Sebastiano (my brother) and treat Renato as family. Because of his being a practicing physician, Zio Renato was deferred from military service during the war. Every time I see the opera 'The Barber of Seville' (Gioachino Rossini) I get goose bumps thinking about how it must have been in those days, when people would serenade or court someone. In the old days, it must have been an accepted practice before engagement. It is remarkable to me that Papa pursued Francesca, although they came from such diverse backgrounds. Papa never visited a farm, let alone a mountain peak, and was not adapted to farming or shepherding. Obviously, their attraction in those days broke the barrier raised by the social class system of the times.

Michele rented a barbershop parlor in 1929. The shop belonged to a former barber who passed away the year before. He served as an apprentice in that shop for over four years, and also apprenticed as a tailor, shoe maker, chef and butcher. In those days, one gained skills through apprenticeships at no salary. Typically, if one could not afford to go to the University, he or she would learn a skill at a local shop or business. However, these apprenticeships were reserved for family members. It was rare for a shoe repairman or barber or bricklayer to hire someone outside the family to do apprentice work. The shop was kept in the family business from generation to generation. In the case of Michele, the deceased barber had no children. After taking over the barber shop, he developed a rapport with his clients in a very short time. Papa would make everybody's business as his own anytime someone came to his barbershop. He would advise "Jack, Jill and Joe" about everything and anything. In short he knew everybody's business and would commiserate or celebrate with them.

There was no control over Papa's behavior or overtures to Francesca. In the end they got married with blessings from both sides of the family, irrespective of the families' initial hesitation and class consciousness. Love had the major call.

The marriage lasted about six years (1934 – Dec, 1940) ending with the death of Papa. Sebastiano was born in 1935 and my sister, Caterina, in 1936. Soon after the siblings reached the age of one and two years they were shipped to Nonno Sebastiano's, our paternal grandfather, house. He still had a grocery store at that time. The only support Francesca had was money sent to her by grandfather Carmine from America. It was enough to support Francesca and Imalda who were helping out in making ricotta and other cheeses for neighboring shepherd families. As a barber, most of the time Papa did not charge his friends who frequented the barber shop. To say that he was a poor businessman was an understatement. The barber shop was more of a social club with no membership fees.

I remember, as an altar boy after the War, the first performance of the opera "The Barber of Seville" played for the first time at the local Church of Saint Peter. The opera was staged by a local musician and sponsored by the church. As an altar boy I was the handyman in helping out with the menial work. In the first act, when Figaro springs out of nowhere to sing that beautiful aria "Sono un Barbiere" (literal translation: "I am a barber"), everybody seemed to enjoy the bravura of Figaro except Francesca. She quietly walked out of the church and never returned to see the opera. Then, I never understood why the sudden exit, but now I do. Figaro's character in the opera was too close for comfort for Francesca. It reminded her of Papa, and she preferred not to reminisce about those times.

I asked Francesca years later how it was to live under the Mussolini's Fascist regime. She said that before the war, living was good. The government provided subsidy for those having children and also perks for attending school at the kindergarten level. She added that we knew that Mussolini was a buffoon and delusional, but as long as his focus was on the welfare of the people, we didn't care how he spent his time with his mistresses. With the government subsidy, father's barbershop and mother tending sheep from time to time, living in Avella was good. For the first time trains were running on time. That was an important factor to the town of Avella. It was the only connection to the outside world, like to the big city of Naples. There were few telephone lines in Avella then.

It all ended when Mussolini entered the war in 1940 [3, 39, 49, 64]. Then, according to Francesca, with the outbreak of the war, Mussolini was lowly regarded and a buffoon (those words are the filtered translations of what she really said) who did not care to understand his people. It was probably the only time that the whole family agreed on anything. Although Francesca went only to third grade, she made a very prophetic comment: "That man (Mussolini) has no balls (no courage) and one day he will regret this decision to enter the war and bite him in his ass (quil si fa o' culo)". Those words were expressed by her well before Italy entered the war. Obviously, she did not mince words. Being a shepherd's daughter, she loved profane words to make her points. To this day I don't know whether it was intuition of a "goat" or a woman to arrive at such a startling conclusion. Historical facts support her conviction or woman's intuition about Mussolini.

At the end of the war, Mussolini was such a timid and cowardly person that he couldn't even save his son-in-law's (Count Galeazzo Ciano) life

[14, 15, 16, 33] from the wrath of Hitler. Mussolini was so much in love with himself and the special image that he cultivated over the years. He was prisoner of his own delusional world. As such, he was not even able to relate to the people suffering from the war and the suffering of his own grandchildren on the death of their father. It is very difficult to understand the mentality of a criminal like Mussolini upholding artificial laws of the Fascist court system in order to put the father of his grandchildren to death.

Besides being a coward, Mussolini proved to be a criminal as it was suspected in Italy. He ordered the killing of Giacomo Matteotti [87], who was the socialist deputy and who fervently tried to prevent Mussolini from coming to power. Mussolini was involved in a scandal in the 1920's whereby Sinclair Oil Company had paid a bribe of one million dollars to the deputy Finzi, a front for Mussolini, for the concession to carry out oil exploration. Matteotti had obtained proof of this and he was going to produce the evidence in the Chamber of Deputies.

Besides Francesca, there were others in Avella, as well as the rest of Italy, who were disgruntled with this man. The question that I have not been able to answer is how one man could coerce 45 million people to do his will? Can it happen again? Yes! If one reads the history of imperial Rome (see the book entitled Cicero by A. Everitt) [44] it was amazing how history repeated itself many times over. The same human atrocities were committed by the same types of tyrannical personalities over and over again, as soon as a political advantage was gained over the opposition. It proves that if past history is forgotten, people are doomed to re-live it. Papa's father ran a grocery store and a wine shop. During the war the business closed down. Supplies were too low to maintain an inventory in the shop. His main competitor, a block away, produced his own wine. He kept his business open even during the War. The grocery and wine store re-opened soon after the war. When I was born, my father's family consisted of grandparents, 3 aunts, 2 uncles and my father who was stationed in El Agedabia, Libya. My grandmother's name was Nonna Caterina and the aunts' names were Anna, Candida and Caterina. One of the uncles (Antonio) emigrated to Everett, MA, USA before the war and the other uncle (Pellegrino) enrolled in religious seminary studies to become a monk. He shortened his name to Pierino. However, the family knew very well that studying to be a monk was a way out of serving in the Italian Army. After the war uncle Pierino enrolled in the University of Naples to study law and eventually became a lawyer, judge and chief of police of Interpol.

The uncle in Everett had left Italy to earn enough money to pay for a tax obligation on his farm. Of the three aunts one (Candida) married after the war and the other two remained single. I believe that the war greatly interfered with their courtships with potential mates. Their two male friends served in the Army and never returned. One potential mate was shipped to the Russian front and never was heard from again, and another was sent to Germany to work in a factory. Again, the latter young man was never heard from. The male population was nearly decimated due to tragedies of war. For example, about 300,000 Italian soldiers were sent to the Russian front, but only about 10,000 ever made it back to Italy after the war. Only one made it back to Avella.

Shepherds have lived in Avella, since the days that Samnite tribes [88] camped there. They resided mostly in the mountains of Avella and rarely lived in town. When they lived in town, they usually lived in the poor sections of town among other shepherd neighbors. There was little mingling between shepherd families and the rest of the people in town. Francesca's family consisted of grandparents (Carmine and Imalda), and one aunt (Giovanna). Giovanna was married to Giuseppe (Uncle Joe) and they had two children, a boy (Carmine) and a girl (Giannina).

Uncle Joe came from a family of construction builders dating back to the Middle Ages. Most of the buildings and palazzos in Avella were built by this family, the only family in town involved with construction. Joe was destined to also be a construction builder or bricklayer. Uncle Joe was assigned by the Italian Army to an artillery battalion stationed in Sicily waiting to be transported by boat to Libya. With lack of ships and the British patrolling the shipping lanes in the Mediterranean Sea, the Italian Army was presented with a difficult problem in transporting troops to Libya. The contingent in Sicily was part of a group of soldiers who were to reinforce the remaining Italian Army in Libya. The Italian Army suffered setbacks at the hands of the British Army in Libya in 1940-1942. With the Italian Army in full retreat in Libya resulting in many deserters, Uncle Joe was re-directed back to Sicily. The rationale for this move by the Italian General Staff was "why pour good money on bad". The Italian army was propped up with the infusion of two armored divisions under the leadership of Field Marshal Erwin Rommel. It was too little and too late to help the Italian army in Libya. Thus, by 1942 the Italian General staff already decided that the occupation of Libya was a lost cause and diverted whatever reinforcements there were to Sicily. That is where Uncle Joe was stationed.

Imalda's husband, grandfather Carmine, owned a large plot of land on the highest peak of the mountain chain, Monte Avella. The family produced wool, ricotta cheese, and hard pecorino cheese. My grandfather owned about 50% of the sheep that crazed on his fields. The rest of the sheep belonged to other shepherds. Grandfather Carmine collected grazing fees or rent for allowing other shepherds to graze on his fields. This was the way to insure year round grazing of the land. However, in some winters, the mountain peaks were snowed under and there was no access to the fields. The sheep were fed from grass or hay stored at the end of summer. The chain of mountains near Avella offered an ideal location for all sorts of crime, because it was a very isolated area and full of wolves and other wild animals. At a young age, Francesca and Giovanna often camped near the sheep on the high mountains in order to guard them. There were huge shepherd dogs to guard them and the sheep as well.

Francesca and Giovanna were not encouraged by their parents with their schooling as they were needed to take the sheep to the grass fields. So, their futures were pretty much chartered by their parents, and their education was terminated after third grade, enough for them to be able to read and sign their names. Due to a lack of a formal education, their language was laced with a variety of profane words that I never heard before or that I will ever hear again. This created many problems for me later on, when I attended kindergarten and elementary school administered by the nuns. At that time every other word was profane, for which the nuns slapped me with a wooden stick. I am sure that every other word was not pleasant to the ear and was cause for the nuns to often put me in special detention after school hours. It didn't help me at all when Francesca tried to complain to the nuns about my treatment in school. Every imaginable invective was directed at the nuns which they did not receive kindly.

Long before grandfather Carmine emigrated to the United States in 1914, the sheep died mysteriously on the high mountains near a watering hole. It is not clear whether they were poisoned by eating clover leaves, or simply that the water was contaminated by a form of bacteria in the grass, or fungi. The upshot of this tragedy was that my grandfather had to pay for half the number of sheep and for taxes on the land. Some of the sheep did not belong to him; they belonged to other shepherds who rented the fields. Since there was no extra income to be derived from the sheep, he emigrated to Ambridge, PA, USA and worked in the coal mines and steel factories. After two years he paid the taxes covering a period of 30 years, paid the shepherds for the loss of their sheep, and retained his fields. However, he chose not to return to Italy. Grandfather Carmine decided to remain in the USA, because life was so much easier for him there. I don't think that he was politically savvy in recognizing Mussolini for what he was, a criminal at heart.

Life as a shepherd was arduous. Typically, one shepherd would tend to his own sheep, as well as those of five or six other shepherds. While he roamed the mountains for grass fields, the others waited their turn in town, resting and/or making cheese. While tending the sheep in the mountains, for a week or so, they lived in small and uninsulated shacks with haystack roofs. Their protection from the many wolves and other wild animals was shepherd dogs (a mixture of German shepherd and Collie) who watched out for the sheep and the shepherds. There was little socializing between the shepherds and the townspeople. They co-existed as two separate social classes. One was primitive and the other urbane, worldly.

I remember Francesca and me spending three to four weeks [47] at a time with our shepherd neighbors. In winter, we and they would sit close to the fireplace to stay warm and to roast chestnuts. I was both terrified and in awe of the huge, ferocious guard dogs that breathed down my neck, fearing that if I turned too quickly, I would be bitten in the face. The many scratches and bruises on their faces, and ears that looked like tagliatelle (pasta strips used in lasagna) attested to their hard mountain guard work. Francesca felt most comfortable and at ease with other shepherd families.

Francesca and other shepherd women devoted themselves to the art of making cheese. There are a number of factors that affect the quality and the taste of cheese: Temperature of the liquid-solid milk consistency, spinning rate of the mixture, condiments, air-to-smoke ratio, aging, and precise timing of addition of condiments to the liquid-solid solution. In solid state physics, this change in solidification is referred to as the liquid-solid phase transition. The transition to a single phase and uniform composition of the solid state occurs at a critical temperature and cooling rate. There is a science in the production of solid compounds. However, the process developed by the shepherds is mostly empirical. The recipe for condiments was handed down from generation to generation and it was usually a guarded secret of a shepherd family. Also, making cheese was a way to socialize. The cheese that they made was very similar to the Romano pecorino (little sheep) cheese which is sold all over the world today. As a child, I was too impatient to wait the required time for the cheese to harden. I loved, when it was still soft. I was like a little mouse who would hunt all over the house for the soft cheese.

Besides the dairy production from the sheep's milk, wool was produced from the sheep fur. Each spring the sheep were steered into a large pool of water to get rid of fleas and ticks in the fur. Once out of the water, they were clipped or sheared. The wool was collected in a raw state and transferred to a storage house where Francesca and/or Giovanna, and other shepherd families, converted the raw material into yarns of wool. There is a sad part to this story concerning grandfather Carmine. Records of tax payments that my grandfather made on the land that he owned on top of Monte Avella were lost soon after the war. That was no accident. It was a pre-meditated act by the local tax collector for the purpose of acquiring land from people who resided abroad. After the war, corruption at all levels was rampant and all records were destroyed. The Fascist tax collector who originally collected taxes from my grandfather left town soon after the British army camped in Avella.

Effectively, it negated whatever tax payments grandfather Carmine made on the fields. The payments were supposed to be good for 30 years or more. Since there were no records of tax payments, the owner was considered to be delinquent! The new tax collector made a bid on the property at an auction of properties that were delinquent on tax payments. No one in our family heard or received notice of delinquency on the property or about the auction. In summary, the tax collector paid very little money to buy the fields on the mountain. In 1920 the property was estimated to be in the thousands of dollars. Today, there is sizeable construction at the foothills, near the mountain's grass fields; the property is worth millions of dollars.

Grandmother Imalda returned to Italy in the mid 1920's. She never made peace with the English language and had a most difficult time adapting to America. The problem was that she was barely fluent in Italian let alone able to cope with another language. Her local dialect was not helpful in communicating with anybody outside of Avella, even with those of Italian extraction in the United States. The dialect in Avella is similar to the Neapolitan, which is a mixture of Spanish, Italian, French and Arabic languages. However, the shepherds of Avella spoke a dialect which was different from the Neapolitan dialect. It was a residue from the Samnite language which expired about 100 BC [88]. The Samnite spoke a dialect derived from the Latin. Over the years their dialect has been intermixed with the Neapolitan dialect, much like slang words introduced in the English language. As far as Francesca was concerned, she was happy that her mother returned and that my grandfather send some money to the family in Italy for everyday living. No one learned skills, other than shepherding and making cheese. She was too old to go back to school and, besides, there were no school opportunities for her, as there were in the USA.

My first recollection as a baby [47] was around the age of 10-11 months. I remember being placed in a cylindrical wooden contraption, sometimes referred to as a "baby walker". The top was enclosed by a hollow circular wooden supporter, 12 inches in diameter. A similar but bigger supporter, with wheels at the bottom, was attached to the top with wooden sticks. This was a standard wooden apparatus to help babies learn to walk. Usually, by the age of nine months most babies begin to walk, but not me. Nonno was worried about it and he babysat me in his house encouraging me to walk while I was pushing this wooden stroller. He didn't realize then that he was inviting a lot of headaches once I began to walk.
Francesca would take me to Nonno in the morning and pick me up in the evening. She and her mother had part-time jobs making cheese or wool yarns. In addition, my brother and sister were also attended to by my aunts, in Nonno's house. There was not enough food to go around in my mother's house so that all of the siblings were fed at Nonno's. Because of the war there was no money sent to my mother from my grandfather in America. Fortunately, Nonno was very loving to me. He kept an eye on me the minute I stepped in his home. I would push the wooden "baby walker" all over the house until I fell down, and Nonno would quickly come over and pick me up from the hard cement floor. There was no basement so all food and wines were kept in a large storage room with no windows.

Lucky for Nonno, the formal dining room was one step higher than the family room where everybody congregated. My stroller simply could not climb over the step. In the dining room there was a big trombone hidden beside a piece of furniture that I loved to blow air into. The trombone was Nonno's pride and joy and he was very protective of it. Nonno was a member of the military band in WW I. After WW I he was employed by the Montefalcione orchestra near Avella. The band was well known and respected in the area and they were often invited to play opera or classical music at festivals. I was as equally determined to get to the trombone as Nonno was protective of it. It was a classic stalemate. He prevented me more than I could get to it. However, once I started to walk, it was no contest. I got to the trombone as often as I liked. Eventually, Nonno tried to show me how to get a sound out of the trombone, but it did not help me. I tried and tried but, eventually, gave up.

I rarely saw my brother and sister. They spent most of their time with the aunts on the second floor. The aunts were seamstresses and most of their work was making dresses for the wives of important functionaries of the Fascist Party in town. The only time I got to see them was in the afternoon, when everybody would gather around the fireplace in the family room and wait for the coffee to brew. The family room was rather large. At one end there was a fireplace where as many as 8-10 people could gather and enjoy a cup of coffee made from dried chicory. The other end of the family room included a kitchen and a small business table counter where wine and pasta were sold. In the middle of the family room was a large table where the whole family shared Sunday meals prepared by Nonno. In a nutshell, that was my world. It was a joyous moment to see people come to the family room and socialize. That was my only interaction with the outside world.

Smell of chicory coffee was as intoxicating as coffee, before and in the early days of the War, imported from African colonies. Nonno saved enough coffee from his grocery store, although it closed down soon after the war started. The coffee lasted for a couple of years before Nonno switched from coffee beans to dry chicory in order to brew "coffee". I would stand in the stroller while all were sipping coffee, as if everybody was in a trance, transfixed by the coffee. With the stroller, it was impossible to get near anyone and "beg" for some coffee just to experience what the excitement was all about.

At that time everybody called me by the name "Michele" for it was the same name as my father. My aunts decided to call me by that name soon after Papa died in Libya. Twelve years later, on the way to Ambridge, PA, before meeting my grandfather Carmine, I was informed by Francesca that my real name was Carmine and not Michele. In order to impress upon me that this was fact, she produced my birth certificate to prove it to me for I couldn't believe her. So, for about twelve years I was misled by everybody in Avella. What a shock!

My brother Sebastiano was given the nickname "capitano" which was an army rank to honor my father. However, my father was a corporal in the Army, but he was promoted to captain through my brother (capitano) as bestowed to his son by the aunts. The impression that my aunts wanted to advance to the town was the notion that my father's rank was that of a captain. Yes, that was absurd, but that was the type of mentality of those days. The truth of the matter was that my father's rank was relatively low and his duties were confined to hospital maintenance, since his experience as a barber was thought to be useful. My guess is that he talked his way into those duties instead of being in a battlefield. My brother's name was Sebastiano in honor of Nonno. My sister's name was Caterina in honor of Nonna. I had a hard time pronouncing the word Sebastiano, so for me it was easier to say Sastianiel.

The aunts were so persistent about my new name that they induced the whole town to call me Michele. Francesca did not mind, because it was a good way to honor Papa at that time. As far as I knew then, my name was Michele. The aunts and mother in unison started to call me the new name. As a child there is not much importance or association with a name until about two or three years old.

The aunts truly loved Sebastiano and treated him like a child of their own. Throughout his childhood, the aunts provided him with financial support and clothes, including school uniforms. As for myself, I was looking forward to the day that I would grow big enough to wear Sebastiano's clothes after he outgrew them, especially winter clothes. In short, he was special, because he represented the next generation and was the oldest of the siblings. In Italian families that is special. Any attention coming from Nonno's family was welcomed by us siblings for none was coming from the shepherd side of the family, since we seldom were with them. They were not in a position to help out in any way, and had to scavenge the hills to survive starvation during the War.

All three of us were living in Nonno's house, since Francesca was helping grandmother Imalda make ricotta and other cheeses and sometimes making yarns of wool. Those were the only skills that she knew well. The role of my sister was to take care of me constantly for I was a handful. I really did not like the stroller for it constrained me. Often, aunts and uncles would come by the stroller and pick me up and cuddle me. It never failed, sooner or later, for one of them to toss me up in the air. I never understood then and now the fascination of tossing babies up in the air. I don't think adults realize that babies are aware of dangers and surroundings. There are real dangers being tossed up in the air. I knew how hard the cement floor was, even falling from the stroller.

In Southern Italy there were no heating or air conditioning systems installed at that time in homes. In the winter time, it can get cold. The wind, blowing from the mountains of Avella, made the cold drafts feel like daggers. Typically, people deployed a heating chamber in the middle of the family room and consisting of a so-called "frisera". The "frisera" contained red hot charcoals and the pot was placed in the middle of a circular wooden supporter. The purpose of the wooden supporter was to keep people away from the hot charcoals. In the evening and nights the "frisera" was activated. Everybody would huddle next to it in order to stay warm at night.

Sometimes my mother would join us, when it was extremely cold outside in the winter. The temperatures in Avella rarely reached below 5 Centigrade (42 F). However, on a cloudy and windy day the cold seemed to reach every bone in the body. I was most happy to see my mother on Sunday, when Nonno would prepare the special pasta meal for the whole family. Everybody would attend including my grandmother Imalda. In fact, I don't recall ever seeing my grandmother Imalda during the war, except for those Sunday meals. Quite often, she would bring those big round goat cheeses smoked and hardened. The combination of Nonno's pasta and grandmother Imalda's cheese was delectable, although there was not much to eat besides that. When pasta ran out the only thing left to eat was polenta (baked corn flour) and cheese.

Most times that I spent with grandmother Imalda was at Nonno's house. However, there were few occasions that I saw Imalda at Fracesca's. Usually, Francesca and Imalda had a set up to produce all sorts of cheese right over the fireplace. They produced soft ricotta to hard cheese and gourmet smoked cheeses as well. All that I can remember was a big pot of milk over the fire in the fireplace. Above the fireplace various sizes of cheese were supported over a perforated wooden plank to allow smoke through the holes. Every so often salt was added on the surface of the cheese. The two ladies would place me in the stroller to keep me away from the cheese and the smoke. At other times the two ladies were required to do their work on the mountains and I was left with our neighbor, Serafina, or another shepherd family.

Serafina and her sister were seamstresses and lived across from mother's house. They were related to Renato, Zio di Roma. I looked forward to Imalda coming over to me during work sessions and feeding ricotta to me on a fig leaf. If I could walk then, I would have gone for the smoked cheese instead. Cheese was sold in town or at market places in Nola. Grandmother Imalda was the sales person for the shepherds at the markets in Nola.

My aunts were very talented in converting the latest style of dresses, as advertised in newspaper ads, into the shape of not so slender clients. They would modify the original fashion designs of Dior or the fashion houses in Milan, to fit the client of "normal" shape. The seamstress work generated the only source of hard cash. The farm owned by Nonno produced only fruits, vegetables and corn. The farmhand employed by Nonno provided farm products to Nonno on a regular basis. The rest of the farm products including livestock were used by the farmhand to feed his family for the year. As the war progressed, farm supplies dwindled.

I would rarely see my aunts, since I was too small and clumsy to climb those long steps to the second floor. I tried a couple of times, but often rolled down the steps and every bone in my body ached. I just wanted to be with my siblings. Curiosity always got the best of me. However, about this time my brother attended the nun's elementary school. I will refer to the private school administered by the nuns as simply "the nuns' school" henceforth. After school, my brother would report to my aunts and work on his homework.
The few times that I saw Sebastiano in school were during a special occasion organized by the local Fascist Party. I believe that the special occasion was the anniversary of that Party on March 23 (1942). I recall

school children dressed in black uniforms with white collars marching around the school grounds in an orderly fashion before and after speeches by a number of Fascist functionaries. Some of the Fascists were dressed in black shirts. Flowers adorned the stage and the walkways where speeches were given and children lined up in front of the stage. Near the end of the festivities, "Bersaglieri" soldiers, wearing alpine hats with feathers on them came running to the stage, blowing their bugles. These special mountain soldiers fought in the Alps during WW I [89]. For kids, that was an exciting and cheerful event. The festivities ended with Fascist songs sung by children and adults. I had no idea what was going on, and I was in the audience with Francesca. There were children of all ages and a lot of people wearing black shirts with red bandannas around their necks. As for myself, I just wanted to see Sebastiano and observe what he was doing there among other children. For the Fascists, it was pure propaganda aimed at the young, much like what was happening in Germany.

In 1942 Uncle Joe was scheduled to be transported by boat to Tobruk, Libya, as part of the Black Shirt division of the Italian army [39, 49, 59, 61, 63, 64 90], although he was not a Fascist. Italian divisions were placed under the command of General Erwin Rommel of the German Army stationed in Tobruk. Historically, at this point in time, Italy ceased to be an equal partner in combat. The Italian army played a subordinate role to German plans for combat in Libya and elsewhere. This was due to the fact that the Italian Army was soundly defeated by the British Army the year before in Libya and Hitler shipped Rommel, with two armored divisions, to rescue the Italian Army from total annihilation.

My cousin Carmine told me that his father, Uncle Joe, falsely claimed to have an appendicitis attack to keep him from going to Tobruk, Libya. Uncle Joe gorged himself with enough bread to harden his stomach simulating an inflammation of the appendix. Upon the doctor's examination, he was placed in a hospital for observation. All of his efforts came for naught, when the Italian General Staff decided to cancel the shipment of heavy cannons and tanks together with artillery troops to Libya. The reason for the cancellation was that the Italian Navy could not protect Italian boats from British attacks by boats and planes. Thus, the early part of July 1943 marked the beginning of the end of the Fascist Army. In fact, on July 25 Mussolini was arrested by the King of Italy. Once the news was announced that Uncle Joe's division was not going to be shipped to Libya, a "miracle" occurred. He had no more inflammation of the appendix. Perhaps, San Gennaro must have heard his prayers. Italian soldiers who deserted and were not captured by the British Army stayed behind in Libya after the war until Colonel Ghaddafi of Libya expatriated them back to Italy thirty years later. In the early summer of 1942 Uncle Joe remained in Sicily to be part of a new army formation to defend the homeland territory of Italy. Most of the remaining troops (German and Italian) who were able to get transport out of North Africa after the El Alamein [61] fiasco found their way to Sicily. However, the crossing from Libya to Sicily was difficult, since the British Navy controlled the Mediterranean Sea, especially in daytime. Nevertheless, as many as two to three German divisions and about three to four Italian divisions made it back to Sicily [1, 32, 39, 48, 49, 62].

Many years later I asked Uncle Joe what it was like to be in the camp with German troops. He said that they (Germans) kept to themselves and in particular they did not like to share their canned meat foods and, in particular, marmalade from Germany. However, they readily bartered their dark bread for the local bread. The dark bread was so hard that it could bounce off a wall. Clearly, there was little fraternization between Italian and German troops in Sicily. Basically, German troops did not have much confidence in the Italian Army willingness to fight, and they were right. For most Italian soldiers, including Uncle Joe, the War was over.

The problem for Uncle Joe was not so much faking the appearance of fraternization with the German troops, but how and when to get away from them. Getting away in Sicily, according to Uncle Joe, was simply ill-advised for they still needed a boat ride to the mainland across the Messina strait. So, they bided their time until the whole Italian and German Armies crossed into Calabria by ferry boats at night. In Calabria (mainland) they had to make their move for freedom from German troops. Two soldiers from Avella (Uncle Joe included) and another soldier from Sperone (a town very near Avella) planned to escape from the clutch of the Germans.

Uncle Joe was assigned to an artillery battalion. I asked him whether they ever shot the cannons at airplanes. He said the only time was when they spotted a British reconnaissance plane flying over Messina where he was stationed. They shot about 10-15 rounds, but the plane was out of range. Historically, this was about the time that the Allies were considering invading Sicily. So, it was no surprise that the British would send reconnaissance planes over Sicily at that time.

During his duty in Sicily, Uncle Joe was "borrowed" by the Germans to do construction work on their camps, since he was a bricklayer by trade. Basically, he was used as a common laborer without pay laying down bricks on fortifications, housing, etc. for the German Army. In fact, Italian soldiers had not been paid since they left North Africa. According to Uncle Joe, Sicilians kept to themselves and kept women off the streets. They were not particularly friendly to Italian troops who were looked upon by Sicilians as occupiers like the Germans. Civilians in Sicily were resentful of Italian troops, blaming them for the predicament that they were in, under German occupation. After all, it was Mussolini who put a lot of their men in isolated islands around Sicily before the war. Sicilians never forgave the Italian troops for exiling 4000 of their men, especially then. Vendetta in Sicily was and is as traditional as time itself.

I never saw Uncle Joe leave Avella to go to Sicily for I spent most of my time down at Nonno's house and little bit of time at mother's house. I say "down", because Francesca's house was located on higher grounds at the foothills of the Apennine mountain range. Nonno's house was in the center of town at the bottom of the valley. Whenever it rained, usually in the spring or fall, one could easily ride the water overflows from the Clanio creek to carry oneself down from the foothills of the mountains to "downtown" Avella.

TWO
BEGINNING OF THE END

It was a bone-chilling winter in 1943 and Mount Avella was covered with snow down to the foothills. The wind blew into town like daggers aimed at your naked body. Nonno, the aunts and I often cuddled near the red-hot charcoal-filled "frisera" to try to stay warm. That was the time I first started walking, which gave me the chance to scout about the formal dining room to continue my quest of the trombone. My sister was about 8 years old and she was baby-sitting me after school. The routine was for her to take me to Nonno in the morning before going to school and then to my mother's after school. Like Francesca, she attended public school, since Sebastiano was attending private school administered by the nuns. The nuns granted only one scholarship per family that invoked casualty of war, like Papa.

One particularly cold day, my sister stayed longer at Nonno's. The fire chamber offered warm spots and not so warm spots. I darted past the red hot charcoal container in order to find a warmer place, and fell in the charcoal pit. My stomach and neck were charred. To this day I have scars on my stomach and neck. Naturally, Francesca was upset and blamed Nonno for the accident, although he was not even in the room. She felt that Nonno should have kept an eye on both Caterina and me. I was taken to a local "doctor" who was actually a medical student attending the University of Naples. He didn't have a license to practice. In those days anyone attending a University was referred to as a doctor. However, he knew some people at the hospital in Naples and somehow arranged for me to see a practicing physician. At this time of the war penicillin was not commonly known or used. It was restricted to important Fascist officials and to real emergency cases and my case was not considered critical. I was in the hospital for about a week. I don't remember my stay, but do remember the welcoming committee of my mother, brother, sister and Nonno. My sister hugged me so hard it confused me. I didn't comprehend the situation. All I wanted to do was go to Nonno's house, smell the aroma from the chicory coffee and blow on that trombone to annoy Nonno.

Francesca promised drastic changes in view of what happened. My siblings and I were no longer at Nonno's house after school. She re-arranged her two-room house so that we remained at home the whole day. One room, consisting of a dining room, kitchen and den, was located on the first floor. The bedroom was located on the second floor. The two rooms were connected by a set of spiral steps exposed outside of the portico and leading to an open air veranda on the second floor. From the veranda it was simple to climb to the roof of the building leading all the way to Saint Peter Church, a block away. All the roofs were inter-connected and lined up from east to west so that the view toward the church, the medieval castle, and the Bay of Naples was truly awesome. The view to the south was toward Mount Vesuvius. The steps were separated from our neighbors' by a high stone wall on top of which Francesca placed her plants. For us siblings, the wall sometimes served as a stepping stone to the dry fruits hanging from our Fascist-tax-collector neighbor's window. Yes, we were that hungry and it was a delight to take it from the tax collector. The dry fruits were sweeter.

The toilet located in a common portico on the first floor was near the family room and the next door neighbor. The toilet was more like a septic tank. It was emptied out by our neighbor about once a year. This facility was shared by two families. Opposite the toilet was a brick-oven used to bake bread and below the oven was a pig sty. However, we had no pigs at that time. Next to the toilet was a deep water well which had been dry for a number of years; it separated our portico from the neighbors. It was covered by a wooden board to prevent little kids like me from jumping or falling into it. Francesca was apprehensive that someday I might fall into the well. Fortunately, that never occurred, although I crossed the well many times to get to the neighbors' courtyard.

We often visited the neighboring shepherd family, who were distantly related to us. Their nephew, Don Camillo, was a cousin of Giovanna and Francesca, and he was active in the Communist movement in Avella. In their younger days, Giovanna, Francesca, the shepherd family, and Don Camillo utilized the same cottage in the mountains when tending sheep. The cottages were spread over 200 miles on top of the mountain chains, from Calabria to the Abruzzi region. They served as an "oasis" for shepherds' stopovers. The times that Don Camillo was grazing the sheep, he used grass fields that grandfather Carmine owned on Monte Avella. The family consisted of two-old time shepherds who availed themselves for shepherding duties whenever someone got sick and could not work on the mountains herding the sheep. Obviously, they were poor, but they were the nicest people. They shared everything they had, including their smoked cheese and chestnuts. The neighborhood near our house was mostly made up of people whose living depended on dairy products derived from sheep. Thus, the neighborhood was conveniently located near the foothills of the mountains.

We children resisted staying in mother's house for it was very small and had no place to play or socialize with others. There was always someone around in Nonno's house. In mother's house Sebastiano spent most of his afternoons doing homework alone in the bedroom. He had a desk facing the balcony to the street, across from Serafina's balcony. He looked very studious and I would stare for hours at my brother admiring how brilliant he must be, especially at that new shiny desk. I couldn't wait to grow up and someday use the same desk to do my homework. My sister Caterina was hovering around me making sure that I did not get into trouble again.

Francesaca and Imalda worked at making ricotta, other cheeses and more dairy products in a nearby farm owned by a friend of the family. They worked in an old building owned by a shepherd. I visited that building with mother once or twice. I remember that as I entered through the huge portone (front door), it was like going to a magical world. Everything inside was at least 500 years old and dilapidated. The passageway from the portone was full of pot holes and lava stones that looked more like obstacles than a paved road. In the middle of the courtyard there was a large grass field in which sheep fed. However, the upstairs quarters were as modern as could be for the times and that was where Francesca worked.

There was barely enough food to go around. The diet was mostly polenta (baked corn bread) sprinkled with cheese in the morning, for lunch and at dinner. On Sunday, tomato sauce was spread on the polenta bread to make believe that it was a pasta dish. The meals on Sunday were a lot better at Nonno's house. When mother worked, the neighbors next door babysat with Caterina and sometimes Serafina helped out. I hated to smell the dog's breadth right in my face when the neighbors babysat me. They were simply ugly and huge shepherd dogs. The trick was to move slowly so that the dogs didn't snap at me. I learned quickly as to what one could get away with those dogs, not much.

Tragedy struck the family again. My sister Caterina scraped her knee when she fell down during recess at public school. That, in itself, was not bad. However, due to the fact that there was no medicine, especially no penicillin, available during the war in Italy turned a minor injury into a major catastrophe. The scraping of the knee developed into an infection which required yellow pus to be drawn from the knee regularly. Every time that I have asked my mother about it, she refused to discuss it and would start crying. The infection was brought to the attention of the local "doctor". He told Francesca that, without penicillin or disinfectant medicine, she had two choices: amputate the leg above the knee or hope for the best by washing the wound clean.

My mother did not want the stigma of a crippled child and chose the second option. Caterina died in my mother's arms. I found out about the choice many years later, not from my mother but from Sebastiano. It was profoundly painful for she loved Caterina so much. Francesca would, from time to time recount in pure agony what Caterina did as a child and her pride in her was obvious. It was the same type of agony expressed by the "Zingarella" (the shepherd gypsy) in the opera Il Trovatore (composed by Giuseppe Verdi), when Zingarella recalls in the aria the time when she threw her child into the fire by mistake. Every time I hear that aria, tears well up in my eyes. Caterina was raised in shepherd tradition and beliefs. Francesca went to her grave with the memory of her lost child in her mind. Caterina was buried in a cemetery where the grave was carved out of a side wall that waited for Papa's remains to be buried as well. After many petitions to the Italian government, Papa's remains were joined with Caterina's in the cemetery of Avella in 1988.

At the funeral, the walk to the cemetery was long and sad. Francesca cried so hard that it terrified me. I thought that something terrible was going to happen to her, as she was held up by relatives. Nonno and I walked together followed by both sides of the family: Sebastiano, the aunts, Serafina and sister, Aunt Giovanna, and her family. Also, all the shepherds of Avella were in the procession to the cemetery, led by grandmother Imalda and Don Camillo. The realization by me as a child that death was so close was a very sobering and traumatic experience. In order to make things easier for Francesca in those painful days, Sebastiano and I were allowed to return to the care of Nonno or the aunts, once again depending on the availability of food. Francesca had no choice for there was no food in her house or in Avella in general. The two chickens that we had in our pigpen disappeared. Things got so bad that butchers would skin cats alive and sell them as rabbit meat. Nonno would tell me to look at the paws of the rabbit in order to determine the type of meat hanging from the butcher's hooks. I remember him visiting the butcher behind the counter and hearing some vicious discussions about meat quality. The butcher bribed Nonno to go away with a piece of meat, for paying customers were getting too inquisitive and impatient waiting in line. The barter system was still operational at that time. Sooner or later the butcher would be looking for Nonno to return the favor in terms of a liter of wine, as soon as Nonno was back in the business of selling wine.

The butcher did not want to educate the customers about the meats in the store, but those discussions were loud enough for all to hear. That was just a show on the part of Nonno. It was a ploy to get people's attention and embarrass the butcher. This was the same shop where Michele apprenticed well before the war. Nonno and the butcher often socialized at informal gatherings of old timers at bocce tournaments. The real truth, in those days, was that there was no meat to be had from the butcher. Even chicory was no longer available anyplace, since it was early spring of 1943.

About this time, I began to hear the name "Mussolini" for the first time. Being a child I didn't particularly associate the name with anyone in Avella or with any connection to the family, but I overheard the name almost on a daily basis. Most of the conversations were animated or agitated among family members and strangers coming by Nonno's. One thing was clear to me, the conversations were not pleasant, by the tone of the words. That much I understood.

These conversations were being held between Fascists and the rest of town who never joined the Fascist party [3, 12, 16, 19, 21, and 47]. Things were not looking good for Fascists anywhere in Avella. The Italian

Army was in total disarray after many defeats in Libya. Most of the conversations dealt with who to blame for the catastrophe of the Army. Deserters in the Italian Army outnumbered regular army soldiers. I am of the opinion now that the early spring of 1943, marked the beginning of the end of the Fascist party, not only in Avella, but also in the rest of Italy [32, 39, and 48]. People were staring at starvation all over southern Italy and morale was low among soldiers.

I am sure that the news from Russia [91] and North Africa was not what the populace envisioned, when people invested their lots with Mussolini before the War. The sad thing about the whole situation was that people knew that the man was a buffoon and vain and, yet, allowed him to cover Italy with misery. Mussolini was also a criminal, but people did not know that. Had they known, would that made any difference? Francesca certainly suspected as much, but she didn't mind as long as it benefited her family before the war. I suppose that must also have been the attitude of non-Fascists. What a price to pay! At least, in early spring, people's attention in Avella turned to going out in the farms and picking anything that was edible and, most importantly, some chicory flowers to make "coffee". There were no more coffee beans from the colonies. Many people stored the flowers and dried them in the sun. I remember the whole family going to the farm and picking any green edible: Dandelions, chicory, and yellow flowered weeds.

In order to shed light on the turn of events at that time, let me review some historical facts. The allies were planning [1, 32, 39, 48, 49, 59, and 62] to invade Sicily sometime in the summer of 1943. The rationale for this invasion by the Allied Army was based on distance from North Africa to Sicily, air coverage, number of troops available, and number of ships to transport the troops to Sicily. I will not delve into the justification of the argument, but simply express my opinion that the strategy or rationale for the invasion was a total mistake then and especially now, knowing more facts about the invasion.

General Montgomery [61] was once asked what he thought of the strategies in WW II and the gist of his reply was as follows: "General Eisenhower never understood the strategies of warfare and never will". When I first heard of that comment, I thought that it was harsh and mean. I thought that General Montgomery was a jealous old man looking to re-write history. Now, after reviewing many WW II artifacts, I am of the opinion that General Montgomery was correct. Another General who agreed with Montgomery was George Patton. These two never agreed on anything, except on this one point. They loathed each other. General Patton [92] proposed occupying both Sardegna and Corsica without ever invading Sicily. His point was that from Corsica or Sardegna it would have been an easy "hop" to invade north of Rome without ever having to climb any hills.

The benefit of such a "hop" would have been the trapping of the whole German Army in the South of Italy. The implication of such a maneuver was that the battles of Salerno [17, 32, 50, 58, 70]], Anzio [5, 32, 52, 54, 55, 68, 70, 81] and Cassino [6, 8, 30, 32, 63, 70, 80] would never have occurred and, hence, many fewer American casualties. The Normandy invasion would have been scheduled much earlier and the war shortened. As far as Avella, there would have been very little collateral damage and no shortage of food supplies. Caterina would have had the medicine for her injured knee.

Here are the facts according to Peter Tompkins' book, Italy Betrayed [20, 21, and 23]. On Sept. 9 General Antonio Basso reported to General Ambrosio in Rome that the German General (90 Panzer Grenadier division) asked to leave the island of Sardegna peacefully. As such, 15,000 German soldiers left there completely on September 10. Thus, without a single casualty, American troops could have landed in Sardegna and planned the invasion north of Rome. Yes, it would have been that easy, just a "hop". Instead, the Americans suffered many casualties at Salerno, Anzio and Cassino later in the campaign in Italy. General Patton was well aware of all the invasions of Rome in ancient Roman times and the outcome of those past invasions. He knew what was coming and he wanted to avoid the disastrous campaigns of the past. Unfortunately, most officers of the American Army were not cognizant of the terrain and past campaigns in southern Italy.

On July 10, 1943 American and British troops landed in Sicily at about 3:00 am [1]. The landing operation was code-named HUSKY. Troops landed at Gela and Licata. There were approximately six to seven Italian divisions, but their morale was rather low. The Germans had two divisions, Herman Goring Parachute Panzer and 15th Panzer Grenadier Divisions, and reinforced with two more divisions later. The Black Shirt Division, to which my uncle Joe was attached, entered the battle about 10:30 am in the morning of the invasion.

Within two to three weeks the Allies drove the German troops out of Sicily. It is remarkable that the German troops were able to cross over into Calabria at Messina with few losses to troops and materiel. Germans utilized ferry boats at night to transport two German Divisions, Italian soldiers and materiel across the Messina strait. About 62,000 Italian soldiers were corralled by the Germans and transported to Calabria. At this point the Italian Army ceased to exist, period.

On July 25, 1943, Mussolini was arrested by King Victor Emanuel III of Italy [3,7, 11, 14, and 16] after the Fascist party council voted for no confidence in the leadership of Mussolini. There were 19 "No" votes and 6 "Yes" votes. Mussolini's son-in-law Ciano was one of the negative votes. Mussolini regarded the voting as some form of suggestion or consent which could be dismissed at will. Delusional! Donna Rachele, Mussolini's wife, warned him to put those 19 Fascist councils in jail and not to visit King Victor Emmanuel III on that fateful day. He dismissed his wife and went on to visit the King, thinking that the King could also be dismissed at will. Before arresting Mussolini the King informed him that he was the most hated person in Italy, see Ref. [11]. When Mussolini was finally arrested at the King's palace, there was jubilation throughout the country.

With bells ringing from church towers, crowds of people gathered to celebrate. For the first time I heard the name of Mussolini mentioned in the same sentence with regard to what to do with some parts of his body (not nice things). Nonno took me to City Hall piazza and I was exhausted getting there. For every step Nonno took, I had to take three. Finally, Nonno got the hint that I was tired and put me on his shoulders while observing the spectacle of people venting their frustration with the war and with the Fascists in town. By this time most Fascists in Avella left for towns where pockets of fanatical Fascists were still running City Hall. Remarkably, few fanatic Fascists stayed behind in Avella with the hope that their fate may improve with the eminent arrival of the German and Italian Armies. The partisan movement was just about to be active in Avella or anyplace else in Italy. Fascists who left Avella knew which way the wind was blowing and headed north of Avella toward the towns of Cervinara and Benevento where Fascist governments at City Hall were still in power.

By the end of August, when the German soldiers occupied Avella, these happy moments came to an abrupt end. By then, Germans troops were chocking the town of Avella. There was no place to hide from German soldiers. The Fascist mayor left town, never to return. It was not clear whether he was running from the Germans or the partisans or the people of Avella. At that time Mussolini was jailed in Abruzzi, Italy. In general, Fascist Mayors (Podestas) began to leave towns under German occupation to other towns still under Fascist rule. Fascist Mayors did not want to be in a position to depend on people's goodwill for their survival. Before and during the war they subjugated people to tyrannical living conditions unmercifully. This period of time marked the end of Fascism governance and the beginning of lawlessness in Avella, and in other small towns in the Naples area.

The occupation of Italy by Germany began. Other books have reported that the occupation of Italy began on September 10, 1943, in Rome [2, 3, 11, 14, 21, 27, 31, 38, and 52]. In this book, it is claimed that occupation occurred a couple of months earlier, end of July. After the King arrested Mussolini (July 25), Hitler put a plan into action by splitting Italy into two occupation zones [20, 21]. The Northern part administered by Field Marshal Erwin Rommel and the Southern by Field Marshal Albert Kesselring. Thus, it was not just a feeling by Uncle Joe that things were different in dealing with German soldiers, when he was stationed with them in Sicily, mid-July. They were treated as prisoners. Italian soldiers were dispersed all over Sicily, if not transported to Calabria. Uncle Joe and two other soldiers from Avella and Sperone were transported to Calabria and placed on a truck with 20 other Italian soldiers heading north via the coastal roads in Calabria, facing the Tyrrhenian Sea. The coastal road led straight into the Salerno and Naples areas from Calabria. It is the same road that ancient Romans traveled to Sicily from Rome toward the salt mines or wheat fields of Sicily. Calabria is located at the boot of Italy, across the strait of Messina, Sicily.

Years later I asked Uncle Joe what right or rule of law the Germans had that demanded that one should go on their truck? According to Uncle Joe there was only one law, "a gun to my head". I was confused by the answer and followed with another question: "why put a gun to your head, if Italy was allied with Germany". "Well, there was a transformation in the treatment by German soldiers toward us. We were treated very much as prisoners instead of comrades". Clearly, Italian soldiers were earmarked for concentration camps, factories in Germany, another war front, etc. They were promised employment in construction companies in Germany and that the pay would be good to support his family. His response in verbatim was, "What a crock". I mentioned to him that if that were true, why was there a need to point a gun at his head. After all, accepting employment was free will. His answer was, "In no fucking way am I going to Germany, even if they were going to kill me". He recounted that the trip along the coastline in Calabria was especially hot. The sun, in the month of July, was truly unforgiving. Temperatures rose as high as 110 F. and in the back of that truck it was even hotter. Ten German soldiers were riding with the Italian troops in the back. It was crowded and hot. In the front seat of the truck, there were three other German Soldiers. The Italian soldiers were handed one can of food to be shared by three soldiers on a daily basis. In addition, one slice of dark bread was handed to them which was so dry and hard that they ate it only to avoid hunger. It took nearly a week to travel about 100 miles north along the coastal road. The coastal road was continuously bombed by Allied planes during daytime. The truck had two flat tires and got off the road when Allied planes were overhead. They set up a check-point on the road, stopping the few passing cars for the purpose of requisitioning food and petrol from passing motorists.

When they arrived near a town on the coastline of Calabria, called Maratea, the truck suddenly came to a stop on a side street facing the beach. Uncle recalled that the street was totally deserted. They stopped at about 100 meters from the sea and the beach was sandy white, and inviting. The Italian soldiers did not like the sudden stop for they feared the worst on an isolated side street. Suddenly, German soldiers totally undressed and started to run toward the beach and the sea! The Italian soldiers stared at each other and soon they realized that there was not a single German soldier guarding the truck.

This sudden change of fortune had three possible explanations. The reader may decide which one was plausible. The first explanation was that it was a gift from God. The second explanation was that someone in the truck was praying so hard that God answered his prayers. The final explanation was that the Italian soldiers or deserters were really a burden to the German troops. For one thing the German soldiers had to share their food with the Italians, and, perhaps, food was running out. Also, the Italian soldiers had no desire to do any more fighting in the war. In effect, they were useless to the German war machine. One other option would have been to execute the Italian soldiers. Obviously, the Germans decided to let them go.

What to do? It didn't take long to realize that this was the magic moment that they had been waiting for. In life it does not come that often and, most often, it is not recognized as such. They all decided to take off, but where? The problem was they didn't know where they were. They knew that they were along a coastline in Calabria. The Italian prisoners were from all over Italy, and not local to the area.

They decided to split in three directions, since, by doing so, logic dictated that the survival rate would be fairly high. The decision to split three ways came spontaneously and quickly to them. They did not consult each other as to who should go where. Germans could not possibly chase them in three different directions – not enough manpower. One group headed south toward Sicily along the coastline. That turned out to be a clever move. By heading south, they were moving toward the advancing allied Armies. There could not have been many German soldiers between this group of Italian soldiers escaping to the south and the advancing Allied Army moving north along the coastal road. After all, the truck that they were riding represented the last German soldiers retreating. My uncle never found out the fate of this group.

The second group headed east toward the mainland and the mountains away from the coastline toward the town of Rossano, Calabria. Many years later I learned the fate of this group. A friend of mine, Natale, about my age, who was born in Calabria and emigrated to USA, recounted the story to me. He told me that after the landing of the Allies in Sicily, many deserters came to their area, Italians, Germans, Russians, Austrians, etc. Fortunately for deserters, local farmers needed help in the farms and these deserters came in handy at that time of the year, since most of the local young farmers had been shipped to far-away lands by Mussolini.

In the fall of 1943 Italian deserters working in the farms of Calabria eventually tried to return to their homes by any means possible, but the foreign deserters tended to stay around the farms helping out until the end of the war. This was an important piece of information from Natale. Perhaps, the group heading south along the coastline must have seen other deserters heading north. Thus, they reversed their directions and headed into the mainland as well, toward farms alluded to by Natale. There was no reason to go further south, for sooner or later they would have to head back north to their homes. There is no historical account of what happened to all of those deserters, at least 100,000 of them of all nationalities.

However, Uncle Joe and two other prisoners (two from Avella and the other from Sperone) decided to head north along the coastline toward Pompeii. This was the route to Avella, circling around Mount Vesuvius from Pompeii, but a more dangerous trek. The retreating German troops were heading in the same general direction and using the same coastal highway. Before they took off, they raided whatever food was left on the truck and found dark bread and some marmalade. They stayed away from the main coastal road and walked within eyesight of the road and the sea, as they climbed the foothills in the vicinity of the coastal road. Fortunately for them, at that time of the year everything was dry and farms were full of fruit trees, but empty of workers or farmhands.

After about 30 km along the foothills they arrived in the vicinity of Sapri where they were surprised to find an anti-aircraft battery manned by Italian soldiers on top of a hill, and they had a broad view of the highway and the sea below. They reported to the commanding officer and explained their plight. Apparently, the officer in charge was not aware of the debacle in Sicily and the fact that German troops were rounding up Italian soldiers. Within 30 minutes the whole operation was disbanded and soldiers were told by the commanding officer to leave and that they were on their own. By this time Uncle Joe's group ran out of the dark bread and water. The commanding officer directed them to a farmhouse on a small hill which was about a mile from the anti- aircraft battery. When they got to the farmhouse, it was empty of people. However, there were watermelons still attached to the vines in the garden next to the farmhouse; so, they helped themselves to watermelons and rested for the next two days.

Finally, they tore off the military clothes and put on some dirty old farmer's clothes. The commanding officer arrived on the scene and offered them a ride along the coastal road toward Salerno. German troops did not yet appear in the vicinity. They drove in a military car on back roads for a while until they ditched the car. It was too dangerous to drive in a military car along the coastal highway, or any road, for fear of being stopped at check-points by fanatic Fascists or by Gestapo police or partisans. In short, it was dangerous even to be near the coastal highway. The worst fear then was that the Germans were rounding up every Italian soldier on the race to Salerno.

They arrived in Salerno traveling at night, in back roads amid the foothills near the coastal highway. By this time they were exhausted from hours of walking along the foothills and worrying about being captured by the Germans. The commanding officer in charge of the gun-battery disappeared into the woods back near Salerno. He knew the area very well and made a dash for his home. For one thing, their shoes were worn out and their clothes were dirty and tattered. They had the look of deserters. They could not afford to be seen by anyone. Also, they ran out of food. According to my Uncle, the soldier from Sperone was mentally and physically depleted. He made a decision to stay behind in Salerno and hide in the foothills, claiming that he had relatives there. That was a disastrous choice for him as in September of that year Salerno was invaded by the Allies, and a major battle ensued. This young soldier from Sperone was never heard of again.

Temptation for the other two soldiers from Avella to hide in Salerno was very appealing, since they both were very familiar with Salerno. It would have been an easy ride to proceed toward Naples by the coastal highway, bypassing Amalfi, Sorrento, etc. Instead, they opted for the land route and along the hilly routes, thinking that the Germans would most likely travel by the coastal highway toward Amalfi as well. The plan was to stay off the main roads and mostly on hills.

Mount Vesuvius was their point of reference on the way to Avella, since it is visible from Avella. They headed east away from the beautiful Amalfi-Sorrento coastal highway toward Vesuvius inland. Once Mount Vesuvius came into view, they circled around it on the right side until Monte Avella could be seen. Monte Avella and the medieval castle appeared to them as beautiful as ever. They became very emotional and took extra precautions to get home, heading straight to Avella, along only the foothills. Via Appia to Baiano was too dangerous even at night, since it was a major highway then. Along the way, they came across many kind farmers who helped in hiding, feeding and clothing the two Avellanos. At that time of the year there were a variety of fruit trees with ripened fruits; there was plenty to eat in the farms. The few farmers who were around to welcome them were very hospitable, and desperately wanted to hear what was happening at the battlefronts. They had no access to even a radio. Once told of the total disaster in Sicily, farmers appeared relieved.

Uncle Joe told the few farmers that it was useless to continue the war for Italy was defeated and being occupied by Germany. The farmers were looking forward to the end of the nightmare with Mussolini. Most of them probably had sons abroad in some strange land and wanted them back. They needed help on the farm. The following towns were traversed on the way to Avella: Vietri, Ravello, Sarno, S. Marzano, Nola and Baiano. However, the pace was less frantic for they were on home grounds and among friends. They knew the lay of the land.

I asked Uncle Joe where they got the food near Avella. He said that once they explained their plight to the local farmers whenever they came across a farmhouse, they were shocked at what was happening to the Italian soldiers and unbelievably helpful and generous with their food. One farmer allowed them to ride his donkeys for quite a long way on the road to Baiano. In another instance, they were able to rest for a couple of days in a farmhouse in Cicciano. The pace was slow, but there was no need to rush, for Germans had not yet arrived in small towns like Avella, Baiano and Cicciano. However, at night it would get cold in the hills even in the summer and the two soldiers were lightly dressed.

View from the castle toward Avella, Baiano, Sperone, Nola and Vesuvius. Photo courtesy of Anmarie Vittoria, 1981.

The object was to get to Nola before the Germans so that they could take the train to go home. The train would have taken them directly to Avella, 10 km away. They were too exhausted to walk the remaining 10 Km. As they approached the station at Nola, to Uncle Joe's consternation, there were German soldiers throughout the station. The Germans may not have won the race to Salerno, but they arrived at Nola before Uncle Joe and his colleague. According to Uncle Joe there must have been at least 50 soldiers that he saw outside the station. German soldiers took over the ridership of trains and busses from Nola. Check points on roads approaching the station at Nola were quickly set up.

The rationale for the appearance of German troops at Nola was because it had always been the center of communication and transportation to the south and north of Italy. Uncle Joe and his colleague retreated from the station and headed for the foothills toward Baiano/Avella the hard way, walking. They traveled on foot along the foothills of these towns. From Nola and nearby towns, one can see the medieval castle of Avella sitting atop a hill. That was their reference point in walking toward Avella.

I never found out where my Uncle was hiding, when he arrived in Avella. Aunt Giovanna and cousins Giannina and Carmine never revealed the return of their Papa. My guess is that he arrived in Avella at the end of August, 1943. It took Uncle Joe about one month to travel about 140 miles mostly on foot to get to Avella from Calabria. The whereabouts of Uncle Joe was kept a secret from the family at that time. The fear was that some local fanatic Fascist might report him to the Germans who were already in Baiano, or a nosy neighbor might gossip all over town about the return of a soldier which was rare in those days. Officially, he was a deserter from the Italian army, since the Fascist government was still in control of local governments. However, in Rome a Royal government was installed under General Badoglio. By this time there was a constant flow of German troops, trucks, tanks and materiel along the main highway through Baiano, a town about one Km from Avella. The two towns were connected by a dirt road by-passing the cemetery and crossing the railroad tracks.

News spread by word-of-mouth that German soldiers and tanks were in Baiano and were using the dirt road between Baiano and Avella. The Avella cemetery was located on this dirt road halfway to Baiano. There were a lot of discussions in Nonno's household as to exactly where the soldiers might be and what their intentions were in Avella. Yes, there was a lot of apprehension of not knowing, and I felt that anxiety from the adults. Nonno was the only one in town who had any idea what we were dealing with when the Germans came. In WW I he was stationed at the Piave River where the German Army annihilated the Italian Army; there were one million casualties. He was captured at Caporetto [89] by the Germans and released six months later. As far as the people of Avella knew then, Italy was still allied with Germany. Uncle Joe went into hiding as soon as he got to Avella and had no time to warn people what the real intent of the Germans was. People were starving for news about the whereabouts of the Germans and starving for food as well. In short, the town was on edge emotionally.

The view at that time among the diehard Fascists in town was that, after all, we were allied with Germany and perhaps there was little hope that they came to help. Most of us were in fear of the next move by the Germans. It did not take long to vanquish the goodwill thoughts. We heard the news that the Germans were in Baiano heading toward Avella. We had a premonition of that move as German motor scooters were already scurrying about town. Nonno and I ventured toward the cemetery with the pretense that he was visiting a relative near there. As we walked toward the cemetery road, a German motorcycle appeared from out of nowhere whizzing by us in a clear gesture of intimidation. As we turned the corner, another one appeared. By this time we got the message; they did not want us on the road linking Baiano to Avella. We were on the cemetery road and no one to help us. We wanted to get out of there fast.

In retrospect, Nonno was wrong in assessing the situation and exposing himself and me to danger. He thought that he could deal with the Germans and decipher what their intentions were. What he didn't realize was that those German soldiers he dealt with in WW I were not of the same mindset as the ones coming to Avella. The ones coming to Avella were indoctrinated into Nazism and that was a totally different beast! Soon we found out. Also, the main escape route to Rome was Via Appia through Baiano. From Avella, there were only two roads that led to Via Appia, the dirt road to the cemetery and a secondary road that crossed the Clanio creek near the "Greek" cemetery. As such, these two roads were constantly patrolled by the Germans. Anyone from Avella or Baiano traveling on these two roads would have necessarily drawn a lot of attention from the Germans.

German soldiers on heavy trucks, tanks and motor scooters with side carriages traveled constantly on the cemetery dirt road to Avella. One tank was so big that it took up the whole dirt road. In order to walk around it, we dropped ourselves into a ditch next to the road. The soldiers moved about with purpose and looked busy. Nonno kept saying to me, "don't look into their eyes" for I could not help staring at them. As a child, I could not comprehend the sudden appearance of new people in town with those big machines and why these soldiers were in town. Why come to town without bringing any food, or medicine that Caterina could have used? It made no sense to me at that time.

My mind was going at 100 miles/hour. What are these big vehicles with long arms sticking out? Why were they here in Avella? Why the special uniforms? They were not very friendly. Why? Why the goggles? So many questions, but no answers. I knew that there was a dramatic change in town and not for the better. I could tell by Nonno's reactions that he didn't want to be stopped by them and he walked very stiffly back home with me. A child can sense danger or ill will without the need to talk or know when to be silent to conform to the new situation, whether scared or apprehensive. The worst feeling was not knowing what was coming next, friendly gestures or the opposite.

Most people in Avella locked the doors to their houses and did not venture outside once they realized that these soldiers were no friends. Nonno went out with me to walk to his farm to scavenge for any farm products or edible wild growth. Those excursions cost him dearly. One of those motor scooters with a side carrier stopped and ordered Nonno to get in the carriage with me. I don't remember exactly what transpired, but they took us near Nonno's farm and talked endlessly. The result of those conversations was that a paved road was built next to Nonno's farm heading behind the cemetery to the town of Baiano, toward Via Appia. Obviously, this was an escape route from their camp in Avella to the main highway, besides the other two escape roads.

Years later I questioned Nonno about the encounter. He told me that the ranking officer asked him if the dirt road alongside his farm was heading toward the foothills and where caves were located. Nonno told him that the dirt road ended at the foothills, about a kilometer from his farm, and the drop-off of the dirt road was due to an earthquake fault-line. As far as the location of caves, he was only aware of the Saint Michael cave below Monte Avella.

This was a lie, for two caves were located about 300 meters from his farm hidden from view of the Germans. The purpose of the lie was to steer the Germans away from his farm and close to Saint Michael cave which was about five miles away. Furthermore, the terrain at the Saint

Michael cave was simply awful due to unpredictable rising waters in the Clanio creek and impenetrable woods. The fact that they camped atop a small hill above the two caves near Nonno's farm tells me now that they investigated the area. They must have discovered those two caves near Nonno's farm.

Apparently, the Germans decided to camp in the vicinity of Via Appia, Baiano and Avella, but the precise location of their camp was discovered long after the war. No one dared to go out and look for the camp at that time. The Germans extended the paved road behind Nonno's farm all the way to Baiano, where the main highway to Rome was running through. Nonno thought that the inquiry about the caves was rather strange. After all, German soldiers were not tourists! In retrospect, I believe that the Germans were looking for air coverage, since the Allies controlled the sky with their superiority in planes. This explains why the Germans were able to hold on to Monte Cassino for so long in spite of continuous bombing by the Allies.

After the exchange, the Germans dropped us near Francesca's house and we returned home. Never again did we go outside to fulfill our hunger for food at that time. I don't believe Nonno informed the family as to what transpired. I did not know enough to say anything. Only through the adults' reaction to these visitors did I began to realize that they were not wanted in town. The point was that German troops were all over our town and surrounding towns, including secondary roads like the cemetery dirt road in Avella. We were occupied by German troops and the mood in town was somber. There was nothing friendly about these visitors. People did not want to be caught in the streets with soldiers, especially when they were drunk. They were drunk most of the time at night. Sometimes they would march from their camp to City Hall and back with their guns at the ready. It was-mind-boggling and frightening. As a child I knew that something was not right. The mood in town was beyond somber; it shocked the town into submission. One could not even breathe air from the mountains without having to share the breath of air with a German soldier. They did not come to help. It was clear that they came to occupy and to intimidate the people.

Farms were raided for livestock as they needed horses to pull heavy equipment up the hills. Even farms owned by the churches were raided. The only company in town that produced wine for the whole region was raided for all of their wines. The wine store next to Nonno's house was always full of soldiers at all hours of the night. Nonno was happy that his wine store was not open during these times. People complained to the local Fascists about the behavior of German soldiers, to no avail. In short, desperation was beginning to set in, and the true nature of their intent was clear to all. The people of Avella were not aware of the disaster in Sicily and the change of attitude of the German Army toward Italy. Neither Uncle Joe nor his family passed the word about the intentions of the German troops. If he did that at the time of his return, he would have been reported by local Fascists and most likely deported to Germany. Also, the other escapee was in hiding.

Nonno's farm was situated next to a dirt road as shown above. The earthquake fault line ran along the other side of the dirt road. The British camped on the farm in 1943. The Goumiers camped 200 yards to the left of Nonno's farm and the Germans to the right of the farm (not at the same time). Monte Avella is in the background. Caves are located behind Nonno's farm.
Photo courtesy of Anmarie Vittoria, 1981.

Uncle Joe's family had built every palazzo in Avella seemingly forever. His grandfather, father and two brothers were in construction almost from birth. One of the brothers, Franco, emigrated to New York City and established a successful construction company in the Queens district, next to Idlewild Airport, now named J. F. Kennedy Airport. After WW II, I discovered a "false" bathroom located on the second floor of the palazzo where the whole family lived. The courtyard was located in the middle of the palazzo and was shared by three families: Uncle Joe's family, brother Vincenzo's and my cousins' grandfather, Enrico's. In the middle of the courtyard was a big fig tree that we all adored and a common toilet.

The hiding place was discovered by accident. One day, when I was visiting cousins Carmine and Giannina, I had to go to the bathroom. As I approached the bathroom on the second floor, my cousin told me that it was not really a bathroom. "Notice, he said, that there is no water anyplace around the toilet". He continued by saying that if one twists the right ear of the angel sculptured above the toilet, the wall supporting the toilet frame is displaced slightly. Behind that wall there was a tiny room with a window facing the garden that was owned by a well-to-do family. Even then, I did not realize the connection between Uncle Joe's hiding place and the false toilet. Only now has it become obvious to me that that was the hiding place. There was enough room behind the false toilet to house one person. The three families shared two bathrooms on the second floor instead of the required three. The third bathroom was converted into the hiding place.

As expected during the German occupation of Avella, traffic increased, with the presence of Germans transporting troops and materiel through town. As a result, another tragedy struck our family. On the way to the railroad station in Avella, grandmother Imalda was run over by a truck carrying German troops on their way to Sperone and Baiano just as she was rounding a ninety degree turn near the train station. She was on her way to Nola to sell her cheese in the market. The width of the road was barely wide enough for the truck to pass through. There were no sidewalks to protect pedestrians. The truck never stopped. The driver was totally drunk. She lay on the ground in pain until people heard her screaming in agony. The truck went on as though nothing happened. To this day I don't know how she ever made it home. I believe that if she received medical attention immediately, she could have survived. She died within a day of the accident. Her collar bone was broken and not much could be done for her. Nonno, aunts, Sebastiano, mother, other immediate family members and I visited her bedside right after the accident. Macabre is not sufficiently descriptive for seeing Nonna Imalda laying in the bed so helpless. It was heart wrenching as we all knew the outcome, even I as a child.

The young doctor simply could not do anything for there was no medicine or emergency vehicles to take her to the hospital in Naples, 21 km away. Besides, the Germans had checkpoints along the main highway from Baiano to Naples. It was impossible to even travel by foot to Baiano, one kilometer away, before being stopped by German patrols with their motorcycles, the same ones that whisked Nonno to their camp earlier.

The motorcycles were seen in every street of Avella. There was not a place unattended. People were denied access to the foothills, except for the shepherds. There were five dirt roads heading toward the foothills and all were blocked by German guards. However, once the shepherds left for the hills, they stayed there until the Germans left. No question about it, the whole area was occupied, and we felt trapped. Effectively, the Germans surrounded the town and there was no way in or out of town or running to the hills. I simply did not comprehend what happened to grandmother Imalda and why. She loved to visit us and tell us stories about wolves and bears in the mountains. I was told by Francesca that grandmother was terribly sick and needed rest.

Every shepherd, of all ages, came to the funeral of the matriarch of their "clan", to show respect for one of their own. A large hearse, drawn by four black horses, carried the body of Imalda. They wore special shepherds costumes appropriate for a matriarch's funeral. The procession to the cemetery was led by the head of the shepherd community, Don Camillo, who was a distant Zio (uncle) to our family, and a second cousin to Francesca. Zio Renato also showed, out of respect for my father. At this time I did not know about the special bonds between Francesca, my father, and Zio Renato. Zio made it clear that he had tremendous respect for Imalda's beliefs and her inspiration to the shepherd clan. To me, as a child, all this made an impression that will remain with me forever.

Zio Renato arrived by overnight train in order to avoid bombing and strafing of the railroad from Allied planes. What should have been a two to three hour ride took the whole night, as German convoys of supplies were streaming south from Rome toward Salerno interfering with normal train schedules. During the funeral procession German convoys interrupted the procession to the cemetery from the church of San Pietro in Avella. Germans were not about to share any road with the locals, especially an escape route to Baiano.

Obviously, there was no recourse for complaints about the Germans' behavior. It simply did not do any good to complain. Besides, where did one go to complaint? Local Fascist officials had no leverage with the German occupiers. The streets were constantly patrolled by the Germans and, soon enough, streets were empty of people. No doubt about it, the town was being suffocated by the Germans. It was such a helpless feeling to have German convoys interrupt normal life in town. People went about town in a state of numbness, resignation, and uncertainty about the future.

THREE
GERMAN OCCUPATION OF AVELLA

The German Army occupied Avella from August to October, 1943. Uncle Joe arrived in Avella about the same time as the German arrival in Baiano by Via Appia [93]. This meant that they must have crossed paths someplace between Nola and Baiano. Uncle Joe traveled by the foothills, and had to cross Via Appia from Nola in order to reach Avella. The German Army was retreating along Via Appia about the same time. There was no time for Uncle Joe to warn the people of Avella about Germans' movements and the possibility of them coming into town. He went into hiding, as soon as he got home.

Caves were known to exist at the foothills near the Avellino area. This was crucial to German strategy in avoiding bombing raids by the Allies. Also, they had a strategic view of the valleys below as well as panoramic views of Avella, Baiano, Vesuvius, Caserta and the Bay of Naples. In essence, Germans could easily see the highway passing through Baiano which served as the main supply line to Salerno.

No one knew exactly where the German camp was located as no one dared to try to find out. For military reasons the Germans wanted to keep the location of the camp secret from the people of Avella. I believe now that the camp was located slightly behind a small hill facing Nonno's farm. Every morning, German soldiers would march from the Fusaro picnic grounds onto a narrow dirt road leading to our house, and turn left toward Nonno's farm to return to their camp. People gathered at the intersection of two streets near our house to view German soldiers march by the two intersecting roads. A check-point near Francesca's house prevented people from going to their farms.

On the slopes of Monte Avella about half way up. Below are the towns of Avella, Baiano, Sperone, Cicciano, Nola and the scenery extends all the way to the bay of Naples. American paratroops landed on this mountain. The landing site of the American troops extended over thirty miles. The cave of San Michele, the Clanio creek, and the Fusaro picnic grounds are at the foothill of this mountain. Photo courtesy of Anmarie Vittoria, 1981.

On one particular morning, when soldiers were marching near the intersection, there suddenly appeared out of nowhere two motorcycles with side carriages that had stopped at the intersection in the midst of people, and one of the cyclists grabbed a teenager by the arms and legs. The screams were so loud that Francesca and I heard them and ran out to investigate. We saw the back of the motorcycles driving onto the dirt road toward Nonno's farm with a howling teenager on one of them. The soldiers disappeared as quickly as they appeared on the scene. People at the intersection went berserk while held back by soldiers with guns ready to shoot. The piercing shouts and crying tormented us then and now. The people were left standing there gawking and wondering what just happened. Why that particular teen ager, since there were at least three other young men there.

People started to run toward the check-point, where they thought they might have taken the teenager. One rumor claimed that the teenager was caught stealing at the German camp. About an hour later the motorcycles and a military truck returned and stopped at a building two blocks from our house. The whole neighborhood was standing around the vehicles including, Francesca and me, to see what was going on, anxious about what was going to happen next, and expecting the worst.

The teenager's mother and sister were placed in the truck under soldiers' escort. The screaming from the crowd and the teenager's mother was unbearable. At that time I had no clue what was going on. It was obvious that the family did not want to be dragged away from home and inconceivable to us that they had committed any crime. They were like us. That was what was so terrifying. The father was away at war in the Balkans. The whole family ceased to exist in a matter of thirty minutes! There was a terrible fear permeating throughout the neighborhood. The fear of not knowing was greater than the fear of the German soldiers in themselves.

After that episode, people ceased to stand at the intersection gawking at German soldiers. Francesca put a plan into action. Every time that we would hear those repugnant songs, " Hupf, Mein Madel", " Skip, My Lassie" or "Lili Marlene" sung by German troops coming from their camp marching toward our house in the morning, we would hide in the pigsty and lock the door. Fear won over curiosity. We didn't care to know what they were up to. It could only be bad!

One evening, we heard shouting and rowdy noise from a distance among German soldiers heading toward the intersection. They were drunk and were looking for adventure in town. We locked ourselves in the pigpen and stayed there until the next day. I couldn't lie down. The ground was moist with wet, smelly, and dirty water draining from the portico floor. Small pigs, chickens and sheep were placed there temporarily from time to time. Rain water drained from the veranda down the steps directly into the pigpen and from the water drainage by the portone. This was no longer a game of hide and seek. I was no longer curious. This was survival and, therefore, a totally different mindset for a child. The Germans were looked upon as persons to avoid at all costs. They were no longer our allies, but our enemies. Thus, a transition in our mindset occurred. I felt that I aged ten years. I could not forget that teenager, sister and mother and the screams of the people. The whole neighborhood was in shock.
The occupation of Italy became a reality, when Kesselring posted rules [11, 21, and 27] of occupation in the streets of Rome on September 11th. The fundamental question to address now is whether Mussolini knew about the partition of Italy by Hitler? There are no historical records addressed to this issue. Mussolini must have known about it, when he escaped from jail on September 10. If he did know, that would make him a traitor, in addition of being already a coward and a criminal.

On September 7, 1943 brigadier general Maxwell Taylor [2, 94] and Colonel William Gardiner were on a spy mission to discuss their plans for landing the 82nd Airborne US division north of Rome with General Badoglio [11, 21, and 27] who represented the Italian government in Rome at that time. They met at Badoglio's villa at 1:00 am to discuss the coordination between the landing of the 82nd American Airborne division and the stationing of Italian troops north of Rome. Badoglio basically told them that the Americans should not rely on the help or assistance of Italian troops near Rome for they were poorly equipped. Therefore, he advised that more American troops land north of Rome, according to Peter Tompkins' book, Italy Betrayed [21].

In effect, Badoglio was declaring to Taylor that the Italian army was in shambles and leaderless, since he was in communication with only few commanders. It was really a shame that this man was at that time in charge of the Italian government. After the jailing of Mussolini, he had 45 days to organize the military defense near Rome with eight Italian divisions already stationed in the vicinity of Rome. There were only 5,000 German soldiers stationed north of Rome. Furthermore, according to Peter Tompkins [21], Badoglio was in communication with a German general in Sardegna requesting to leave the island. It is not clear from historical records whether or not Badoglio informed Taylor about the communication with the German General in Sardegna. In retrospect, landing American troops in Sardegna and north of Rome at that time would have changed the course of history. More importantly, casualties for all concerned would have been far fewer.

The same sentiment was shared by none other than Field Marshal Kesselring of the German Army South. When he heard from SS Colonel Eugen Dollmann [38, 66, and 69] that General Taylor was visiting Badoglio, Kesselring was apprehensive. He related to Dollmann that "if the Allies land north of Rome by sea or air, all is lost" (Peter Tompkins). Dollmann was a German spy who, together with Father O'Flaherty, mingled with the aristocrats of Rome and often were invited to parties of the affluent and the powerful. According to Peter Tompkins, an American spy in 1944, he suspected that Dollmann was a double agent [20, and 21]. Robert Katz [11] confirmed in 2003 that Dollmann was indeed a double agent. Dollmann enjoyed "La Dolce Vita" long before Fellini embellished on it. He loved Rome and spoke fluent Italian.

Potentially, there could have been one American division [51] and eight Italian divisions facing 5,000 German soldiers north of Rome! At 4:00am the two American officers informed General Eisenhower to stop the landing of American troops north of Rome, although troops of the airborne division were already loaded on planes and waiting to go that morning. I believe that with a small amount of organization on the part of Badoglio, a lot of bloodshed could have been avoided in the whole region of Southern Italy and suffering in Avella from the occupation by German troops.

At 6:30 pm, September 8 [2], General Eisenhower [95] announced on BBC radio that Italy had surrendered unconditionally. This part of history is often glossed over. The official version offen quoted in books was that Brigadier General Castellano [26] of the Italian Army, under orders of General Badoglio, contacted the British Ambassador in Portugal to sue for peace or the surrender of the Italian Army. This rendezvous was partially true, but there were many other potential contacts in Portugal, the Vatican, England and all over Europe by Italian diplomats and government officials suing for peace at much earlier times than Castellano's contact. Even Mussolini's son-in-law, Ciano, who was Foreign Minister in 1942, was advocating a conspiracy [15] to sue for peace and was in communication with the Vatican.

Each approach by Italian diplomats was rebuffed to the point of being insulted and disrespected by British diplomats. The rebuffs were orchestrated by British royalty for the sole purpose of restoring a royal government in Italy after the war. British diplomats were not going to "lift a finger" to help italian diplomats out of their predicament in forming a democratic government in Italy. The only reason that they helped Castellano was that it was clear by then that the people of Italy wanted nothing to do with the monarchy, because the King was lowly regarded by Italians in general. The monarchy in Europe was inter-related and protective of one another.

Once the American shield vanished in protecting Rome, Badoglio [2], the general staff and the King's family left Rome along via Tiburtina toward the East coast of Italy (Brindisi-Bari) on the Adriatic Sea [11, 21, 42, and 72]. The convoy of 20 cars was stopped at a German checkpoint about five to six miles east of Rome at 5:00am on September 9. It is remarkable to me now that the convoy was allowed to go through the checkpoint in view of the well-known fact that Hitler wanted so much to capture both the King and Badoglio and bring them back to Germany. This episode has not been fully explained in historical records as to exactly how the convoy was allowed to pass on through. Royal connections throughout Europe played an important role in this episode, allowing royalty to survive in Italy with the hope that a resurgence might occur later. Italians, in general, (regardless of what affiliations) have never forgiven the King for running away from Rome to avoid the responsibilities of a leader to protect Rome. He will always be looked upon by most Italians as a coward who shirked his responsibilities.

On September 9th at 3:00 am American and British troops landed at Salerno [17, 32, 50, 58, and 70] beachheads. The code name for the landing was AVALANCHE and the General in charge was Mark Clark. By this time there were German troops all over Campania, including in Avella. The resistance from the Germans to the Allied invasion was strong. On the next day, September 10, Rome was occupied by German troops. Approximately half a division of German troops withstood and captured most of the eight Italian divisions stationed near Rome, with the King having run away from Rome the day before. The cowardly King and Badoglio never recovered from this embarrassment.

The point is that whatever element of surprise a ttack that m ay h ave existed from July 25 to September 10th it vanished not only in Campania but also in Rome. On July 25 Mussolini was jailed and on September 10 the Germans occupied Rome. In between those two times, there was a vacuum of enemy troops stationed in Rome and vicinity. There were only Italian troops under the command of Badoglio, but he never exercised control of his troops. For example, if the 82nd airborne [51, and 94] division had landed north of Rome in early September with air support coming from Sardegna, they would have met no opposition whatsoever. By diverting the Salerno invasion north of Rome instead, German troops positioned south of Rome would have been trapped and most likely taken prisoners. As Kesselring was quoted saying to Dollmann at that time "all is lost". Bloodshed and misery would have been drastically reduced in the Naples area and American casualties reduced to very minimal.

After September 10, reinforcement of German troops, armaments and food arrived in Salerno from all over the territories occupied by them. On September 10, 1943 German paratroops under the leadership of Major Skorzeny [14] in eight gliders landed on the Gran Sasso, Abruzzi, to "liberate" Mussolini from Italian police guards and fly him to Munich to be reunited with his wife Donna Rachele.

Mussolini would never see Rome again. He established a neo-Fascist regime in occupied North Italy called Italian Social Republic (RSI) with the capital at Salo on Lake Garda. On September 14, 1943 Peter Tompkins [21] landed in Salerno with the 82nd Airborne Division. He later established the first American espionage network in Rome under the auspices of the OSS (Office of Strategic Services), the pre-cursor to the CIA (Central Intelligence Agency), which was established after the War.

In Avella, about this time we heard loud explosions that never seemed to stop, early in the morning of September 9. At first we thought that our "old friend", Vesuvius, was at it again. There is a love-hate relationship between Vesuvius and the people of the area. Vesuvius is blamed for good and bad omens. The explosions lasted until evening hours. No, it wasn't Vesuvius' misbehavior. The direction of the explosions and booming cannon shots came directly from the south of Vesuvius, but we in Avella did not know exactly where they came from. We guessed that they came from the other side of Vesuvius. We and many others climbed on the roofs, but we couldn't see anything happening in the bay of Naples. We gathered that the explosions were south of Naples. I tried to get a better view by climbing over (with the help of Francesca) the shed on the roof, to no avail. Our view was blocked by Mount Vesuvius when looking toward Salerno. However, we could see smoke rising on the other side of Vesuvius. Again, no visible explosions were seen in the Bay of Naples.

The next morning we heard a rumor that long columns of German soldiers, tanks, materiel and trucks were on the main highway from Baiano to Nola. Rumors in Avella traveled from door to door. It seemed that the whole town went to Baiano to see the spectacle of German soldiers, trucks, and Tiger tanks. Nonno carried me on his shoulders to see the spectacle. From a distance, we could see that the soldiers looked very tired with white dust on their uniforms and machine guns at the ready. The tanks appeared to be unreal. They were huge with big 88mm guns on them. These troops were headed to Salerno via Nola and circled around Vesuvius, much like Uncle Joe's odyssey from Salerno but in the reverse direction.

Clearly, the troops marching on the highway must have come from far-away places. They were not the Germans stationed at the foothills of Avella. Germans troops stationed in Avella were the ones that retreated from Sicily more than a month before and were in reserve.

In the afternoon of September 11 we saw an awesome airplane dog-fight over the skies of Avella, extending from Naples to Vesuvius and Salerno (toward south of Avella). There must have been at least 50-60 small planes in the air shooting at each other. Every minute the planes were flying closer and closer to the Avella area. I was at Nonno's house and he grabbed me and ran toward Francesca's house with my aunts, Sebastiano, Nonna and friends of the family trailing us. Nonno decided to run toward the foothills past his farm.

We were desperate to get to the farm quickly. Once there, Nonno pointed to the location of two caves. I ran as hard as my legs would move toward the caves, as my life depended on it. Fear and desperation were evident on people's faces. It felt like the end of the world was at hand. We were exhausted by the time we reached the caves. It seemed that the planes were getting closer and closer to the farm, but we were relaxed in the caves watching the spectacle. I estimate now that about 200-300 people were in the caves. Thank God, my family was among them.

In retrospect, there was no evidence that the Germans used the caves, although their camp was nearby on top of the small hill. The entrance was about 50-60 square feet and 200 feet long, but there was no evidence of habitation. The fact that we were there implied that no German troops were around the area. Before the Salerno invasion, no one got within one hundred yards from Nonno's farm before being escorted back to town by German soldiers. I surmise now that the German troops stationed in Avella must have been rushed to the Salerno front. The common denominator between the battles for Sicily and Salerno was the deployment of the 15th Panzergrenadier and Herman Goering Divisions in both battles. This leads me to believe now that these two divisions, or one of these divisions, camped in Avella. In order to avoid detection of their whereabouts, they took a secondary paved road to Baiano built by them, circumventing the old cemetery road. Nonno was made aware of the German's disappearance from the caves via his parsonale (farmhand). The planes involved in the dog-fights were spread from the Bay of Naples to Nola inclusive of the Vesuvius area. Planes were dodging and shooting at each other drifting toward the Bay of Naples and the Caserta Valley area, north of Salerno. Anti-aircraft fires from the ground could be heard from those area. However, one dog-fight between two planes was drifting more and more toward us, and we all ran deep inside the cave. One of the planes crashed only 200 yards from the farm, toward the Clanio creek. The air battle lasted from the entire afternoon into evening. We could not identify the origin of the planes on the ground and in the air or who was winning the battle. However, no one dared to go back to town or investigate the downed plane. All of us remained in the caves during the night, and no one slept. The adrenalin was simply too high. By morning tranquility had returned. One could even hear birds chirping. So, we headed back home sleepy, and worried, too exhausted to look for the downed plane. We just wanted to go home and sleep.

The downed plane belonged to the German Air Force. After the air skirmish witnessed by us the German Air Force ceased to be effective in the air for the remainder of the Salerno campaign, sealing the fate of the German Army there. The corpse of the pilot was picked up from the wreckage by the soldiers of the 15th Panzer division who were camped near the caves. The pilot was not buried in Avella cemetery, but in the foothills of Avella, near the German camp. It took years for the locals to remove the wreckage. After the war the countryside from Salerno to Avellino, including Avella, was strewn with all sorts of wreckage of war. In particular, the main supply highway from Baiano to Nola and the railroad line from Avella to Nola were bombed almost on a daily basis in daytime, especially in good weather. Nola had always been the center of communication to the south, via Salerno, for the past 2000 years. Every imaginable vehicle was stranded on the highways emanating from Nola. At the railroad crossing near the Avella cemetery two 1000 pounds bombs did not detonate. It was not until after the war that the bombs were defused. However, the shells remain there even today, as well as a cannon stranded in front of Saint Anthony church in Avella. Most of the mementos of the war have been cleared of explosive materials, but some of them are still standing there, reminding the locals of those frightful days.

Two days later a squadron of bigger planes returned and headed south of Vesuvius (toward Salerno). Again, we all ran to the caves. It seemed like the whole town was inside the caves and everybody rushed to the front of them to see the spectacle. The skirmish between planes never materialized for there were no small planes in the air whizzing by each other. By evening, exhausted from the anticipation, we decided to return to our houses. Our nerves, even for a small child like me were "on pins and needles".

Our family could not handle any more personal disasters. Fortunately, there were no more air battles over Avella for the remainder of the Salerno battle. In the next few days we heard cannon shots from ships off shore south of Naples. Those shots were from American and British ships for there were no German or Italian ships in the whole Mediterranean Sea. In fact, it was this barrage from the sea and air that turned the tide in the battle for Salerno. It seemed that every day brought something new, different and dangerous. We were anxious, to say the least. We were starving for news. No one in the family owned a radio. I do not recall anyone in Avella who had a radio.

About this time Giovanna came to visit Francesca and appeared to be distraught. Hysterically, she told Francesca that a German officer and two-black shirt Fascists came to her house and asked the whereabouts of Joe. No one, not even our family, had a hint of where Uncle Joe was; so how could the enemy know. I have put together a reasonable scenario of what occurred in those security searches. Uncle Joe's colleague, who escaped the Germans with Joe, celebrated his freedom soon after he returned from Calabria. At that time, it became public knowledge in town of his and Joe's escape from the Germans. Local black-shirted Fascists informed German security of the escape. When German troops showed up in town. Joe's colleague was soon apprehended and never seen again.

The next day the Gestapo returned and ransacked the house looking for Uncle Joe. Our family was terrified to say the least then. Giovanna was hysterical before, but by then, she was shaking all over. She came to my mother's house with cousins Carmine and Giannina to get away from the search party at her house. Her children and Giovanna were taken to another "safe" house, our dear shepherd neighbor's house, where they slept for two nights. Next to the neighbor's fireplace was a false wall that led to a tunnel where they slept. For us children, we were more fascinated with the hidden tunnel than anything else that was going on. As a child, I did not understand why Giovanna and children had to move from one place to another. Nothing made sense to me, but I could tell that the adults were extremely upset, anxious and apprehensive. I understood that the aunt was upset, but from what? Now, I know. The good news was that the Gestapo never discovered the whereabouts of Uncle Joe, although they spent the morning looking for him at his residence.

The German Army left or retreated from Salerno and the Naples area in late September, black shirts were no longer fashionable any place including in Avella. In fact, the Fascist Mayor had left town a month earlier. Local Fascist fanatics disappeared from Avella. Few returned after the war, but most of them simply disappeared, and never returned. Prior to the Germans' departure, we would hear explosions emanating from Salerno almost on a daily basis and sometimes in the afternoon planes would fly over places like Nola. However, we would no longer run to the caves. For some odd reasons we felt safe, because explosions and planes were sufficiently far away from Avella. However, one evening a squadron of large planes was flying in the opposite direction of the usual flight pattern of the past month. The planes were heading toward Avellino, in a direction away from Salerno, the battlefront. Suddenly, the sky was full of parachutists that we observed from my mother's house. The drop of parachutists was spread from Avellino to Cicciano (about 30 km apart). Cicciano is near (5 km) Avella, closer to Naples.

Most of the parachutists were picked up by the German troops stationed at the foothills of the mountain range near Avella, the epi-center of the drop. From their view on top of the hill near the Fusaro picnic grounds, the Germans could see it all. The men of the American 509th Parachute Battalion were dropped on the mountains near Avellino and Avellla on the night of 14 September, 1943. About 600 men were parachuted for the purpose of blowing up or sabotaging the supply lines over bridges and a tunnel in Avellino, but the drop was spread more than 25 miles off target. Some parachutists landed on roofs, mountain tops and ravines. It was nearly disastrous. Some did make it back to Salerno and survived. Some parachutists avoided being captured by hiding in towns like Avella and were able to carry out sabotage acts against German troops. In one particular case, American soldiers were assisted in their mission by local partisans in Avella.

In the year 2000 I met a fellow scientist at a scientific conference in San Antonio, Texas, who was, indeed, one of the parachutist who landed on Mount Avella, part of the 509th Parachute Infantry Battalion. His name was Richard Richter and he described his ordeal at that time. He told me they were supposed to be dropped near Avellino, within 1km circle area, but the pilot never flashed the green light for the drop. As a consequence, some parachutists from other planes were dropped earlier and some later. Fortunately, he landed on the highest peak, Mount Avella. I told him that he was one lucky man to have landed on the peak. First of all, he landed among friends. I estimated that there must have been at least three to four shepherds in the vicinity, second, being at the peak, the Germans did not have the manpower to climb from their camp at the foothills to the treacherous top.

No sooner had I said that, he mentioned a shepherd by the name of Camillo who helped them a lot in terms of hiding places and food. I explained to him that that shepherd was none other than a distant relation, Zio or uncle, who was the local partisan leader and communist who was grazing his sheep on my grandfather Carmine's grass field on the mountain. What a small world! His order was to set up an observation post and radio communication with Navy ships off the coast of Salerno. According to my friend, the view from the peak was stunning. One could see the whole bay of Naples, the valley extending to Caserta and south beyond Mount Vesuvius. Most importantly, they had a clear view of the highway through Baiano, the major German supply route to Salerno. He and three other parachutists set up the observation post and radio communication in a matter of days and remained on the post until the Germans left camp in Avella and headed north toward Rome.

The medieval castle in Avella built in ~ 800 AD. In the background is the mountain chain that includes Monte Avella. It is noticed that the terrain is much drier than the terrain near Monte Avella. The view from the castle extends all the way to Mount Vesuvius.

Besides Richard's group there was another group who got away from the Germans and landed near a medieval castle located on a small hill about five km south of Mount Avella. The castle was built as a stopover for crusaders who were on the way to or back from the Middle East. Nowadays, it is not the type of place to stop at for a picnic, as it is full of rattle snakes. The town of Avella was sacked in 455 AD by invaders. The population took refuge in the mountains. The city rose again under the Lombards creating living quarters or districts around a castle which held a strategic position on a hill (326 meters) at the foothills of Monte Avella overlooking the valley below and the town of Avella. The castle is formally known as the "Lombard Castle of Avella". The Clanio torrent cleaved a creek through the town. Due to its strategic position, the castle played a role in numerous wars, including the Saracen invasion of 884, the Magyar invasion of 937 and the invasion of Allied troops in Salerno of 1943. The castle was rebuilt by the Norman, Aragon, Angevin, and Swabian families, but lost its military functions in medieval times. It was turned into an aristocratic residence thereafter. In 1465 the castle was partially destroyed by an earthquake and renovated in 1553. By the 16th century the castle was totally abandoned.

The other American group of soldiers hid in the castle. They decided to blow up an important bridge on dried-up Clanio creek. This story is relayed to me by Don Camillo's nephew, Andrea, who resided near the bridge. Andrea was my classmate at the nuns' school. His father was also a shepherd drafted into the Army at the same time as my father. He was captured by the British army in Libya, where he was badly injured. The British were not able to save him and he died in Libya. Like my father, his remains were returned to the family in 1988. Andrea had older and younger sisters. The mother and the older sisters helped Don Camillo shepherding the sheep. As far as I know, the two sisters were not in private school like their brother Andrea. Probably, the nuns could provide only one scholarship per family, as with our family. Most likely, the two sisters attended public school, which was free. Their academic careers ended after fifth grade and the family had plans for them to be out in the fields with the sheep.

View from the blown up bridge by the Americans over the Clanio creek. Saint John church is on the right. The O'Vicolo district is to the left of the creek.

Andrea qualified for scholarship to the nuns' school on the basis of hardships and his father's death in Libya. He was a very good friend and an excellent student. Like me, he loved to play with numbers. In some sense he may be characterized as a numerologist. However, he was indoctrinated in communist ideologies by his uncle, Don Camillo. He would tell me that he aspired to travel to Russia and continue his schooling in Russia. Of course, he tried very hard to convince me about all those free things that were available in Russia. I did not bite. In fact, we would argue almost on a daily basis about the pros and cons of Russian living in big farms. Our argument always turned into stalemates but we have remained best of friends to this day. It is obvious that his uncle, Don Camillo, who was a partisan and communist diehard, must have done the indoctrination.

In the year 2000, I saw him again at the University of Miami, Florida. He was visiting the physics department at the same time as I was. He never left Italy to attend universities in Russia. He remained in Italy to become a professor of particle high energy physics at the University of Naples. The chairman of the physics department arranged for us to get together. Interestingly, the chairman resided on the island of Crete during the war, when the German Air Force bombed that island back to the Stone Age according to the chairman.

I asked Andrea directly what happened to his dreams and a professional career in Russia. He said that as a university student at Naples he did visit Moscow Institute of Physics with the idea of attending that Institute. He was told that a new Institute of Physics was opening up in Siberia and they were looking for good students to attend. He emphatically told me that there was no way for a Neapolitan like him to end up in Siberia. So, that was the end of Communism for him. Besides, according to him, Communism is incompatible with the Neapolitan laissez-faire temperament. As is well known, Communism as practiced in Italy, has little to do with the Karl Marx theory of Communist ideology [84].

The title of "Don" was bestowed to someone who was important in the shepherd "clan" of families in Avella. Don Camillo resided in the part of town that was relatively poor, consisting mostly of shepherd families. As we would say in the USA, he lived on the "wrong side of the tracks", in this case the creek. The Clanio creek is dry in the summer but starting in the fall and early spring it looks like a full blown river. Sometimes it is referred to as the Clanio River. At some places it is as wide as 300 feet and, near the foothills, waterfalls as high as 40 feet are prevalent. It is tricky to navigate across the river in the spring and dangerous, for the water level can change significantly within a few hours and the water currents are very strong. On one side of the bridge is Avella's poor district; on the other side of the bridge the road leads to the medieval castle. The road over the bridge was one of two roads to Baiano and the highway through Baiano was vital to German supplies.

Most of the locals near the bridge were and are into shepherding. Also, on the other side of the creek were the foothills where the Germans were located only 1000 feet away. The bridge was important to the Germans. It was wide enough to allow transport of tanks. The castle was located behind German positions.

Don Camillo and his brother owned a grass field near the castle and were well aware of the Americans. The two of them led the sheep back and forth across the bridge and across the German checkpoint. They knew the lay of the land and the whereabouts of everyone near the bridge and the castle. The two brothers guided the Americans to the bridge at night, where the American soldiers placed dynamite underneath the bridge. After the placement of the dynamite the American soldiers were whisked inside the church of Santa Candida, 50 feet away from the bridge. The bridge was blown to smithereens. I remember the explosion very well for we were awakened from sound sleep in the middle of the night.

Early in the morning, the Americans were led to the jailhouse of Avella by Don Camillo. The distance between the church and the jail was only 100 feet. When the Americans arrived at the police station, they were worried and suspicious of Don Camillo, but they were re-assured by the Maresciallo (chief of police) that the incarceration was temporary and only until the Germans left the area in the afternoon. Jail would be the last place the Germans would be looking for American soldiers. Each time Andrea recounted the story to me, he would always embellish the role of Don Camillo and the partisans and claim that the real heroes of that night were the partisans. I was obliged to defend the role of the Americans, because I could not stand the thought that partisans, or Communists were the heroes. He and I would argue about who the real heroes were, the American soldiers or Don Camillo and his brother.

As the Maresciallo predicted, the Germans were not able to find the Americans after the explosion. The American soldiers were then led by Don Camillo via the valley toward the Naples-Caserta area which was safe for the Americans. They were in the hands of friendly shepherds from one hill to another. Don Camillo was the perfect guide, as he knew those mountains and the treacherous river route as well as any shepherd. Noise from the explosions on the bridge and the earthquake tremors were nerve wrecking and we would have preferred almost anything to being in this situation. We tried to sleep between door entrances to avoid getting hit by rubble.

The Germans were then in a very precarious and vulnerable position. Their main highway of exit (Via Appia along Baiano) was being bombed on a daily basis by Allied airplanes. In addition, Navy gunships, with their big cannons, were able to reach secondary roads, as well as anything moving on the roads. The exit roads from Avella were reduced from two to one. Slowly but surely German troops started to move out. Their exit from Avella was glorious and we felt that we were escaping from purgatory. The German occupation was over and our release from Fascism and Nazism gave us the long-awaited feeling of freedom.

Valley between Monte Avella mountain range and the castle. The burning of the fields indicates that farmers are preparing the ground for the following year's crop. The valley extends all the way to Caserta and Naples. Photo courtesy of Anmarie Vittoria, 1981.

Nothing went right during the Germans' exit from town. That day finally arrived with our hearing, from a distance, German troops singing "Hupf, Mein Madel", very loud. As soon as my mother heard that song, she rushed us into the pigsty once again, like it or not. We stayed there until the street was quiet. In hurrying to the pigsty, we didn't secure our rooster that Francesca was fattening up. It was left in the portico. Her plans for that bird, maybe to serve it for a dinner, never came to fruition because it disappeared. We later learned that not only the rooster was missing, but mules, horses, cows, pigs, etc. were also missing from farms in the town of Avella. Yes, then and now, I would make that trade anytime given the circumstances, freedom versus occupation. For two or three days the town went numb. The town people wanted so much to believe that the Germans left town. They dared not celebrate for fear that they may be back. They refused to talk about who lost what. As a child I was tired of getting in that smelly pigsty, but I could tell that something was brewing in town. The character of the town was changing. Once it hit home that they were gone, a lot of people came out of their homes and engaged each other in the streets. They talked about their experiences and other horror stories during occupation.

As far as the shepherds were concerned there was no change in their lives. They were up on the mountains and they still were there taking their sheep for grazing during the German occupation. However, starvation was still with us but more so, since the German troops took a lot of the livestock from town.

FOUR
FROM PURGATORY TO HELL ON EARTH

By October 1943, the German Army was in full retreat heading northward to Rome from the beaches of Salerno. There must have been at least 200 "tiger" tanks on the highway passing through Baiano heading north. Soldiers looked tired and distraught and a lot of them were injured riding on trucks or other forms of transportation. All the residents of Sperone, Baiano and Avella, including Nonno and me, were standing on the side of Via Appia, the main highway. We dared not look in their eyes for we could not express relief or happiness we felt. We were afraid to do so. At Salerno, the German Army increased their strength from approximately two divisions to more than ten within two weeks, drawing strength from army groups in occupied parts of Europe.

It seems that the only reason people went to Via Appia in Baiano was because they wanted so much to believe that the Germans were leaving for good. The people wanted to turn the page over and start a new journey in life without Fascism and Nazism. For the next couple of months, things were far less than ideal.

Two of the ten German divisions consisted of veteran soldiers involved in warfare for at least two years, as in the Russian and African campaigns. They were replaced by younger and younger inexperienced soldiers barely out of High School. German troops retreated to form defensive positions from the Tyrrhenian to the Adriatic seas, referred to as the winter line, anchored at the San Pietro-Venafro area and later, the Gustav line anchored at Monte Cassino [6, 39, and 58]. Basically the German army took the high ground and forced the Allied army to move in terribly wet and soggy terrain conditions along narrow uphill corridors in the fall. At places, mud was knee high.

The weather in mid-October begins to change dramatically toward more rain, especially on the hills of the Apennines. The mountain ranges in Italy run from east to west for about 300-400 miles in the north (the Alps) and from north to south for 700 miles (the Apennine). The Apennine range runs in the middle of Italy much like bones in a sardine so that there is little land around the coastlines. The Allied troops were forced to climb those Apennine Mountains in mud and inclement weather.

After all these years I still find it incomprehensible how an American army could be suckered into such a trap. Never mind that people were starving and suffering and the bad weather made things even more difficult to search for food. This type of misery usually falls under the category of "casualties of war" or "collateral" damage. Obviously, ambitions won over common sense for many generals, and, believe it or not, they were promoted in those days, in both armies. The bottom line to all of this absurdity and killing was that it had no effect whatsoever on the outcome of the war. This opinion is shared by most of the military community.

We had so-called collateral damage in Avella. My sister, aunt and grandmother Imalda died as result of collateral damage. Accidental death is still permanent. No labeling of those events can change that. Other collateral damage included the lack of food, basic necessities and medicine. Typically, we would have polenta for breakfast, lunch, and dinner. On Sunday the polenta meal was masqueraded with a touch of tomato sauce in order to give a semblance that one was eating spaghetti. A second dish it included a chicory salad or some wild green plant and, to this day, I could not tell you what it was. An egg was worth its weight in gold. The few farmers did very well in those days. They had plenty of chicory in storage and demanded pretty much what they wanted or bartered. People were rummaging farms for anything green like chicory, wild daisies, dandelions, etc. The whole town was hooked on chicory. You could smell it all over town.

The biggest problem was that there was no medicine in town and no doctor who was licensed. One could not afford to get sick; even a scratch was considered serious. The local "doctor" was no help for he suggested the usual worthless remedies – keep warm, rest and liquids. There was no anti-biotic medicine. So, it really was not the fault of the local "doctor". He didn't have the tools to practice his profession. Francesca's cousin had an apartment next to ours, sharing the same open air veranda on the second floor. My visit to the sick aunt was traumatic for I did not want to be there. Everybody coming out of her apartment was crying. I could tell that aunt Esparanza lost a lot of weight and it was such a hopeless feeling. I can never forget the pale and expressionless look on her face. In a matter of two years my family suffered three casualties: sister, grandmother Imalda and aunt Esparanza. Besides those mentioned abovewas the loss of Papa.

It turned out that aunt Esparanza's son in-law was a prominent Fascist in the town of Benevento. The name Benevento is derived from the fact that there is always wind in that town even in the summer. The translation of the name is "good wind". It is located on the other side of Mount Avella (north of Avella) about five miles away. It was remarkable that when he showed up in Avella, in November, no one knew that he was a Fascist. Had they known that, people of Avella would probably have lynched him next to his mother in-law during the funeral, when he first showed up in town. By then, partisan and Communist activities picked up and Fascists were being pursued all over Italy.

All of sudden, there were no more local Fascists in Avella. In fact, the Fascist Mayor of Avella disappeared right about this time. Disguised Fascists like Esparanza's son in-law began to arrive in town incognito. My guess now is that the Mayor must have traveled to a nearby town, where he had family connections or friends, for support until things got back to normal. As the Allied Army was marching north liberating towns, Fascists who resided in these newly liberated towns headed south nearby towns and hid there until the war was over. They did not want to be caught by partisans, dead or alive. The rationale for former Fascists moving into liberated areas was because there were no partisans in liberated areas. Partisans operated in areas where there were still Nazis and Fascists to combat.

Esparanza's son in-law did exactly the same disappearing act in Benevento. This type of behavior is not strange to me. For example, in Roman times (see A. Everitt's book, "Cicero") during Cicero's tenure in the Senate there were many civil wars. Usually, the winner would make up a list of adversaries to liquidate. This was to eliminate potential political foes and take over their properties as some sort of reward. The ones on the list who could afford to travel by ship to Greece, the Middle East and North

Africa and join a political friend or relative would survive the purge. After a couple of years they would return to Rome to turn the tables on their foes. The ones who did not get out on time or could not afford to travel or had no connections abroad were slaughtered. It is remarkable to me how history repeats itself. Here we are 2000 years later with the cycle re-kindled over again and Fascists running away and waiting for a better time to return. Obviously, society is doomed to relive terrible indiscretions, if we ignore past history. The only difference in WW II was that the distance traveled by displaced Fascist officials to a new place was a lot shorter.

It should be pointed out here that Uncle Joe was still in hiding. His fellow escapee disappeared from Avella, never setting foot in Avella again after he was captured by the Gestapo. At that time, I did not know that I had an Uncle Joe, although I often visited cousins Giannina and Carmine. Their grandfather would tell stories about dragons, monsters, princesses and the castle in Avella, while roasting chestnuts at the fireplace. About 8-10 children would gather around the fireplace. The grandfather must have been in the seventies and loved having children in his house. As soon as the children gathered in front of the fireplace, he would start with "C'era una volta" ("Once upon a time") and began telling his story. He soon had our complete attention. He loved to shock us with stories about gnomes, half man and half goat and mythical heroes on white horses searching for princesses in faraway castles atop tall and treacherous mountains. Typically, the hero would have to solve riddles to win over the princess, much like in the opera Turandot (Puccini), and avoid three-headed dragons spitting fire, flying monsters, giant snakes, etc. We kids looked at each other as if to say: is this for real or what? Some kids just could not stand it anymore and ran out of the room. Over the years I have wondered whether or not those stories were fairy tales handed down from past generations. It seems that every country in the world has similar fairy tales [96]. We sat in rapped attention at his every word.

My cousins did an excellent job of not alluding to their Papa's hiding place. In fact, the word "Papa" was never mentioned by my cousins to my brother and me. We were totally in the dark about the situation. With the departure of the Germans I questioned why Uncle Joe didn't come out of hiding? I believe that he did not want to be rounded up by the carabinieri (Italian Police) as a Fascist, since he was associated with a

Fascist Division before the war, although, I repeat, he was not a Fascist. The division was made up mostly of stragglers from other Italian army divisions stationed in North Africa during their stay in Sicily. There were three Fascists divisions in Libya that were wiped out by the British Army at Tobruk [49].

It was not until near the end of the war, in 1945, that Joe finally emerged from his hiding place. When he did come out, the first thing that he constructed was a "presepio", a nativity scene with Jesus, Mother Mary and Joseph in the manger, during the Christmas holidays of 1945. As a child then, I was not aware of anything like the special preparations people made during these holidays. Perhaps, people were not in a festive mood before 1945. The presepio caught the spirit of the time and I was ready for it after all those gloomy days. We children were so happy. My uncle happened to be a talented sculptor, painter and builder. That must have been in his mind for a long, long time, and the creative spirit just exuded out of him.

After the departure of the German Army in early October 1943, there were no foreign troops anywhere in Avella, but still the people of Avella were numb and apprehensive. The war was still around the corner. However, one day we were awakened by the loudest explosion ever. Our fears were re-kindled. We climbed on the roof of our apartment and could see that the explosion came from the bay of Naples and not from Salerno. When I was on the roof, I was able to place the explosions on the waterfront of Naples. Sebastiano had a hard time making sure that I didn't trip and fall to the ground, a sixty feet drop.
Our fears were eased when we heard what happened in Naples. A group of scugnizzi were raiding a department store. A scugnizzo was usually an "almost" orphan whose father died in war and who lived in the streets. The mothers, who were not able to provide for the boys, threw them out of the house. They begged, stole, bribed, and pimped to survive, and ranged from six to twenty years old.

The Fascist and German security police surrounded the department store and demanded surrender or else. Masaniello, leader of the scugnizzi, showed up with about 200-300 scugnizzi and counter-demanded that the Germans surrender [13].

What makes this story so remarkable was that Masaniello and a group of children were staring right into two tiger tanks. To this day I don't know whether Masaniello's response was an act of courage, foolishness or simply a bluff. It was a life and death situation and this teen-ager was the epitome of calm.

It was a classic stalemate leading to only one conclusion – a shootout. Soon after the stalemate, every street in Naples was barricaded. The people of Naples rallied behind Masaniello. Fifteen to twenty tiger tanks were blown up, and molotov cocktails (explosives) were thrown from roofs, windows, and barricades. WW I rifles were the weapon of choice by the scugnizzi. Unbelievable as this may seem, the Germans were chased out of Naples by the scugnizzi and the populace. However, before the Germans left town they blew up every ship in the Harbor. That was the sound that we heard in Avella. To my knowledge, Naples was the only city in Italy where its citizens chased the Germans out of their town.

Before the Germans left Naples, their demolition squads went around the city blowing up anything of value or in operation. There was no water or electricity. People were experimenting with sea-water for cooking and trying to distill it. Also, there was no food and Neapolitans went out in the fields along the roadside to search for edible foods. There were about fifteen different kinds of plants which were edible, but bitter in flavor, including the chicory plant. Inexplicably, no boats were allowed out to fish in the fall of 1943.

Butcher shops displayed chicken heads for five lire (10 cents), chicken intestines were five lire, a gizzard was three lire, a large piece of windpipe was seven lire. Coincidentally the cat population declined in the Naples area. Allied soldiers were charged for looting. Officers of the King's Dragoon Guards, who entered Naples first after the Germans left, removed paintings from frames in Museums, and made off with fine pottery collections. These items were crated and shipped to England.
Germans planted delayed-action explosive devices in Naples before departure. As a result, a number of buildings were pulverized in late October of 1943. Colonel Scholl of the German army had mined buildings located 300 meters from the sea front. A million and half people left their houses and crowded into the streets in order to avoid potential explosions of their respective streets. Fortunately, the bombs

never exploded. In late fall, most restaurants in Naples were open but the clientele was mostly Allied officers.

The black market reigned supreme and prices were outrageous. At the famous restaurant Zia Teresa the price for a fish dinner was priced at $20. That is equivalent to about $1000 today. The black market was controlled by the Camorra in collaboration with the local Italian police marshal (Maresciallo) who wielded huge and tyrannical power in towns as well as in cities like Naples. The Camorra was an organization of thieves, equivalent to the Mafia in Sicily. By this time of the year things were coming back to normal, except for telephone communications and electricity. People were stealing wires and selling the copper to small shops to melt. In the town of Cicciano, near Avella, the AMC (Allied Military Commission) [40] caught a number of wire cutters in the act of stealing copper wires and they were sent to Military prison. At least, the prisoners had something to eat regularly.

General Mark Clark [13] came to Naples to take credit for "conquering" Naples. What a fool! The fact that he was the youngest field general and declared himself as liberator of Naples should tell you something about his ambition and vanity. He never acknowledged the role that the scugnizzi played in the liberation of Naples. To General Clark's thinking, children's efforts in war counted for naught! The historical fact remained that there was not a single German soldier in sight when General Clark entered Naples. The only thing that he captured was a totally destroyed city. Nevertheless, celebration of the liberation was held at the restaurant called "Zia Teresa" near where all the ships were sunk.

The problem was that there was no meat or fish meal to offer the general. One astute chef had a brilliant idea. He went to the aquarium located at City Hall in Naples, about a mile from the restaurant, and raided a large bass fish from the aquarium. He then cooked it with vegetables and, voila, a dinner was served to General Clark. According to the general it was the best fish meal that he ever had. The resourcefulness of the people of Naples in those starving days was truly unbelievable. When the whole population was starving and the scugnizzi were pimping even their mothers, they produced a four star meal for a three star General! The general was so egocentric and pompous that he didn't have the capacity to see the misery and starvation of the people of Naples or try to do something about their plight.

By the end of October, 1943, the rainy season started and lasted about a month. The British troops arrived in Avella just about when the rains began to stop. The contrast in arrival of British and German troops could have not been more different. Whereas German troops appeared menacing and intimidating with pointing guns, the British troops came in a parade atmosphere and with no guns. Scottish bagpipe playing soldiers led the parade playing their instruments. Nevertheless, the town was being occupied by foreign troops, and people were fed up with any soldier in town. The soldiers were marching in an orderly fashion toward the foothills near the Fusaro, past Francesca's house. None of us paid attention as to exactly where they were heading, as people were resigned for the worst.

We assumed that the British troops were going to take over the German camp until one day in November 1943 when the "parsonale" (farmhand) came to visit Nonno's house during the coffee or chicory break. By this time I was allowed to taste chicory coffee. It was bitter and I never drank it again. The visit was unusual for these visits were usually around Easter and Christmas as part of the farmhand duties to pay his respect – to bring a rooster, fruits, vegetables, etc. from the farm. I could tell from watching Nonno and the parsonale that they were involved in animated conversations. The sense was that something important was happening. Indeed it was.

It turned out that British troops had arrived on Nonno's and adjacent farms and decided to camp there without informing anyone or securing anybody's permission. Unknown to the family, the British had cleared land to secure an asphalt road behind the cemetery leading directly adjacent to Nonno's farm, complementing the paved road built by the Germans. They moved tanks, heavy trucks, and cannons on Nonno's and adjacent farms. On the farms, they constructed sleeping quarters for non-commissioned and commissioned officers as well as cafeterias and a field hospital.

It was also a mystery as to why it took so long for the parsonale (farmhand) to report to Nonno about British intentions on the farm. One bright and cold morning Nonno came to Francesca's house to pick me up on the way to his farm. It was nippy cold and, frankly, I would have liked to stay home. For the life of me I didn't understand why Nonno dragged me along to the camp after he found out from the parsonale. Mother was happy to see me go as it freed her to do chores around the house. We walked along a dirt road to Nonno's farm, the same road German troops marched on every morning on the way to their camp a month earlier. That morning British troops were also marching on that road; nothing changed, only the color of the uniforms. The British wore drab tan and the Germans drab dark green uniforms. Sometimes there was no distinction, since soldiers would scamper in the nude in the summer. When we got to the farm, soldiers in shorts were doing calisthenics. We stopped at a check point entrance to the farm. Nonno was trying to tell the guards that they were on his farm. Jokingly, he said that either they had to pay rent or get out. We might as well have been from the moon for they didn't understand a single word of Italian. They ushered us aside and told us to wait for an officer. The farm looked busy with small tent buildings all over, delineated from each other with stones marking small passageways to buildings. The stones were painted white. Army barracks were lined up parallel to each other with smoke coming out of each one. Every tree was cut except for the cherry tree in the middle of the camp. It seemed that we waited forever for the officer, with the cold breeze from the mountains chilling us. Finally, he showed up and led us inside a large tent. He was meticulous about not stepping on the stones marking a passageway. It looked like they were playing house, but Nonno was playing survival. We were introduced to at least 8-10 sharply dressed officers with shiny shoes. I noticed the shoes for I compared them with the ones Sebastiano wore. The only other time that I saw Army barracks was at the University of Toledo (USA) in the chemistry laboratory and it was a traumatic experience for me. I did not expect Army barracks on a University campus and it reminded me too much of the past.

In the British camp, I remember the aroma of their cooking being so inviting. I smelled fried eggs, potatoes and bacon and that alone was like being in heaven. The British sent us from one office to another and politely requested that we wait each time. I now believe that was their way of tiring Nonno, diffusing the situation, and cheating him out of his farm. Many years later, I asked Nonno what he was looking for, when we went to the camp. He related that he wanted to know how much the British were willing to pay for the rent of the farm and when the first payment would be. The British understood very well what Nonno was saying. Even I understood what he wanted. The loss of the farm meant less food for the whole family, making a dire situation hopeless.

We stayed there the whole morning and afternoon and into the evening, when an officer showed up and handed a loaf of white bread to Nonno. I was ecstatic seeing the big loaf of bread. For the first time in a long time we had bread for a change instead of polenta from morning to night. That was the payment for renting the farm! The poor man, Nonno, took the bread home and shared it with the rest of the family.

The next morning Nonno and I again went to the camp to collect another loaf of bread. This time we didn't have to wait long. Apparently, we must have registered with the military authorities the day before. Also, they saw our pathetic look the day before. Bread was baked early in the morning at the camp. In fact, one could smell the aroma from Francesca's house, which was close to the camp. British bread was nothing like Italian crusty bread, but given the circumstances, we ate it. It was about 6x6x18 inches and as white it could be, very little crust to it. On another trip to the farm, or camp, as we were waiting for the bread, Nonno noticed that the soldiers were about to cut down the cherry tree. That was sacrilegious to him. He started shouting like a mad man at anybody he might get attention from, but everyone ignored him. The days before, being nice and polite did not help. As a child, I was not aware of all these innuendos, for all I wanted was to get the bread and get the hell out of there. The outcome of this outburst was that he saved his beloved cherry tree. In retrospect, I doubt whether he could get away with that behavior with Germans in camp. They would have shot him next to the tree. However, a lot of fruit trees were cut to make room for tents or temporary quarters, as more soldiers were appearing every day, including Australian and New Zealand troops. More and more farms were simply taken over without permission and more bread handed out to farm owners.

Barracks were not the only things the British built. They built a swimming pool with dimensions of 150 x 60 square feet along with cabana housings next to it. In between the pool and the creek, a Roman aqueduct ran alongside the pool to bring water to it and to the town as well. The pool was located next to the Clanio creek and about 200 yards from Nonno's farm. It didn't do the town any good at that time for no one from the town was allowed. In fact, I was not aware of the pool until some nude British soldiers were running along the dirt road to the pool. There were guards posted at the entrance of the pool and a barbed wire fence, 6 feet high, all around.

The British used the water from the Roman aqueduct to replenish their water needs at the camp. As a result water was in shortage in town. Also, they built a paved road from mother's house to the foothill of Mount Avella, passing by the pool and the picnic grounds near the foothills of Fusaro. Before the war Neapolitans would come to the Fusaro in droves after the Easter holidays, the first Saturday in May. Neapolitans, who wanted to get away from the polluted city air and breathe the clean mountain air, used the Fusaro grounds for picnics and usually staged a singing festival of old and new Neapolitan songs. Years later some of those Neapolitan songs were also sung on the radio during the San Remo festival in the fall. This tradition holds to this day. The people of Avella scheduled the picnic one week after the Neapolitans.

The routine was the same every day. Nonno would get up early in the morning and go to the camp to receive the loaf of bread and it was excruciatingly painful for me to walk through the camp and smell that wonderful cooking in the morning. Also, it was a long, long walk for me and I didn't always accompany him. I tried to avoid that long walk as much as I could, especially in the winter. Besides bread, nothing was ever offered to us in the morning, like a cup of real coffee. At least, the British occupation was more pleasant than the German. No one in town would run and hide, when British soldiers came to town for no one feared being sent away.

However, one winter day   (January, 1944) Nonno was so excited that he came to Francesca's house wanting to tell us something important. He told Francesca that he discovered a secret passage from the British camp (his farm) to his house. It reduced the walking distance from 8 to about 4 city blocks. I knew what that meant for I had purposely stayed at mother's house to avoid going to the camp and walking that long distance in the cold wind. I had worn-out shoes and was wearing hand-me-down clothes for winter. I was in no mood for experimenting. Still, I dreaded that cold breeze from the mountains in the winter.

The next day, bright and early, Nonno came by mother's house to pick me up, and Francesca just shrugged her shoulders. Bread lines were already in place with Nonno's name on the loaf of bread. They no longer bothered to hand it over. Apparently, there were other people picking up bread from other farms that the British occupied, as more colonial troops were coming and camping in nearby farms. We left the camp and headed toward a neighboring farm across from Nonno's farm. This was supposed be the new way toward town. That farm was separated from the camp by a dirt road and a drop-off in level of about six feet. I realized now that it was an earthquake fault line. We knew the other farm was unattended for we walked past it a number of times before.

We slid down the drop-off clutching the bread for dear life. The farm was full of hazelnut and olive trees but no fruit trees. Clearly, this was a business farm selling hazelnuts and olive oil commercially. Today, the European Union sets the quota on how many tons of hazelnuts Italy can export to other European countries. Ironically, today no hazelnuts are exported from Avella for the first time in 2000 years! One of the 18 species of hazelnuts is referred from the Latin word Avellana which in the Roman days implied the special hazelnuts grown in Abella (today Avella). Since the farm was unattended, we were not afraid of getting shot at by the owner. In Avella hazelnuts were and are the only big business in town, exceeding wine. A thief may steal anything on a farm in Avella, but not hazelnuts or olives; one can get shot for that.

As we walked south on this farm, we came across a very large stone and brick construction with an entrance door about 90-100 feet high. Usually a portone to a palazzo in town was no more than 30-35 feet high. The strange thing about this big portone was that it was not attached to any "palazzo", like downtown Avella. It led to an empty space. On closer examination, the empty space was the location of a field resembling a soccer field. There were wild hedges at the entrance and ivies growing on the walls of the corridor leading to the field. At the entrance and in the corridor, there were broken statues. A pile of marble columns, complete statues, and bricks so high that it was very difficult to get to the entrance. One had to climb over the stones and broken statues just to get to the hedges in front of the portone. I realize now that they were statues from ancient Roman times. After a couple of hours we cleared a path to the front entrance. We (really Nonno) pried the door open so that we could get to the other side of the corridor. I was surprised to see the energy coming out of Nonno. He was determined and on a mission to find out what was on the other side of the portone.

The whole scenery was surreal. It was like entering an ancient world. A circular road, paved with red bricks and lava rocks, led to an immense oval "playing field" (the size of a football field) about ten times the size of the pool built by the British. The large construction was only 100 yards from the British camp.

What made it surreal was that, along the side of the entrance and corridors, there were large steps all around the oval recessed field, going up, for people to sit on, like in a stadium. The corridors circled all around the field. Furthermore, there were broken steps connecting the corridors to the field and below the field. The difficulty was that everything was covered partially by grass, ivies, hedges, chicory plants, and broken statues. Unbeknown to us at that time, underneath the ivies there existed cavities or holes in the wall containing vast treasures of antique art dating to Roman times. Apparently, in Roman times Avella was a big city and important enough to the ancient Romans to build another colosseum or amphitheater south of Rome.

The colosseum in Avella with Monte Avella in the background. The entrance to the colosseum with the large portone (door) is shown at the opposite end of the colosseum. Nonno's farm is about 50-70 yards to the left of the entrance beyond the trees. All foreign troops camped at the foothill of the smaller hill in front of Monte Avella. The town of Avella is on the left of the entrance. The cave of San Michele is above the gorge separating Monte Avella and the smaller hill. The Fusaro picnic grounds are at the foothill of the smaller hill (far left). Photo courtesy of Anmarie Vittoria, 1981.

Historically, Emperor Sulla of Rome (see Everitt's book, Cicero, ref. [44]) built this colosseum or amphitheater in 89 BC as a reward to the people of Abella (Avella) for being loyal to Rome in their battle against the Samnite tribe of Nola. It is interesting to note that in one of the many museums in the Vatican, Abella (Avella) is depicted in an ancient map of Roman territories as a colony of the Roman Empire. The capacity of the colosseum in Rome was about 50,000-80,000 spectators; the one in

Avella seated about 20,000-30,000 spectators. It is interesting to note that both the colosseums in Avella and in Rome lacked toilet facilities. This explains why the exits were built all around the colosseums to facilitate exits. Besides colosseums in Avella and Rome others were built in Verona, Pompeii, Naples, Pola, Nimes, Arles and El Djeem (Carthage). The amphitheaters or colosseums were adaptations of Greek theaters which were considerably smaller.

As a child at that time (1944) the amphitheater in Avella left no impression and, to me, it was just another building. Broken statues were quite common in the town of Avella. Everybody had a Roman statue placed in a courtyard. It never occurred to me as a child that it was a big deal to Nonno. I was more interested in the black ants all over the place, building huge anthills and to be aware of snakes in the hedges and ivies. I would plug one hole with dirt and soon enough another anthill was formed. I soon concluded that it was useless to try to make life miserable for the ants. They were too smart and quick for me.

Nonno must have been trying to figure out what the special construction was all about. I believe that he figured it out and never told anyone about it. After this escapade we crossed to the other side of the neighboring farm and into another dirt road. We turned right and, pronto, we were at Nonno's place within five minutes. I was not even tired or cold from the walk, as promised.

At Nonno's house the white bread was cut into approximately 1/2 inch slices. The slices were grilled at the fireplace until they turned light brown. The choice in eating the bread was either to place slices of tomatoes and olive oil on the toasted bread or ricotta. Sometimes the toasted bread was used to dip into the chicory coffee. Interestingly, grated cheese was never combined with the tomatoes to toast the bread simultaneously and make what we know today as pizza. Just a small change in the old recipe would have produced pizza as we know it today.

In the late 1990s I visited my cousin Peppino, the son of my aunt Candida, the seamstress. His younger brother was named Michele in honor of my father. Candida had died about five years before. Half the young people in Avella were unemployed, but Peppino got a job with the railroad system soon after finishing high school (scuole media). Those types of jobs are more like political appointments. Peppino had been involved with local politics from the time he was a teenager. His mother was influential with local politicians, whose wives had their dresses tailored specially for them by my Aunt Candida. This was during my sabbatical leave from Northeastern University in Boston. My wife, Anmarie, and I stayed with my cousin Peppino.

Peppino mentioned that there was a famous museum of antiquity in Avella and that we must see. The museum was attracting people from all over the world. I could not believe that finally Avella was "on the map" and recognized for something besides its white onions and hazelnuts. Vidalia onions sold in the USA are one by-product of onions from Avella and hazelnuts are exported throughout the world. It was on a Sunday and the museum was closed, but my cousin was undeterred. He called someone at City Hall and argued his way into having a personal guide escort us at the museum. Ever since that episode I have had new respect for my cousin.

As he drove us past Francesca's house toward Nonno's farm, the old dirt road grandfather and I often walked to the British camp was widened to look like a boulevard. The earthquake fault line was leveled to make way for the road. I am afraid that one day it will not be so leveled, when the next major earthquake hits the town. Across from Nonno's farm, we arrived to the grand entrance to the museum.

It was so familiar to me that I almost cried (and did cry secretly). Those scenes were so emotional to me! He drove us right into the farm where Nonno and I stumbled onto that big "portone" in WWII. That monstrous portone discovered by Nonno was the entrance to a colosseum. Finally, there was closure to that discovery. I never told my cousin about Nonno's earlier discovery of that colosseum in 1944 as he was happy to tell me all about the museum and all the statues uncovered under the ivies!
The entrance led to a large portone and was cleared of dirt and debris. Also, it was adorned with Roman figurines somehow stuck on the portone. Remarkably, the portone looked as good as new after 2000 years. This time there were no wild underbrushes, hedges, ivies and smashed statues at the entrance. One could actually see Roman paintings adorning the walls to the entrance. Also, statues of famous Roman figures were placed alongside the entrance.

Years later, rumors in Avella claimed that soldiers of the British Army camping in Nonno's farm carried most of the interesting art away from the colosseum during their occupation. I would venture to say that a lot of the museums in England may be depositories of art looted from the colosseum in Avella and similar places. I believe that this is another form of hidden collateral damage which is often under-reported. With art carted away in WWII by soldiers, the identity of the town of Avella and the pride or soul of the people who lived in the town was taken away with just a loaf of bread as payment!

On entering the colosseum, past the tunnel or part of the corridor, there was a spectacular view of the colosseum facing right into Mount Avella. Spiritually, it felt like sitting on top of the world, and as if the rest of the world were irrelevant. It was truly spiritual, me and nature. The ground floor of the colosseum was the stage, or the field, and it was full of grass and spots of daisies and chicory flowers were still growing. The walls surrounding the stage were adorned with busts of statues covered with ivies. The sitting arrangement was oval shaped around the stage. The colosseum in Rome had canvas or awning arrangements to shade the spectators from the sun. The one in Avella had no such structure in place. I surmise that the colosseum in Avella was used for both gladiator matches and as a theater setting. We never got to view the dungeons below. It was remarkable to me that this massive structure was obstructed from view by the wild undergrowth of bushes, ivies, hedges, and trees when Nonno and I walked on the dirt road. The owners of the farm must have encouraged this growth of plants around the structure in order to hide it. Farm owners, in general, did not want to sell their farms to the antiquity bureaus in Rome. On further observation of the location of the colosseum relative to the foothills of Avella, I came to the conclusion that the colosseum was at the center of "old" Avella, Abella. I base my conclusions on these facts. First, the colosseum in Rome is located near the center of "old" Rome. Second, an old cemetery of Greek origin was discovered long after I emigrated to America. There are plans by City Hall to build another museum dealing with Greek antiquity. As it is well known in Greek and Roman times, cemeteries invariably were found at the perimeter of town, never in the center. Third, recently underground housing and tunnels have been dug up in a farm near the colosseum giving credence to a town setting next to the colosseum. Clearly, the farm owners did not disclose earlier the discovery of underground dwellings to anyone for fear of being forced to sell their farms to the state for little compensation.

Finally, as a child I knew of a stone and brick wall separating one farm from Nonno's farm. The wall consisted of bricks and stones dating from ancient times surrounding the whole area much like the forum in Rome. As a child, I didn't pay attention to that wall for it was just another barrier for me to climb over to get to Nonno's farm. Unfortunately, I was never able to put two and two together, to realize that that particular wall separated the inner city from the edge of town.

The same stone construction that separated the two farms near the colosseum can be found exactly the same as in Rome. Indeed, there must have been living quarters right next to the colosseum. Thus, "old" Avella was converted into farms, probably in the middle ages. The fact that Greeks settled in Avella well before the Romans implies to me that the site of the colosseum must have also been the site of a theater, where Greek plays were performed. It was inconceivable to have a major Greek settlement without a theater.

Wherever major Greek settlements were discovered in Calabria and Sicily, there was always a theater at the center of the settlement. With the arrival of the Romans in Abella, they simply constructed a colosseum on the same site or on top of the Greek theater. However, the center of modern Avella is built near the Greek cemetery which was on the outskirts of Abella, the "old" town of Avella. Thus, farmers were able to hide the main city of Abella for centuries.

A Greek cemetery dating back more than 2000 years. The location is about 100 yards from the bridge that the American soldiers, with the assistance of Don Camillo, blew up in Avella in 1943. Photo courtesy of Anmarie Vittoria, 1981.

This means that excavations around the perimeter of the colosseum in Avella should reveal some interesting artifacts of antiquity from the Greek and Roman times. I would not expect much antiquity to be found near the Greek cemetery, since, in the old days, it was at the edge of the town of Abella. In addition to our visit to the colosseum, we visited a local artist who painted landscapes of local scenery. We bought a painting of the market place near where the bridge was blown up by the Americans. In the studio I noticed a black marble sculpture about 18 inches high which preceded Roman times; perhaps, it was Greek. It was truly beautiful and I was told that it was dug up near the colosseum. Everything was for sale in that studio. Obviously, I am not the only one in Avella to have surmised where to dig in Avella for antique Roman and Greek artifacts. My cousin tells me that a number of people in town have established businesses connected with the discovery of antiquities from the diggings.

For years the owner of the farm next to Nonno's was trying to hide the existence of the colosseum by putting a high fence along the dirt road separating the two farms. He was fearful that, if the national antiquity department of Italy heard about the finding, the government would confiscate the farm or pay minimally for it. Government assessors would have evaluated the farm at the lowest price possible. In essence, there were different levels of corruption in government for the owner to deal with. Ultimately, the owner could have been a two-time loser with the loss of the commercial business in the sale of olives and hazelnuts and the price of the farm itself. It was unavoidable that the colosseum would have been discovered, since it was too huge a structure to hide indefinitely.

At this point in time let's review where we were, historically, in the rest of the Italian campaign in WWII in the winter of 1944. The Allied army was bogged down at Monte Cassino where a Benedictine Monastery was located on top of the hill. Actually, there are two peaks separated by 200 yards and the Abbey was located on the lower peak. It was a steep climb from the town of Cassino below the two peaks. American, British, Australian, Indian, Polish, Canadian, among others, tried to climb to the peaks, to no avail. Monte Cassino was the epi-center of the so-called Gustav line formed by German soldiers [6, and 29].

The monastery itself was bombed by the Allies many times, but the Germans held out. The religious leader of the monastery was allowed to leave for Rome. The allied brain trust (mostly at Churchill instigation) decided to outflank Monte Cassino by landing British, colonial and American troops at Anzio and Nettuno [5, 32, 52, 54, 55, 56, 58, 68, 70, and 81], within one km of each other. They are on the Tyrrhenian Sea and located 20-30 miles southwest of Rome near the old road called Via Appia (route 7) and 45 miles northwest of Monte Cassino. The name of the operation was SHINGLE. In addition to this outflanking maneuver, the Allies brought more reinforcements to attack Monte Cassino; they were 8,000 mountain troops, referred to as the Goumiers, who were from Morocco, Algeria and Tunisia [30, 57, and 68]. The French Free Army in North Africa trained them, under the leadership of General Alphonse Juin.

The Goumier troops first showed up in Avella in the winter of 1944. The thinking in town was "another day another Army; we are still in purgatory". We were all wrong in our estimate of things to come. There was no parade or such when they arrived. In fact, no one in town knew that we had a new tenant in our farms. They were part of the contingent of colonial troops streaming into Avella. Their camp was on a farm located between the pool and the British camp, next to Nonno's farm. For about a month, both British and Goumier troops were camped next to each other. The British presence in town was like being in purgatory, and in a holding pattern until they left. On one hand it was euphoric to be rid of the Nazis and Fascists; on the other hand, it was agony to be starving with no means to improve our lot. It was truly tormenting to smell the aroma from the kitchens of the camping grounds. We could tell from the aroma what they were eating. Our house was located only two hundred yards from the camps.

The Goumiers appeared in town in bizarre uniforms – not like the British and German soldiers. The uniform looked like a loosely fit pajama with vertical brown and white streaks. Soon, we heard from various sources in town that their behavior was unlike that of the British and German soldiers. The British soldiers got drunk once in a while, but didn't bother the people. German soldiers went around town to round up able bodied people to do work for them at the camp or to send people to Germany or elsewhere. The Goumiers got drunk, rounded up people on the premises and raped them. They did not discriminate between men and women, or young and old. Anyone on two legs was fair game to them.

Typically, a group of Goumiers would enter a wine shop, consume all the wine in the store, and not pay. The British and German soldiers always paid. To add insult to injury the Goumiers would drink all the wine and payment consisted of raping the owner or clients who were in the premises. It was shocking behavior and defied all standards of civility. The reputation of these soldiers quickly circulated around town and, of course, people tended to embellish the worst behavior.

Fear prevailed. Nobody was seen on the street again and every store in town was closed. Shopping was done by appointment. The first time I saw the Goumiers marching in the street near my house, they looked menacing, waving their long knives and unshaven. I knew, even as a child, to stay away from these people. Often, they would come from the pool area nude, running up the dirt road to their camp. We scurried to our hiding place in the pigpen on sight of them.

One day around noon from a distance Francesca and I could hear them coming from the general direction of the pool. They made that unique shrieking and piercing sound that sent shivers up our spines. We could hear them from a distance, running like wild beasts in no particular direction but drifting toward town. The shrieking sound was getting louder and louder. No question about it, trouble was brewing and coming toward us fast. Francesca and I ran into the common portico connected to our house and, once inside, double locked the portone door. Francesca put a scarf around my face covering my nose and she did the same to herself.

This time we did not hide in the pigsty. We hid below the black slate slab that covered the toilet. This was the typical design of our toilets in those days, where a black slate slab covered a cesspool. A big hole was drilled through the center of the rectangular slab to simulate a regular toilet. The slab was lifted and we descended into a side space where we crouched into the empty cavity. Yes, the odor was terrible, but this was survival. Fortunately, the toilet was emptied out a couple of days before by our neighbor who shared the same portico and toilet. That was part of the maintenance requirement for our neighbor's entry into the portico. A false door was cut out from their single room to allow access to the portico and toilet. Fortunately, our neighbors left for the mountains to help with sheep grazing.

Their flooring had no tiles or anything else to maintain a dry floor during the rainy season. In order to stay warm in the winter they burned wood in the corner of the room. The room was always full of smoke for there was no chimney, but there was a small window to the street. These living conditions were the same as when our neighbors were tending the sheep on the high mountains. At that, he sensed danger and escaped to the hills in order to get away from the Goumiers. In fact, most of the shepherd community left town for the hills once word got out about the Goumiers.

The Goumier soldiers came knocking on our portone. After a brief interlude, they demolished the portone by blowing it up with hand-grenades. The thickness of the portone was about six inches, but the explosion blew the door out and made a huge hole through it. We heard the explosion as it reverberated throughout the entire building. It was a miracle that I did not fall into the filthy slime. My mother grabbed me by the scarf, almost chocking me. The shrieking voices were getting closer and closer until we heard footsteps leading to the pigsty. They kicked in the door to the pigsty. The brick oven furnace above the pig sty was empty of any bread, fortunately. They must have seen us in the street running toward our house and gave chase. Obviously, they were stymied and there was a lull and dead silence.

Suddenly, they resumed their pursuit by descending the dry well next to the toilet room. The well adjoined our portico and that of the neighbor's open-air portico and courtyard. The other neighbor also left town for the hills. In essence, we were alone. We could hear shouting and arguing among them about our whereabouts.

Trying to draw our attention, they ransacked the downstairs and upstairs parts of the house and took whatever little food there was as well as mementos from Francesca's wedding, mostly silver items. Once they got to the open air veranda on the second floor, they were able to climb on our roof and run to other people's roofs and surprise some neighbors. In retrospect, we could not have stayed there any longer. I could not breathe and was covered with sweat. I needed to come up and get some air. It seemed like we were in that cesspool forever. We waited until we couldn't hear any voices or sounds. Time was irrelevant. Life and death were definitely relevant. Although we suffered down there, we were not about to come up for air.

However, we heard commotion in the background and a faint voice coming from the portico entrance. Francesca recognized the voice of our neighbor Serafina. We slowly pushed the black slab out of the way. When we opened the door to the toilet, she could not believe that we had survived the ordeal. Our house looked as though an earthquake had hit it. Items were thrown all over the place. Neighbors on the other side of the toilet door, were asking us what happened. We were too numb, shocked and simply overwhelmed as to what really happened to answer any questions. To say that they were apprehensive was an understatement. They just milled around taking in the damage done to our house. Remarkably, the living quarters of our next door neighbor were untouched.

There were still fumes from the explosions and one huge hole through the portone. The door to the dining room was off its hinges and whatever little food that we had was scattered all over the place. The special cabinet in the second floor bedroom, containing all of the mementos from Francesca's wedding, was shattered with all the silver items gone. Most ceramic items were smashed against the walls. These mementos in themselves were not important to us but, to Francesca, they were important for one sentimental reason; they were delicately preserved by Francesca for the day Caterina would be married. However, it is puzzling to me today as to why Francesca didn't barter those mementos for food at that time, in view of the fact that Caterina died the year before. All the flower pots that had adorned the steps to the bedroom were also smashed to pieces against the neighbor's wall. We smelled awful and ran to take baths many times over until we couldn't smell foul odor any more. We were lucky, because, while the Goumiers were searching for us, none of them had the urge to use the toilet. By now, I was four years old, but I felt like forty. I saw two extremes, life and death, in front of my eyes. Whereas Dante Alighieri, in his "Divine Comedy", talked about atrocities in the journey from purgatory to hell as an abstract or imaginary idea, here it was, a real journey on this earth, to hell. We were in a state of purgatory with the appearance of British troops in town and just entered hell on earth with the Goumiers in town. Under these circumstances we had no desire to be liberated by the Goumiers or the British or from any other foreign Army.

My wife and I have often visited the museums in the Vatican. Hell is depicted in the paintings as occurring in some mystical world, not of this earth. There was nothing mystical about the Goumiers. They violated every code of human decency or moral and religious ethics that civilized mankind ever invented. Yet, General Alphonse Juin (General of the French Expedition Force) was never indicted at the Nuremberg trials after the war. They violated the 1907 Hague convention on rules of war by their behavior to civilians. There was enough evidence in Avella and many other towns to be presented in court and to convict General Juin. There was so much outcry about this behavior that the Goumiers were not allowed on French territory during the Normandy invasion, a half-year later

Mother's house was on the right side of the road at the corner of the intersection. The road led directly to the dirt road and Nonno's farm. Our balcony was facing Serafina's balcony on the other side of the street. At the intersection the teen-ager was apprehended by German soldiers. Foreign troops usually approached town from the road to the left of the intersection. Our portone (door) leading into the common portico and toilet was just below the second balcony from the intersection. The next two residences belonged to shepherd families and the dry well was located in between our portico and the shepherd's portico. Photo courtesy of Anmarie Vittoria, 1981.

Clearly, the French Army deployed the Goumiers in Avella not as liberators, but as evil doers. The Goumiers were never looked upon as liberators for they were never allowed on French soil. They were unleashed on the locals as a form of reprisal for past transgressions of Fascists on the French Army. However, all the Fascists in Avella left before the Goumiers appeared in town. Even if Avella were full of Fascists, it did not justify the behavior of the Goumiers who were under full control of the French expeditionary command. The Goumiers were just terrible soldiers who did terrible things and basically did not adapt to modern civilization.

Lucky for Sebastiano, he was in Nonno's house, never aware of what was happening at home. The day after the attack we had visits from Nonno, all the aunts and more neighbors. Francesca's cousin Don Camillo came from the hills to check on us. Apparently, word spread all the way to the mountains as to what happened to us. It was decided that our family could no longer stay in Francesca's house. The fear was that the Goumiers would be back. For us to hide in the mountains was out of the question. Sebastiano and I would not last more than a couple of days due to the terrible winter winds on the mountains. Shepherds like my mother could manage. The only option was Nonno's house. The three of us slept in one room no bigger than a large closet for three months. It was either that or live in fear of the Goumiers. It was great for me, as I no longer had to commute between Nonno's and mother's houses looking for food.

I shudder to think of what happened to those poor people on the other side of our building. Our neighbors on the other side of the roof were my friend, Stefano, his mother, grandmother and brother Nicola. As I previously said, their father died in Libya, like my father. The town was subdued and worried about living from one day to another. We were nervous and apprehensive, continuously looking over our shoulders to make sure that the Goumiers did not sneak up on us. The neighbors kept a vigil over the comings and goings of soldiers camped on the farms. Our house was an ideal observation post to see soldiers approaching the town.

Whereas German and British occupation troops rarely ventured into the shepherds' territory in the mountains, the Gourmiers had no qualms about going there and helping themselves in slaughtering sheep or goats to have a feast. After all, they were basically nomads whose special skills were in the use of knifes and they were at peace up in the mountains.

A trap was laid out by the shepherds. Two Goumiers were enticed to visit a shepherd family in the hills for wine, roasted goats and sex. The Gourmiers were drugged as more shepherds joined the so-called festivities. The two Goumiers were tied on the flat surface of the table and the shepherds performed surgery for the first time in their lives. The Goumiers were castrated and allowed to bleed to death. The bodies were carried back to the entrance of the Goumiers' camp. The message was delivered as both the shepherds and the Goumiers understood the same unwritten language of nomads.

FIVE
TURNING POINT

In the winter of 1944, British troops camping on Nonno's farm left town led by a marching band of Scottish bagpipers. Infantry soldiers left by the dirt road, passing in front of the cemetery toward Baiano. Artillery troops, heavy tanks, trucks and cannons left by the paved roads routed behind the cemetery toward Baiano. Australian, New Zealand, Nepalese (Gurkhas) and British troops marched on Via Appia heading north. With me on his shoulder, Nonno and I watched the infantry soldiers and the Scottish bagpipers, who were resplendent in their colorful uniforms. In contrast to retreating German troops, the Allied troops looked rested and did not point their guns at anybody in the crowd.

For next month or two, we were stuck with the Goumiers in Avella. The whole town dreaded the situation of being left alone with the Goumiers. That was truly a depressing state of affairs. The thought of being left alone with uncivilized soldiers must have driven a lot people to near insanity, including my family. However, the number of incidents involving Goumiers with the locals seemed to quiet down. For one thing, the shepherds were still hiding in the mountains, especially after performing surgery on the Goumier soldiers. News of the "surgery" must have inhibited the Goumiers' activities in town.
Although Gourmiers left behind a bad reputation and legacy in the Naples area, few of them were good samaritans. Some of them were shepherds who loved to be on the mountains and owned sheep back home. According to Francesca, some of these Gourmiers showed up at the mountain shacks, where shepherds from Avella rested at night, wanting to come along with the locals roaming all over the hills with the

sheep and help out. Of course, the locals were frightened to death upon seeing these "shepherds" at the shack early in the morning, but soon the locals were re-assured of their good intentions.

The art of shepherding is as old as time itself. All that is needed are fields of grass. After each grazing sessions they actually paid in Lire for milk and baby goats to take back to their camp. It was good business for the local shepherds for they made money, got help and did not have to carry milk into town to sell it.

In early March, 1944, the Goumiers left, heading north of Avella. They must have gone in the middle of the night for I never saw or heard them. The only indirect evidence that they left camp was when shepherds began to return from the mountains. They brought the news of the Goumiers' departure. Apparently, the townies were not the only ones keeping an eye on the Goumiers.

There was no celebration or even acknowledgement that the Goumiers left town. It was one big relief. For us, it removed that one major worry about being tracked down by them, since that episode in our portico. We could now sleep at night without worrying about them coming back to our house. The portone door to our portico was still missing. Since Joe remained in hiding, the portone was not going to be fixed soon. Uncle Joe wanted to put some distance in time, before coming out of hiding. He was afraid of possible remaining Fascist or Communist activists in town.

When the shepherds returned from the mountains, they found their homes intact, remarkably. Our shepherd neighbors thanked us profusely, but we didn't feel we had done anything. I suppose that since we were the targets, the Goumiers did not bother with their homes. Don Camillo and other shepherds in the neighborhood helped us put things back in order and do repairs on the furniture in the house. Nonno helped the neighbor who was owner of the wine store which was raided by the Goumiers. Nonno was very handy with repairing equipment used to make wine. Before the war Nonno also owned a wine store and he was getting wine produced by the same neighbor. During the war, Nonno did not have money to purchase wine from him, but after the war Nonno resumed buying and selling the wine. Their relationship was one of friendship rather than competition.

Nonno waited a couple of weeks, after the Goumiers' departure, before he visited his farm, taking me along. By this time I could get around much better and ventured into the next farm where the Gourmiers camped before. He immediately put the fear of God in me by saying that at no time was I allowed to step into that farm. He was stern and meant business, and I knew when he meant business.

Nonno's farm looked like a tornado came through it. The farmhand's (parsonale) living quarter was demolished and the livestock gone. All the fruit trees were cut except for the cherry tree. Interestingly, the cherry tree was adorned with stones painted white circling the tree. I never understood the significance of that. All the Army barracks disappeared, but there were side boards, wooden frames and doors strewn all over the farm. What had once been neatly arranged white painted rocks, there were then randomly white rocks strewn all over the farm. The farm was a total mess in no condition to produce anything, especially in the middle of winter.

Further examination of the caves next to Nonno's farm revealed that the British dumped everything including all kitchen items, office tables, beaten up generators, parts of jeeps, paper supplies, benzene cans, petrol items, but no food, not even a single egg! That was a big disappointment for I vividly remembered the smell of bacon and eggs, when we visited the camp before. Nonno did not get paid a single shilling for all that mess that the Brits produced. Yet, in the farm below Nonno's, not a tree was cut and all foliage was ready to burst into blossom. The contrast only proves one thing: life is not fair. To add insult to injury, British soldiers were well aware of the colosseum. It is certain that some of the Roman antiquities were carted away, when they left town. It did not take long for all of the items found in the caves to disappear. People from all over town scavenged the caves for whatever they could find. Even out of towners came by to see what could be scavenged. The German plane that was downed in the farm next to Nonno's farm during the Salerno invasion disappeared by winter time, 1944. Times were desperate for our family and everyone else in town. It took about a couple of years to get Nonno's farm in condition to be productive and build up the livestock for the farmhand. The farmhand utilized a lot of the wood and metal scraps in the caves to build his living quarters.

Towns in the vicinity also suffered during occupation. After the Germans left camp in Avella, they blew up the railroad station at Nola. As noted earlier Nola was and is the center of transportation and communication in the whole area. In effect, a lot of little towns were isolated from the rest of the world for about a year. To this day there are mementos of the destruction caused by the Germans Allied bombing at the railroad stations from Baiano to Naples. Tracks, unexploded bombs and damaged train wagons are on display at railroad stations.

British colonial troops were shipped to Anzio and Monte Cassino to reinforce the Allied front, and the Goumiers were sent to the Monte Cassino front. The Goumiers s pecialize in mountain warfare and used knives, bazookas and hand grenades as weapons. German soldiers suffered heavy casualties confronting the Goumiers up in the mountains near Monte Cassino. It was rumored that some German soldiers on Monte Cassino, who were veterans of the Russian front, wanted to be sent back to that front, when they were attacked by the Goumiers with knives at night. In many ways the failures at Anzio and at Monte Cassino directly introduced the people of Avella to the Gourmies. There would have been no military reason to bring the Gourmiers to Italy, if the allies had succeeded at Anzio.

The General in charge of operation SHINGLE (Anzio beach landing) was John Lucas. His commander was General Mark Clark who was overall commander of the American Fifth Army. General Clark was a former student of Lucas at the military academy in West Point, NY. Whereas General Clark was ambitious, General Lucas was less so and more cautious. The field command was a favor by his friends in the General staff for the purpose of promoting him to the rank of Lieutenant General (three star General). His expertise lay in the training of soldiers, management and shipments of materiel to and from combat zones. Anzio represented the first major combat mission for him. However, the mission called for an opportunistic or aggressive General who could capitalize or seize a military opportunity, if it presented itself. There was a small window of opportunity. From the Salerno invasion, it was learned that the Germans could amass as many as 8-10 divisions in a matter of 7-10 days which was significantly more soldiers than allocated by the Allied General staff for the invasion of Anzio. This meant that the Allies had to land all of their troops, about three divisions and tanks, in less than a week and take advantage of the short time superiority. The most crucial part of the plan was to achieve complete surprise in the landing. The opportunity did indeed present itself.

The landing at Anzio caught the Germans with their pants down, literally. In fact, some German soldiers were awakened at about two or three in the morning of January 22, 1944. In their haste to try to get dressed and go to the beach to investigate the landing, they ran there undressed, no pants. Most of them were killed. The element of surprise was total. In the history of military tactics dating back to Roman times, the greatest goal of an attack is to achieve the element of complete surprise and the invasion at Anzio achieved the ultimate goal in warfare! In fact, the road to Rome was open from Anzio. Only two SS-police battalions were defending Rome, and they were not in a position to do combat but police work (not part of any infantry division). They were the equivalent of our MP (military police).

Lieutenant John T. Cummings of the US Army was ordered to take a reconnaissance ride in the area toward Rome (see Robert Katz' book, THE BATTLE FOR ROME, [11]). Around 9:00 am on the day of the invasion, he drove his jeep along the Appian Way, the old Roman road, nowadays called Highway 7, all the way to the Tiber River in Rome and back. He did not encounter one German soldier. Yes, this story has been re-told many times in other books. It is worth repeating it, for it was unforgiveable for what happened after that ride. Paul Revere's ride on horseback in 1775 changed history in America, but this ride brought disaster to the American Army at Anzio. Also, the failure to take advantage of this military opportunity allowed for the entry of Goumiers into Southern Italy. Cumming's scouting report was ignored or conveniently lost.

There are two schools of thought as to what General Lucas should have done. One plan was expressed so eloquently by General Clark, when he was quoted as saying: "Don't stick your neck out, Johnny". As a matter of fact not only did Lucas not stick his neck out, his soldiers were ordered to do the same. It cost his job about 10 days later and led to the fiasco at Anzio with which he is identified. Lucas' assumption was that he could increase the beach-head in terms of men and materiel at a faster rate than the Germans. He ignored the lessons learned at Salerno. Clearly, he was biased toward what he learned to do best, the control of flow of soldiers and materiel from and to the combat zone. He was a victim of his training as a supply officer. It was difficult to defend this premise of Lucas due to the fact that the pool of American soldiers and materiel was 4000-5000 miles away (USA) and the German pool of soldiers was within a radius of 400miles away (Balkans, North Italy, France, and Austria). The British Army was maxed out ever since the retreat at Dunkirk. Mostly colonial troops made up the British Army contingency. Sitting around the beach waiting for the German buildup and onslaught was clearly not the solution, and it came within 7-10 days after the landing. In view of Salerno, this was no surprise.

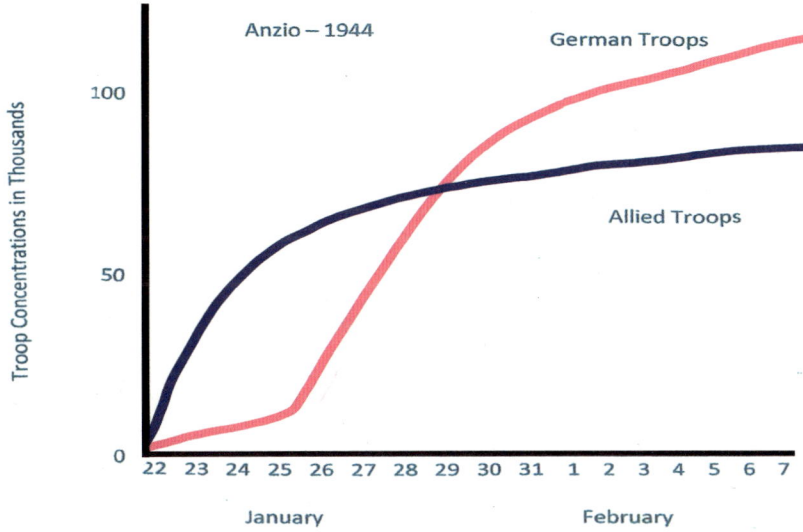

The above plot was deduced by this author on the basis of war reports at the time of the invasion of Anzio by the Allies. The reports are readily available in published books on the Anzio invasion in WW II.

The Germans were able to increase the number of soldiers at Anzio and exceeded the number of Allied troops on the beach area (see the chart above). Thereafter, the Germans amassed troops at a much faster rate than the Allies. Obviously, Lucas' assumption was incorrect and it cost a lot of American lives at Anzio. The Germans almost "drove" the Allies back to the sea. Bombardment from the US and British Navy boats and air supremacy stabilized the front on the beach.

It didn't have to happen that way. The landing at Anzio never provided the necessary military support to unlock the Cassino stalemate. Hence, the need for the Goumiers. Ironically, as it turned out, it was the other way around. With assistance from the Goumiers, the breakthrough of the Cassino front by the Allies in late April was possible and, therefore, relieved the pressure by the Germans at Anzio in late May, 1944. The proponent of the other school of thought was led by the architect of the SHINGLE operation, Prime Minister of Britain Winston Churchill

[28, 41, and 64]. His strategy called for the seizure of the high ground at the Alban hills as soon as landing was secured. The argument against this approach led by the American General Staff was that the Allies did not have enough manpower in the Mediterranean arena in terms of shipping, men and materiel to seize both the beach and the high grounds. The Americans won out in the internal debate, since they basically provided more shipping, planes, etc. than the British. Furthermore, Americans by now were more preoccupied with the Atlantic invasion at Normandy so that most of the investments were allocated for the preparation of the Atlantic invasion. So, about 3 divisions were designated for the Anzio invasion. As such, the Churchill plan was to have approximately one division take the Alban hills and the remainder of the divisions take up defensivee positions at the Anzio beach head.

The basic difference between the two plans was the number of troops to be deployed on the Alban hills. One plan (American) called for zero [68] amount of troops and the other (British) about 15,000-20,000 soldiers. Let's address the fundamental question: was there a number in between those two numbers that would have been sufficient to accomplish the mission. Let's bring some facts to light so that the readers may conclude for themselves.

According to the German General [70] in charge of the military occupation of South Italy and German strategies, Field Marshal Albert Kesselring, he was dismayed and pleasantly surprised that the Allies did not go for the Alban hills. In his book, SOLDAT, written after the war he stated that had the Allies landed as few as 300-400 soldiers on the Alban hills he would have to think long and hard to dismantle the Cassino front. In a reverse order, when the Germans had the high Alban hills ground and the Allies tried to climb up the Alban hills, the American 36th Army division was bogged down at the foothills of the Alban hills near Velletri. These hills were manned by no more than 300 German troops!

The implication here according to German thinking at that time was that with only 300 troops they planned to neutralize a whole Allied division! Indeed, German troops achieved exactly that with minimum deployment of their soldiers on the Alban hills. He, Kesselring, could not afford at that time to tie up a division to climb up the Alban hills, had the Allies occupied them with a minimal force. Kesselring simply did not have the manpower to attack the beach head and the Alban hills at the same time. Furthermore, Kesselring would have had no knowledge how many Allied troops were deployed on the Alban Hills. It would have been this unknown factor that would have driven the Germans out of Cassino and Anzio.

In summary, fate handed the Allied Army a complete surprise and the high grounds at Anzio and they did not know what to do with it. American military leadership was not creative enough to exploit the situation and really did not understand the German mentality about warfare. The prevalent thinking of the German General Staff was that high grounds translated to deployment of a large number of troops. General Mark Clark enjoyed the celebrity of being the first general in military history to have conquered Rome from the south. Yet, it was ironical that the generals he was comparing himself to (in Roman times) all understood the advantages of high grounds and the element of military surprise.

The American soldiers paid a heavy price at Salerno and Anzio for his lack of understanding the fundamental military credo of high grounds. In the words of Churchill: "I thought we had flung a wildcat into the Alban Hills, but, instead, got a whale floundering on the beach". Churchill was half right. There are no whales in the Mediterranean Sea. Personally, the failure at Anzio allowed for the introduction of the Goumier soldiers in Avella and that was a painful disaster for the people of Avella that they will never forget or forgive. Success at Anzio would have meant no need for the Goumier troops to rescue the Allies at Cassino and, thereby helping the breakout at Anzio. The Naples area and the American soldiers suffered the consequences of the errors at Anzio.

German troops at Monte Cassino were veteran soldiers of the Afrika Korps and Russian campaigns under the command of General Frido von Senger und Utterling (General Senger) [63]. They positioned themselves on top of two mountain chains separated by the Liri valley running north-south. More importantly, they used caves as a cover during bombing raids by the Allies, much like in Avella during their occupation. Again the Germans occupied the high grounds. The approach to the valley, by any military means, from the south was utterly suicidal, since the firepower from the high grounds on both sides of the valley was precise and strong.

Highway 6 (Via Casilina) ran through the valley parallel to the Liri River. The Garigliano River flowed west-east from the Tyrrhenian Sea up to the town of Cassino. East of Cassino the river changed its name to Rapido River. Allied troops crossed the Rapido River and there were many futile attempts to climb the hill to the monastery. The Garigliano River was never crossed for the mountains across the river were too steep to climb until the Goumiers showed up at the scene in April. The Goumiers swarmed all over the mountains east of Cassino and reached the top of the mountains within two days.

In the villages of Patricia, Pofi, Isoletta and Morolo females were violated. In Lenola alone fifty women were raped as well as children and old men. Sometimes there were multiple rapists. In Castro di Volsci doctors treated 300 victims of rape and at Ceccano British troops built a fence to protect Italian women. Many Goumiers had deserted the army and were attacking villages well south of Monte Cassino, toward the Naples area near Avella. These Goumier deserters never made it back to Avella. Shepherds of Avella would have taken special medical care of the Goumiers in practicing surgery again. The word was out in town to look for Goumier deserters. For example, the inevitable had happened with the murder of five Goumiers in a village near Cancello, three miles from Avella. They were again enticed into a house with the offer of women, and then given food or wine containing paralytic rat poison often used by farmers. While fully conscious they were castrated, and then beheaded. The bodies were buried under cabbages, which were dug up and then replanted over them in several village gardens. These crimes committed by the local people were never reported in local or national newspapers.

Within a week the Goumiers reached the outskirts of the town of Pontecorvo, behind enemy lines east of Cassino. The battle for Cassino was over. The Goumiers took no prisoners, and advanced past the Monte Cassino front held by German soldiers. However, the Germans controlled access to the Liri valley below, since they occupied the high grounds on both sides of the valley. In order for the Germans to secure an exit on Highway 6, General Kesselring ordered withdrawal of troops from Monte Cassino in late-april, 1944. Via Casilina is a direct route to Rome and it was built after Via Appia in Roman days. Of course, the news was welcomed in Allied capitals and especially at Anzio where they were still hemmed in on the beach. It was time to go on the counter-attack as the Germans were retreating on Via Casilina in the Liri valley or on the run toward Rome.

The German army was trapped between Cassino and Rome provided the breakout from Anzio reached via Casilina and the nearby area of the town of Valmontone (near Rome) before the German army arrived there. However, the lure of entering Rome first was too great for General Clark. His army at Anzio (Fifth American Army) cut across the Alban hills to reach the outskirts of Rome on June 3, 1944 and never tried to cut off the retreating German Army on Via Casilina. In fact, in the haste of getting there, General Clark was shot at by a German sniper. The sniper shot at him while holding a road sign of Rome in his hands. General Clark ordered a small group of soldiers to the Valmontone area (Via Casilina) to give the appearance of obeying orders in turning back the Germans there. However, American troops arrived too late to trap any German troops. This allowed the whole German Army to retreat intact north of Rome safely away from the pursuing Allied armies from the south. Eventually, these troops were deployed in Normandy to oppose the invasion, only to delay the War. In Rome, General Clark spent most of his time giving interviews of the great battle for Anzio and the conquest of Rome while standing next to a statue of Aurelius.

In the pursuit of the German army from Monte Cassino there were troops from Poland, India, Brazil, New Zealand, Canada, USA, Britain, France, Italy, Morocco, Algeria and Tunisia (Goumiers). The Goumiers chased the German troops in the town of Frosinone and introduced hell again on earth in this town. Let me quote two victims from that time [11]. "They came here by the thousands coming down the mountainside, looking like tiny ants from far away. Really it was like a plague going through and creating hell for three days. They were an ugly, filthy lot, rings through their noses, long robes, eyes bulging. All over the mountain you could hear the screaming and the groans. Two of them threw me to the ground, but when they realized I had my period, they ran off. They were beasts and that's how they conducted themselves. Germans took animals and destroyed everything, but were better behaved. And these Moroccans were supposed to be our liberators! They took children and had their way with them. Our husbands, brothers, fathers were beaten back and killed".

Another victim's quotation follows. "We were expecting the liberators and what we got was something else, a people of another breed. How ugly they were! They seemed possessed by demons. They robbed what little we had left and ran havoc over the people. They had been given a free hand and they did all those dirty things to the men and women. It was a slaughter. They came out of every nook and cranny, taking all the women they saw and carrying us off into the brush. There were officers with them, white men, the French, and they didn't do a thing to stop them. We were a joke to the commanders. They told us that the only way you could make the Moroccans go away was to let them do what they want."

The same atrocities were committed in Rome, when the Goumiers arrived. However, the trail of their whereabouts grew faint after that. Certainly, they were not allowed in France or to participate in the Normandy invasion. Perhaps, there was no need for mountain troops in the Normandy invasion. An ulterior motive for excluding them was that French officers could not afford to submit the French people to the Goumiers' indecencies.

Was there any possible way to avoid all the suffering, killings, rapes, and battles in Salerno, Anzio and Cassino? Yes, all was avoidable. First of all, Mark Clark was not the right man for the job as he never learned the lessons of military history, although he attended a military school. Secondly, according to General George S. Patton [92] who advised, after the landing in Sicily, that an invasion of Italy North of Rome would neutralize all of the German troops retreating from Sicily. Airport facilities in Sardegna and/or Corsica would have provided the necessary air cover required for the invasion north of Rome. Those two islands were poorly defended by the Italian army. The latter mission could have been achieved even with the limited resources available at that time. For example, German troops left Sardegna on Septeber 10, 1943 and the Islands were there for the taking.

The Germans had no other choice but to leave the Island of Sardegna. As in Sicily, 16,000 German troops left the island of Sardegna by ferry boats at night to Italy. It would have been extremely difficult for German troops to be reinforced on the island. The Allies controlled the skies and the sea in the Mediterranean theater and the ferry boats was the only transportation to escape the island. Thus, German troops were not in a position to take a military stand, since they were isolated. The fundamental question to address now is: did the Allies recognize the bad predicament that the Germans were in the island of Sardegna? I believe that the Allies knew that, but chose not to do anything about it. Since Allied planners were committed to the Salerno invasion, the Allies could not commit any other troops elsewhere. Besides, the Allies assumed that without reinforcements, the effectiveness of the German troops on the island as a fighting force would whither away with time. That wishful thinking did not materialize, as the Germans did not wait around in Sardegna to be captured.

By August and September, 1943, the Italian government was in shambles and everyone knew that, including Hitler. As such, Hitler already set in motion the splitting of Italy into two zones [14]. The northern zone was to be under the command of Field Marshal Rommel and the Southern to be commanded by Field Marshal Kesselring. By invading North of Rome it would have 1) cut off supplies to the South and 2) forced the German Army to fight uphill from the North and South of Rome. The side benefit from this invasion would have enrolled all those Italian soldiers who saw no purpose in defending a bankrupt government, either Fascist or Royal. There were eight to ten Italian divisions in the vicinity of Rome. Also, there were as many Italian troops (10 divisions) in the Balkans who would have aided the cause once the invasion was in place, coordinated with Italian troops north of Rome.

Brigadier general Maxwell D. Taylor risked his life to discuss with General Pietro Badoglio of Italy the possibility of landing the 82nd Airborne Division north of Rome in September 8, 1943. He was driven in a medical ambulance hundreds of miles behind enemy lines. The plan was to invade simultaneously both the beaches of Salerno and north of Rome. General Badoglio suggested that more than one American division be deployed north of Rome. Taylor decided to pull back the deployment of the 82nd Airborne Division. The plan was flawed for a number of reasons. First, the air coverage would have been weakened north of Rome; planes had to fly from Sicily which was a long distance to north of Rome. Second, Americans had to rely on the Italian army near Rome for assistance in case German troops began to appear in the vicinity of Rome. One American division alone would not have been sufficient to hold off any counter-attacks by the Germans. The German Army was very skillful in amassing large numbers of troops anywhere in Italy on a short notice. In summary, the plans for Salerno were deeply flawed as the invasion should have been diverted to the island of Sardegna instead of Salerno in order to shorten air coverage for an invasion north of Rome.

Generals Taylor and Badoglio meeting in Brindisi, fall of 1943 [108].

The idea of invading North of Rome would have been feasible, if planes were to fly from Sardegna, rather than from Sicily, as suggested by General Patton. It was reprehensible for these planners not to recognize the advantages of taking over the island so near to Rome. The deployment of more than one division in Rome under the protection of air fields in Sardegna would have encouraged the remnants of the Italian Army to participate in the battle for Rome and to trap the German army in the South of Italy, according to Peter Tompkins' book, "Italy Betrayed", [21]. Furthermore, there would have been no incentive for the Germans to occupy Rome, when airfields from Sardegna would have been so close to Rome.

History books have parroted [59] the party line put forward by the American General staff that Sardegna was too far away from Sicily to provide air coverage for an invasion of the island. This party line reminds me so much of the Neapolitan proverb that states: with a little bit of truth one may hide the big lie. The little truth was that the distance from Sicily to Sardegna was slightly beyond the air coverage needed for an invasion there. The big lie was that Sardegna was occupied by German troops. Historical facts have shown that Sardegna was void of a single German soldier in early September [21]. Hence, there was no need for air coverage to invade Sardegna. As such, the cost of human lives would have been minimal or none. American decision makers were hell bent on Salerno no matter what costs and it resulted in heavy American and British casualties.

General Patton advocated the taking of Sardegna well before September 8, when collaboration between the Italian and American armies was possible, after Taylor's visit to Rome. Patton's plan did not even have merit as a contingent plan by the General Staff. Historically, General Patton's plan was rejected for personal, rather than military reasons. The unfamiliarity of the Italian terrain in the winter and poor logistic use of airfields in Italy resulted in 1 million casualties of soldiers and countless atrocities to the people of southern Italy. Obviously, it mattered not a bit to the American General staff or Government officials as to how the war was planned as they never had to shed any blood of their own and experience the atrocities of war at the hands of soldiers like the Goumiers.

Historically, the islands of Corsica and Sardegna were occupied by the Allies in late September of 1943. Corsica and Sardegna are neighboring Islands close to the Italian and French coastlines. This shortened the air coverage for the invasions of Southern France and of Normandy [95]. It was pivotal for Generals Patton [92], from the west, and Devers, from the south of France, to approach the Battle of the Bulge simultaneously to relieve Bastogne [95, 59]. General Clark [68] argued that by keeping a standing Army in Italy, it tied down German troops in Northern Italy which otherwise could have been deployed in France. Historical facts do not corroborate this argument. The Germans were able to siphon off troops from North Italy to France. Even their Marshal, Kesselring [77], was transferred to France. In early 1945, there were at most two to three German divisions stationed in Northern Italy compared to more than twenty-five divisions available in the heat of battles at Anzio and Cassino [77, 68, and 81]. Clearly, the utilization of those two islands for air coverage helped immensely in the invasion of France, not the stationary Allied troops in Southern Italy. It would have shortened the war even more, if the same air coverage from Sardegna would have been provided during an invasion into north of Rome by the Allies.

SIX
VIA ARDEATINA MASSACRE

Let me now recount events that led to the massacre at the Ardeatina caves in Rome and how our beloved friend, Zio Renato, was abducted by the Germans in their reprisal. This story has been reported many times before, but it is worth bringing it up again, since new evidences, as divulged by Zio Renato, who has revealed for the first time the true intent of the Gestapo during those events. After receiving his medical doctor's degree from the University of Naples, he apprenticed for two years as a heart surgeon at the University hospital in Naples before the war. After the apprenticeship, Zio was employed permanently at a Hospital in Rome near Via Appia. He practiced as a surgeon during the war in Rome and, as a medical doctor, he was exempted from military duty. Zio met his wife-to-be, Sarah, at the hospital, when he was a surgeon there. Most of what I am about to tell you was related to me from him, but the events leading up to the massacre at Via Ardeatina can be researched in many books, including the book entitled: THE BATTLE FOR ROME by Robert Katz [11].

March 23 was an important date for the Fascists, because in 1944 it marked the 20th anniversary of the Fascist government in Italy. However, the Nazis let it be known that there was not going to be any Fascist celebration that year in order not to provoke the partisans in Rome. But no matter, the partisans were planning an attack on German troops on that day. A partisan cell of eight to ten partisans planned to attack. One member of the cell was a woman who played a pivotal role in the plan. Her fiancé was a medical student at the University of Rome. The plan called for an attack on the 11th Company of the 3rd Battalion of the SS Polizeiregiment Bozen. The soldiers were from Bolzano, South Tyrol, which had been part of an Italian province in the Alps since 1870.

The inhabitants of Tyrol were and are German-speaking, but Italian citizens. The province was annexed into the Greater German Reich (Alpenvorland) in 1943. After the war, they voted in a referendum to return to the original province as Italian citizens.

However, the partisans were not aware of the fact that soldiers of the 11th Company were from Bolzano (Bozen in German), an Italian province. It is an interesting question now to ask the following: had the partisans known that the soldiers were from Bolzano would they have attacked? In my many visits to Rome I have repeatedly asked that question of my esteemed colleagues at the University of Rome and elsewhere. Most of the answers were in the negative. Some people today in Rome argue that the action by the partisans on Via Rasella constituted as an act of civil war. There remains no proof to this day that the partisans knew the identity of the soldiers.

The 11th Company consisted of 160 men under the leadership of Lieutenant Fritz Volgast (translates to "full of gas"). The battalion commander was Major Hellmuth Dobbrick. The Company was not part of an infantry division. Basically, they were military policemen keeping civil order in Rome. Their immediate supervisor was Colonel Herbert Kappler of the Gestapo in Rome. Kappler was an ambitious man who loved his stay in Rome. Before the war, he vacationed there often. This was not unusual for there were many Nazis in Rome then who were Italophiles roaming in Italy. There was a love-hate relationship between Kappler and the Romans. He loved the weather, the food and the ancient culture, but hated the deceitful behavior of Romans, according to him. Every day, the Company from Bolzano marched in a column of twos through the heart of Rome led by "full of gas", armed and looking menacing and repugnant to the people of Rome. As they marched they would sing a song called "Hupf, Mein Madel" (Skip, My Lassie). They would march from approximately Piazza del Popolo to Via Rasella, bypassing Piazza di Spagna. An armored vehicle mounted with a machine gun trailed the policemen up on Via Rasella. The Company arrived at the bottom of Via Rasella at exactly 2pm each day. Once they marched up the incline at Via Rasella they would continue through historic Centro Storico to the living quarters at the Viminale barracks, their camp.

Via Rasella in Rome as viewed from the North end of the street. Palazzo Tittoni is the tallest building on the right side of the street. Photo courtesy of Anmarie Vittoria, 1981.

Via Rasella is located in the middle of the commercial district near piazza Barberini and Teatro dell'Opera. In Rome there are many districts whose main piazza is the center of social gatherings of residents and, thus, assume a character reflective of the residents. Usually, in districts located in the outskirts of Rome, residents consist mostly of new arrivals from other parts of Italy. Districts in the inner city of Rome, like the one in Via Rasella, residents are longtime residents and their ancestors go back many generations. For example, Romans who resided near Teatro Marcello, formerly known in the past as the Jewish Ghetto district, their ancestors date back to 100 BC. Via Rasella sits in a tranquil enclave surrounded by heavy traffic and shoppers frequenting nearby department stores and bistros. The Germans chose to march in this street to cause the least disturbance to the residents and vice-versa. After all, the German battalion of policemen were in the business of quelling disturbances or insurgencies instead of inciting one. The street was inhabited by middle class working people and it was kept relatively clean. Four to five bakery and butcher shops are located along the way, and it is about hundred meters long. One third of the way up from the bottom of the incline at the south end of Via Rasella, two side streets intersecteVia Rasella.

The German military police would be marching from south to north. Two thirds of the way up, Palazzo Tittoni was located. The plan was to place a cart full of explosives (used by street cleaners) in front of the Tittoni Palazzo. If and when the troops appeared on the scene at the south end, a partisan would remove his cap to signal both the coming of the troops and lighting of the fuse to explode the bombs in the cart. The bombs would explode 50 seconds after being lit. That was enough time for the partisan lighting the fuse to walk away toward the north end exit, Via Delle Quattro Fontane. His girl-friend and future wife would be waiting for the "street cleaner" with a hidden machine gun on hand. The timing of the fuse was such that the bomb would explode, when soldiers would be at the north end of Via Rasella. At the time of the explosion three partisans would appear from the side street to shoot mortar cannons. After 20 seconds four more partisans would appear at the south end of the street to protect the escape of all on the scene.

On paper everything works, but in reality nothing ever works according to plans. This is also known as Murphy's Law of experimental physics - nothing works on the first try. The German troops did not show up at 2:00 pm as expected. They showed up at 3:45 pm. As the fuse was to be lit, the portiere (concierge) from Palazzo Tittoni came out onto Via Rasella. He was told by the partisan (street cleaner) near the cart to get out. "Hell is going to break loose". The portiere disappeared very quickly. The entire attack took less than five minutes. The 11th Company ceased to exist. There were 32 dead soldiers and about 60 injured. There was a brief scuffle between the partisan's girl-friend and two Fascists on Via Delle Quattro Fontane, but as soon as she flashed her machine gun the Fascists ran away like rabbits. The mortar attack from the side streets by the partisans confused the German soldiers into thinking that they were being attacked from windows high on the sides of the buildings. The Germans began to shoot at windows hitting the side walls. The bullet holes on the wall are still there to this day.

Round up of civilians after the partisans' attack on Via Rasella.

In 1976 I visited Via Rasella and noticed those bullet holes on the side of the buildings. I inquired at a bakery shop as to why there were bullet holes on the side of the building? The answer came in the form of a question. "What bullet holes?" The word was mum. Of course, I knew what happened, but I wanted to get first-hand information about those events. Basically, the residents of Via Rasella still do not want to talk about that fateful incident. That is how controversially that episode in history is treated by Romans.

I did not give up on going back to Via Rasella. In 1980 I inquired again about the incident from an elder man who might have lived during that tragedy. Again, the same reaction. In the year 2000 the City of Rome asked their citizens to spruce up their buildings for the 2000 Jubilee year, sponsored by City Hall and the Vatican, by painting them. The residents of Via Rasella refused to cover up those bullet holes on their walls. Obviously, what happened in 1944 was very important to the residents, but not to the Vatican and the City of Rome.

When Hitler was telephoned about the Rasella attack, he demanded reprisal, to blow up the entire quarters of Via Rasella and vicinity demanding the killing of 30-50 civilians for each German soldier dead. After much wrangling [38, 66, 69, 71] among the Gestapo and German General Staff, General Eberhard Von Mackensen reduced the ratio to 10 civilians for each dead German soldier and no destruction or razing of buildings at or near Via Rasella. General Mackensen was in charge of the German Army defending against the Allied invasion at Anzio and Rome itself.

The German General staff proposed to execute persons who were condemned to death, and/or to life sentences by the courts. Criminals, who were most likely to be condemned to death, were included in the list of civilians to be executed. Gestapo chief Kappler was ordered by Field Marshal Albert Kesselring to make up the list of people to be executed and to carry out the executions within 24 hours. Again, the Marshal proceeded only after getting approval from headquarters in Berlin. This was important to all the German Officers involved in the reprisal. They knew that it was morally wrong, but they desperately wanted to wash their hands of the dirty affair by demanding higher authority each time. On the other hand, pressure from Berlin was mounting to follow through with the reprisal as quickly as possible. The Nazis in Rome fooled themselves into believing that they were just following orders or they were simply "covering their asses" in the future. Following orders was never accepted in military courts after the war, as a defense for their actions.

According to Kappler (Gestapo chief in Rome) [11], he was holding 290 prisoners at Gestapo jail on Via Tasso [43] in addition to the ones detained on site. After deliberating over the list, 280 prisoners were destined for execution at Via Tasso. Of the 280 prisoners, they included 70 Jewish prisoners who were destined for Auschwitz, far short of the required amount of 330. None of the prisoners were criminals condemned to death or to life sentences by the courts. Hence, they did not qualify to be on the list, according to General Mackensen edict. One more soldier died from wounds on the night of the 23rd. Kappler demanded from the warden of Regina Coeli jail, Italian prison on Via Lungotevere, 50 more "candidates" for execution. However, none of the 50 prisoners were condemned to death. Thus, Gestapo police went out in the streets of Rome to round up more "candidates".

In order to protect himself legally, Kappler demanded written approval from his superior to go forward with this madness. This request has perplexed me for years. If Kappler didn't believe in the execution of innocent people, why do it? I believe now that it was a sinister plot by him to transfer the culpability of the execution toward the General staff irrespective of the outcome of the war. Either way, he could claim to the Allies after the war that subordination to duty allowed only one action on his part. Indeed, that is what he claimed as a defense at his military trial after the war in Rome. On the other hand, he could claim to a Nazi inquiry, by written orders in his possession, that it was imposed on him by the General staff to make up the list. Either way, he washes his hands of the affair. There was no sympathy whatsoever toward those poor civilians selected for execution. They were innocent of any crime. His up-bringing as a Nazi from youth simply emptied out any feelings of sympathy that he might have felt for these poor souls.

Similarly, Pietro Caruso of the Regina Coeli jail also requested approval from his superior in the Fascist government to hand over 50 prisoners to the Gestapo. In the meantime the partisans were laying low waiting for the German reprisal.

By the morning of the 24th, Kappler completed the list of 330 civilians to be executed. The Vatican newspaper, L'Osservatore Romano, reported on the same morning that there was going to be the killings of 320, not 330. This meant that the Vatican was aware of the killings as of the 23rd. These facts have been reported by Robert Katz, page 241 of his book [11] which was de-classified by the Vatican in 1980.
In 1974, Pope Pius XII's niece, Countess Elena Pacelli Rossignani, charged Robert Katz, film director Carlo Ponti and director George P. Cosmatos with "defaming the memory" of Pope Pius XII who died in 1957. The three defendants claimed that there was enough evidence for the Pope to have known about the executions at Ardeatina and chose to keep silent about it. The final outcome of three trials against Katz, Ponti and Cosmatos was that the defendants were totally absolved of any wrong-doing or claims by the Pacellis.

By mid-morning of the 24th of March, 1944 an executioner was to be assigned. General Kurt Malzer [4], German General in charge of security in Rome, turned to Major Dobbrick as the commanding officer of the military police to avenge the fallen soldiers at Via Rasella. Dobbrick outright refused. Malzer and Kappler were shocked by the direct insubordination.

In retrospect, I understand this fully. If Dobbrick survived the war, he was going to go back to Tyrol and most likely he would have to explain his actions to an Italian audience. This sentiment was probably shared by most of the policemen of the 11th Company. Dobbrick was subsequently placed under house arrest by General Malzer for insubordination. The charges against Dobbrick were later dropped as the German Army was retreating in Italy. Dobbrick was killed by the partisans in Veneto and buried in Costermano (Verona) on July 5, 1944. He was portrayed in the film "Massacre in Rome" directed by Carlo Ponti and George Cosmatos. General Malzer turned to Colonel Hauser, of General Mackensen's staff, to do the honor of the execution. Colonel Hauser simply stated that the execution was strictly a police or Gestapo matter and not an Army matter! By default Kappler, Gestapo chief in Rome, was stuck with the execution at the Ardeatine caves.

It was macabre the way in which the Gestapo officers went about shooting the victims in the head and piling one by one on top of the other, inside the Ardeatine caves. Captain Erich Priebke of the Gestapo had the list of names and he was responsible for checking off the name of the person murdered. He also participated in the killing as well. Crammed into trucks, the prisoners were transported from Gestapo headquarters on Via Tasso to the Ardeatine caves in early afternoon. Shooting started at 3:30 pm and ended at about 10:30 pm.

Like Dobbrick, another soldier from Tyrol also refused to do any shooting of the prisoners inside the caves, although he was a Gestapo police officer. German engineers immediately mined the entrance to the caves and the tunnels leading to the entrances. The hope by the Gestapo was that the caves would serve as the burial grounds for the victims and it would never be revealed to the world. However, Silesian monks residing 200- 300 yards away from the caves heard two loud explosions coming from the caves. The next morning, the 25th of March, some priests went to the caves to investigate. Within a week, the atrocities of the Fosse (caves) Ardeatine came to be known to the rest of the world.

With all the meticulous checking and cross-checking of names on the list by Captain Priebke, 335 civilians were killed instead of 330, although two prisoners escaped from the trucks carrying the prisoners to the caves. The guards were sloppy in accounting for the names on the list due to the fact that most, if not all, of the Nazis were drunk. However, the two missing from the list have had a lasting effect on the history of the massacre at the Ardeatine caves. In order to make up for the missing two, the Nazi sent two trucks out in the streets of Rome to round up anyone in order to replace them. The problem was that they over-compensated for the missing ones by rounding up more than two, seven more civilians. Ironically, all of the German and Italian officials involved in the massacre were prosecuted by military courts in Italy not for the killing of 330 civilians but for the extra five! At one of the trials, Captain Karl Hass in 1996 revealed the mystery of the "extra" killings of the five innocent civilians.

According to Hass, Captain Priebke was at the Ardeatine caves with the copy of the list. He crossed out the name on the list as the prisoner got off the truck. At one point he discovered that one of the prisoners was not on the list and by the end of checking off all the names on the list, there were five extra prisoners beyond the 330. Thus, seven new prisoners were not on the list, since two escaped. It was decided by someone (unknown to this day) that they should kill all the prisoners, including the ones not on the list, in order to "destroy" evidence.

However, Captain Hass did not explain why there were extra prisoners whose names were not on the list. He conveniently forgot or avoided mentioning the escape of the two prisoners which was the impetus for generating more prisoners. Thus, the extra prisoners came from trucks roaming Rome in the evening of the 24th of March randomly picking up people off the streets whose names were not on the list, people like Zio Renato. Germans were so concerned about being precise in carrying out their dirty deed that they went around Rome rounding up people off the streets. Unbelievably, the Gestapo officers needed "insurance" in carrying out this terrible deed. In fact, the truck that Zio was riding in was just around the corner ready to be delivered to the Ardeatine caves in case the number count fell below 330. This, I believe, explains the discrepancy discovered by Captain Priebke and the reason for sending out trucks in the streets of Rome.

The Gestapo purposely created a false impression of events taking place at the Ardeatine caves during the military trials after the war. The impression that they wanted to create for the world to believe was that (1) the extra five prisoners killed at the caves was simply a result of a clerical mistake that anyone could have made and (2) that the Gestapo killed only prisoners condemned to death in the jails at Gestapo headquarters and at Regina Coeli. Assertion (2) by the Germans has been proven by historians to be blatantly false. For example, not a single Roman Jew nor many others committed any crime.

The temerity and the gall for Marshal Kesselring to claim that all the prisoners executed at Via Ardeatina were criminals is beyond belief. He fooled no one. L'Osservatore Romano (Vatican newspaper) correctly reported on the 24th of March, 1944 that the victims had been innocent hostages. Obviously, the Marshal was not aware of the fact that innocent people were indeed rounded up randomly in the streets of Rome in the evening of the 24th of March or, perhaps, he didn't want to know.

This points to an interesting possibility and that is, perhaps, that the Marshal was either lying or didn't think that it was important to know. In either case, it makes him a complete liar about the murder of 330 civilians. Thus, impression (2) created by the Gestapo was blatantly false. Based on the fact Zio was picked up, it was inconceivable for Kappler not to know why the extra five victims showed up at the Ardeatine caves. Impression (1) created by the Gestapo was not a clerical mistake but an overzealous carriage of duty by a warped mind man, Kappler, who was hell bent on saving his career. It is interesting to note the Pope's response after the massacre as reported in L'Osservatore Romano, and it stated:

> *"In the face of such deeds every honest heart is left profoundly grieved in the name of humanity and Christian sentiment. Thirty-two victims on the one hand; and on the other, three hundred and twenty persons sacrificed for the guilty parties who escaped arrest. Yesterday we addressed a sorrowful appeal for serenity and calm; today we repeat the same request, with more ardent affection, with more fervid insistence. Above and beyond the strife, moved only by Christian charity, we call upon the irresponsible elements to respect human life, which they have no right whatsoever to sacrifice, to respect the innocence of those who as a consequence are fatally victimized; from the responsible elements we ask for an awareness of their responsibility, toward themselves, toward the lives they wish to safeguard, toward history and civilization".*

The Pope refuted the notion that the prisoners were criminals by alluding to their innocence. However, he condemned the action of the partisans and indirectly condoned the action of the Nazis who maintained law and order in the streets of Rome. The Pope implied also that it was normal for the Nazis to occupy Rome as long as they kept the partisans away from the Papal State, and Vatican properties. According to the Pope, the partisans were responsible for the killing of the 320 civilians at the Ardeatine caves. The above statement also revealed that the Pope was well aware of the killing of 320 civilians before the morning of March 24, and well before the actual killings. On the morning of the 24th, Kappler was preparing for the execution of 330 prisoners, not 320. The Pope chose not to do anything about the reprisal and to keep silent. Those are the facts. Controversies, opinions and judgements have followed to this day.

In 1996 my wife and I visited the Fosse Ardeatine. The city of Rome dedicated the Fosse Ardeatine as a museum in honor of the deceased. Each cadaver was placed in a casket with the name of the victim on the casket, 335 of them. It was a very somber view, when walking through the maze of tunnels within the caves. One floor above the caves there was a small museum exhibiting the pictures of various people from Rome at the time of the war. The pictures depicted faces of Italian Army Officers, priests, nuns, politicians, etc. I assumed that those were the pictures of the victims. I was curious to see who the victims of the Ardeatine massacre were and what they did for a living. I wanted to know who they were.

However, to my surprise, they were not the pictures of the victims. So, I asked the curator or custodian if I could see the pictures of the victims just to see who they were. I was told that they had no pictures of the victims. It made no sense to me. I explained to the curator that the reason those people died at the Ardeatine caves was because the ones that they had pictures for in display were the ones responsible for what happened to the victims. The whole scenario was mystifying. I wondered what the meaning was or historical implications of these monuments all over Rome. Can one believe anything that museums purport to exhibit? After the German Army left Rome, Romans of all ages seethed revenge. The warden of Regina Coeli, Donato Carreta, and Questore (chief of police) Pietro Caruso were soon apprehended after the Allies left Rome. Only Caruso had the benefit of a trial. Carreta was murdered by a lynch mob. Within 24 hours Caruso had a trial and was shot at Fort Bravetta. The other Italian conspirator, Pietro Koch, in the Ardeatine massacre who actually made up the list of the 50 prisoners in Regina Coeli to be executed was also brought to trial and shot at Fort Bravetta.

Generals Eberhard Mackensen and Kurt Malzer [4] were brought back to Rome from England in November 1946 in order to stand trial. Since the International Military Tribunal and the Nuremberg trials of major war criminals, both Mackensen and Malzer fell under the jurisdiction of the British military tribunal. Field Marshal Albert Kesselring of the German Army served as a witness for the defense and Gestapo chief major Herbert Kappler for the prosecution. As mentioned earlier, the defense was based on two points: (1) the killing of civilians, as in a reprisal, in an occupied country was condoned by the Hague Convention of 1907; (2) only prisoners that were condemned to death were on the list to be executed.

Both defendants contended that they had nothing to do with the killing of the extra five prisoners, because it was Kappler who miscounted the number of prisoners. They claimed that it was a clerical mistake. Therefore, Kappler was the guilty one. Mackensen made the point that it was he who reduced the killing ratio from 25/1 to 10/1 with the approval of Kesselring. Malzer took the position that he did not have any authority to carry out the reprisal. Finally, he said that this was strictly a Gestapo matter and had nothing to do with the Army. Kesselring's position was that if Mackensen and Malzer were guilty, so was he. They were found guilty and sentenced to death by a firing squad.

Marshal Kesselring was also tried by the British military court in Venice instead of Rome. He was charged with complicity in the Ardeatine caves massacre. Kesselring's defense again was based on the two premises outlined above. He claimed that the reprisal was a police or Gestapo matter and not an Army matter, and, hence, Kappler was guilty of the crime committed. He also stated all of the prisoners were criminals who were condemned to death. He was either lying or forgot. His point was determined to be irrelevant upon further examinations. He was found guilty and sentenced to death by the firing squad.

The verdicts were correct in sentencing all to the death penalty, but the reasoning for the verdicts was at best shoddy. Now let me present facts that have come to light since. Premise (1) as presented by the defense at the trial in 1946 should not have been applicable, because soldiers of the 11th company were Italian citizens. Thus, the attack by the partisans constituted a civil war attack, not an attack on German troops invalidating premise (1). Unfortunately, the issue of nationality of the 11th company never came up at the trials. It is an historical fact that none of the soldiers of the 11th company participated in the reprisal and for good reason. They did not want to execute one of their own citizens. Premise (2) was also a lie at the time of the trial. The Pope stated as much in the Vatican's newspaper the next day after execution. The only person who knew the truth was Kappler and he was not about to reveal the truth. He had no incentive to do so, because he would have incriminated himself. The truth was that some of the prisoners were picked off the streets of Rome as an insurance in getting to the 330 count of civilians. Zio was picked up in Lungotevere Street and taken to the Ardeatine caves. He was no criminal. Thus, those poor five souls as well as the other 330 civilians were innocent people of Rome. In fact, a handful of the 330 civilians were petty thieves. In summary, premise (2), by which the defense based their case, could have been easily refuted had criminal records made available to the Court. Clearly, there was no sharp distinction between the 330 and the extra five in terms of them being criminals. Thus, it was not a clerical mistake to account for the killing of the extra five civilians. It was an insurance plan to carry out the injustice. All of that was hidden by the defense team at the trial.

The sentences were never carried out and were commuted to life incarceration. The sentences were further reduced to five years and Mackensen was released in 1952. He died in 1969. Malzer died right after his release in 1952. The British establishment (British royalty and general staff) were influential in reducing the sentence to five years in jail and Kesselring was released in 1952. He died in 1960.

Kappler and his associates were tried by the Italian military tribunal. Kappler spoke for eight straight days detailing the executions at the Ardeatine caves. His main defense was that he was obeying orders from superiors. He claimed that the attack at Via Rasella by the partisans was illegal and the reprisal was legally condoned by the Hague Convention of 1907. All co-defendants were found not guilty as they were obeying orders from Kappler, but Kappler was found guilty. The court decision in Rome made no sense, because the Nuremberg trials of German officers had rejected the idea of blind duty and obedience at all costs. The judges also cited the reprisal as a war crime. Kappler was sentenced to life in prison.

In 1977 Kappler escaped Regina Coeli jail with the aid of his wife. He was visited by his wife at the jail and somehow Kappler was "packaged" inside a large suitcase. According to the New York Times story line it was not clear who produced the suitcase on the premise at Regina Coeli. The wife walked out of the jail with the suitcase and Kappler inside. Kappler died a year later.

The final culprit of the massacre at the Ardeatine caves was SS Captain Erich Priebke who was caught in Argentina in 1996 and extradited to Italy to appear in court for the murder of the "extra" five civilians in the caves. The CIA and Israeli intelligence were responsible for his apprehension. Priebke escaped from a British prisoner-of-war camp in Rimini, Italy, in 1946. He hid in a monastery near Rimini for a month until false documents were produced by Vatican staff. Using the so-called Rat line run by the Vatican staff, Priebke was able to escape to South America. The Rat line was justified by the Vatican as a humanitarian gesture on the part of the church as helping people of all religions and political affiliations from war travesties, much like earlier when the church helped Jews escape Nazi persecution [24, 25, 27, 35, 46, and 60]. However, after the war most Nazis and Fascists were criminals running away from justice, whereas, before the end of the war, Jews and people running away from the Nazis, were just ordinary people, not criminals. That is one major difference that the Vatican failed to recognize. About 60,000 Nazis and Fascists escaped to South America via the Rat line.

The Rat line was created after the war initially to protect Croatian Catholic priests from persecution by the Protestant Serbs under the leadership of the Communist leader Josip Broz Tito (see the book by Branko Bokun "Spy in the Vatican, 1941-1945") [4]. Pope Pius XII expressed public anger over the convictions of half a dozen Croatian Catholic priests by the Yugoslav War Crimes Commission. The Vatican appointed Krunoslav Draganovich as the Apostolic Official for Pontifical Assistance for Croatians. Croatians were mostly Catholics and Fascists, while Serbs were mostly Protestants but anti-Fascists. He was a member of the Ustasa, an anti-Semitic, anti-Serb and anti-Communist party. The Ustasa organization was in power during wartime in Croatia. Draganovich supervised elaborate escape networks through which hundreds of criminals found safe haven in South America and the Middle East after the war. Besides the transport of people and priests, the special Rat line connection moved large amounts of money and gold to the Vatican banks [18].

Helping Nazis flee was not an official policy established by Pius XII. However, the Pope was well aware of it. The Vatican became a mandatory post war stop for many Nazi and Fascist war criminals fleeing Europe. Bishop Alois Hudal, rector of the Pontificio Santa Maria dell'Anima, was energetic in helping Nazi war criminals escape. He established the

Austrian Liberation Committee for that purpose. Here are examples of who he helped out with false passports in the escape to South America: Franz Stangl was the commandant of the Sobibor and Treblinka death camps, where an estimated 1,000,000 to 1,250,000 Jews and Gypsies were gassed to death; Gustav Wagner was camp Commandant at those two camps. Walter Rauff engineered the mobile gas vans before the gas chambers; Adolf Eichmann was in charge of all the trains that carried Jews to Poland's extermination centers [18].

Sister Pascalina Lehnert [74, 76], who served as special assistant to Pius XII, burned a tremendous amount of documents generated by Pius XII during the war. Apparently, Pope Pius XII ordered sister Pascalina to burn his documents after his death. Sister Pascalina's bedroom was situated next to the Pope's chamber for emergencies. The burning of the documents also would have revealed the Pope's knowledge of the Ardeatine affair and, in particular, shed some light in the trial cases between the Pacelli's family and Robert Katz and film Director, Carlo Ponti, as well as other pertinent facts of the Nazi occupation of Rome. At the first trial in Rome, Priebke claimed that he was obeying orders and was found guilty but not punishable. There was an appeal and another trial and, finally, a special witness was produced by the prosecution: SS major Karl Hass who was Priebke's boss. The reader should note that in between the time of the massacre and the end of the war, Hass was promoted from Captain to Major. According to Major Hass' testimony, all of sudden one prisoner showed up who was not on the list. Then, two and three and so on showed up. Since they were witnesses as to what was going on, the Gestapo had no other choice but to shoot the extra prisoners not on the list.

This was a very subtle testimony by Hass. Had he said that the extra five were picked up randomly from the streets, in order to make up for the two escapees, he and Priebke would have been sentenced to death by the firing squad right on the spot in the courtroom. In contrast, the warden of Regina Coeli jail was hanged without the benefit of a trial after the war. By alluding that it was a clerical mistake that could happen to anyone, assured the lighter sentence. I believe that there were ten more extra ones who were not on the list waiting in the truck where "Zio di Roma" was in a holding pattern with the possibility of dying. The strange thing was that these people waiting in the truck were not aware that they may be killed at any moment. Even after all these years I can feel the anxiety of those poor souls in the truck waiting for something to happen.

Priebke and Hass were found guilty on July 22, 1997 and the Military Tribunal of Rome rejected the defense of obeying orders, as it was rejected in the Nuremberg trials. They were sentenced to life without parole. However, the sentences were reduced for both men to five years. In summary, there were eleven Nazis involved in the massacre of the Ardeatine caves. None of them were shot by the firing squad. They all died of natural causes. Yet, for the same crime, two Italian Fascists were shot by the firing squad and another one was hung from a tree near the Tiber River. At the very least, there was miscarriage of justice for the same exact crime.

Let's examine the articles of the 1907 Hague Convention [36] pertaining to the executions carried out at the Ardeatine caves. The Germans interpretation of Articles 1, 2, 22 and 43 of the Hague Convention allowed them to address only the belligerents who attacked the Germans on Via Rasella, but not the civilians. In Article 50 it stated that no general penalty shall be inflicted upon population (civilians) on account of the acts of individuals (belligerents or partisans in this case). The Hague convention or articles condoned the execution of belligerents (partisans) but not civilians.

The partisans who exploded the bomb on Via Rasella were the belligerents. The people who were executed in Via Ardeatina were civilians, not belligerents or partisans. Hence, the Gestapo soldiers were in violation of the Hague convention in carrying out the executions of civilians. Also, the Germans were in violation of Article 45 which stated that "it is forbidden to compel the inhabitants (people from Tyrol and warden at Regina Coeli) of occupied territory to swear allegiance to the hostile power (the Gestapo)". The Gestapo coerced the warden of Regina Coeli jail to produce a list of civilians to be executed, when they had no desire to do so. Yet, it cost their lives when forced by Gestapo to provide the list. The 11th company police troops from Tyrol, were forced to serve in the German Army. None of the soldiers from Tyrol wanted any part of the execution. In conclusion, the Germans had no legal right to execute civilians at the Ardeatine caves, and the execution had nothing to do with the Hague Convention which was the legal document that was applicable in warfare.

The indelible mark of the Rasella affair is that the people of Rome are still divided as to whom should be blamed for the massacre at Via Ardeatina.

On one hand some blamed the partisans for inciting the violent reaction by the Germans. This is exactly the position of Pope Pius XII. On the other hand, others say that the partisans were the true patriots and risked their lives to carry out their deed. The reprisal had nothing to do with law and order. It was simply an act of brutality and outright murder.

The partisans anticipated reprisals to be on them, not on civilians. However, had the partisans known how barbaric the Germans were going to be to civilians, would have they struck? It is hard to predict now what they would have done. However, if one accepts the notion that the Germans were occupiers of Rome and not policemen to maintain law and order, then the partisans had no choice but to attack at all fronts. It is nonsense for some Romans to claim today the attack was an act of civil war. The partisans did not know the police officers were from Tyrol, Italy.

This discussion will never go away in Rome for it strikes to the soul of every Roman, even today. However, the residents of Via Rasella have spoken, not in words but in deeds. The residents of Via Rasella left the bullet holes on their walls to remind the people of Rome that it was another German invasion that put the holes there. It is well known there are many mementos in Rome to remind people of the many invasions from foreign countries that have resulted in violent atrocities. There is no physical evidence today in Via Rasella of the explosion damages caused by the partisans. The message of the Via Rasella residents to future generations is quite clear to me. Rome was invaded by one more Army from the North in 1944 and they wanted to leave a memento behind as a reminder and nothing else. Fuck the Jubilee year 2000.

The Vatican blamed [46] the partisans for the massacre at the Ardeatine caves. Furthermore, German subjugation of Romans in daily life was referred to by the Vatican as police work to maintain law and order and preserve the papal state from Communist intrusions. Basically, the church viewed those events in terms of a repeat of the Italian revolution of the 1860's. At that time the Vatican ceded 20,000 square miles of land to the new Republic of Italy. The church was allowed to keep only one square mile in Rome, the Vatican. Understandably, the Vatican was apprehensive of the Communists, since the Communists were advocating sharing of farmlands with the church.

However, the Communists or partisans had no intention whatsoever of taking over Vatican City. Communist doctrine and dictates from communist leaders in Russia and Italy forbade partisans and/or Communists from engaging in any activities infringing upon territories of the church, including the Vatican. Communist leaders, especially in Russia, did not want to antagonize America for the Russian Army was receiving tremendous amounts of heavy-duty war materiel from America. Partisans and communists in Italy took orders directly from Russia via Palmiro Togliatti [79] who was the Italian Communist leader. He spent the war years in Russia under the tutelage of Joseph Stalin, the Russian leader.

History has shown that the partisans' activities were confined solely to territories occupied by the Nazis, nothing to do with the Vatican state. It raised a tremendous controversy to this day as who to blame for the massacre. The only preoccupation of the church at that time was that of self-preservation, and the fear that the Pope may be deported to Germany, as threatened by Hitler early in the war.

A detente was struck between the Pope and Hitler (the devil). The details of the deal were that the Pope was allowed by the Nazis to remain in Rome and keep the riches of the Vatican. In return, the murderous activities of the Nazis in Rome were labeled or declared by the Vatican officials as police activities to maintain law and order in Rome. The Vatican turned a blind eye to the atrocious behavior of Nazis in Rome and diverted attention away from the Nazis to the partisans' activities. In effect, the Nazis were absolved of any wrongdoing, according to the church. Thus, it was obfuscation of the nth degree. It is this double standard by the church that was the genesis to the controversy to this day.

One day in the future, Pope Pius XII may be bestowed Sainthood by the Curia in the Vatican. A proper name for [60] this future Saint should be "Sanctus Pio Silentium".

SEVEN
WITHOUT WARNING OR PROVOCATION

Without any warning or provocation from the people of Rome, Zio Renato was apprehended by the Gestapo on that fateful night of March 24, 1944. He was not aware of the German reprisal on Via Rasella the day before. Correlating the time sequence of events and researching the facts of that day, the following story can now be told. I became aware of the Via Ardeatina massacre as early as 1949.

In 1949, I was an altar boy at Saint Peter church in Avella. Usually, each spring the church sponsored a competition among altar boys to recite prayers in Latin at a resort town. However, on this particular spring season, the church sponsored a trip to the Vatican instead. Sebastiano wanted to come along with me, as we liked the idea of getting out of Avella and see a big city like Rome. The priest at Saint Peter church paid for the round trip bus ride between Avella and Rome, including board and food. The group consisted of altar boys in the Naples area. Sebastiano was never an altar boy but somehow he was able to come along as a chaperone.

The purpose of the trip to Rome was to have Pope Pius II bless all of the altar boys of the Naples area and extoll the virtue of priesthood. In public appearances, the Pope always seemed to appear distant and aloof. This was an occasion to "humanize" the Pope in front of all those children and put him in a favorable light toward the day when he was to be canonized. As a child, I was in total awe of the Pope for he represented the Catholic Church as its leader. It was only later in life that I learned about the Pope's views toward Jews and Axis governments in World War II [12, 35, 45, 46, and 60].

When I told Francesca about it, she was confused about why I wanted to go. Again, I re-assured her that I had no intention of becoming a priest. Going to a big city like Rome was a big deal to the family and, like any other mother, she was protective of us. She knew that Renato lived in Rome and had a feeling that he would keep an eye on us while there. She needed that kind of assurance before letting us go. After all, we were very young among many strangers. She immediately contacted Serafina (Renato's sister) and made arrangements to contact Renato in Rome. Serafina was a willing partner in making our trip safe and enjoyable. Sebastiano and I vaguely remembered Zio from the time of grandmother Imalda's funeral.

Serafina and her sister owned a seamstress shop making dresses and sweaters. There was really no competition among my aunts and our neighboring seamstresses for they catered to different clientele and lived on opposite ends of town. My aunts catered to the so-called avant-garde in the fashion world who wanted to keep up with the latest style in fashion. Our neighbors catered to clientele who needed repair jobs or slight moderation of a dress as well as sewing wool sweaters. Francesca was the "middle person" in providing Serafina with the wool produced by shepherds. Francesca replaced Imalda as the contact person with shepherds in procuring the wool, since Imalda's death in 1943. Payment from Serafina for this service was usually a sweater sewn for one member of our family. Securing extra wool from the shepherds was no problem for Francesca.

The role of "Zio di Roma" was an important one at funerals in the Naples area. Neapolitans are obsessed with elevating the importance of the deceased in life even in modern days. A man who may have been a near-pauper all his life was certain to be put away in a magnificent coffin. Nothing was spared to increase the prestige of the deceased by having his "Zio di Roma" grieve at his funeral. Typically, the Zio came to the funeral in an Alfa Romeo with a Roman number-plate and an SPQR badge wearing a well-cut morning suit. On the jacket, he sported the ribbon of a Commendatore (cavalier) of the Crown of Italy to show his restrained and dignified condolences. The "uncle from Rome" has always been a popular character in this little farce in the area of Naples. However, the "uncle from Rome" referred to us by Serafina, our neighbor, was related to Serafina, and not an actor.

He was none other than our own adopted Zio Renato, Papa's best friend. He was a medical doctor working in a small hospital on the Tiber River. The hospital was located on an island on the Tiber River. However, he still held a position at another hospital near Via Appia, where he was originally employed. He was not a blood relative, but he was treated by our family like a real uncle. Francesca told us all about him and the special bond with Papa before the war. We felt secure and confident that we were in good hands once in Rome. Francesca outlined for us what to do once we arrived in Rome. We were to be picked up at Saint Peter Square where the bus would arrive in the evening hours. From there the uncle was to take us to their home. Serafina gave us an old picture of the uncle so that we could recognize him at Saint Peter Square. Also, Zio was informed by post to wear placards with our names inscribed on them. The problem was that we did not know the arrival time precisely, ID number of the bus and where exactly the bus was going to drop us at Saint Peter Square. We didn't even know the color of the bus. As such, we were somewhat apprehensive. At worst we thought that we could accommodate ourselves with the rest of the altar boys group in the same sleeping quarters. For one thing, Francesca had no idea how big Saint Peter Square was, since she never visited Rome. The bus could have parked near the Square and be quite a distance from where Zio could have been waiting. As it turned out, we were lucky that we were able to find each other.

Naturally, Francesca arranged, with the help of Serafina, for us to stay at Zio Renato's house in Rome for two nights and return home. There were six boys from Avella who participated in the pilgrimage. The rest of the group consisted of altar boys and chaperons from Sperone and Baiano. Besides the altar boys, priests from Saint Peter and Saint Anthony churches in Avella came along to chaperon the group. All together there were about 30-40 people from Avella, Sperone and Baiano. A bus picked up the contingent from Avella in front of Saint Peter church at six in the morning. We packed one spare set of clothes and food for the trip.

The next stop was in the town of Sperone where we picked up some altar boys and I recognized one as Raffaele, who also attended the nuns' school with me. I was surprised to see him, because I had not seen him before at conventions of altar boys. He must have joined recently in order to qualify for the trip. On to Baiano, where another group was picked up. There were about twenty children, ranging in ages from 6 to 14 years, and ten adults. Most of the kids were altar boys except for my brother. We fibbed and said that he served as an altar boy at Saint Anthony church, a Franciscan order church, instead of Saint Peter church, a Salesian order church. The trip to Rome was sponsored by the Salesian order.

The bus headed north from Nola. There were two ways to reach Rome from Nola. One way was by the old road sometimes referred to as "Via Appia" or, now, designated as route 7. From Naples it hugs the coast line until Gaeta and then goes straight into Rome, away from the coast. The other route has been designated in the past as route 6, or Via Casilina. Nowadays it is referred to as highway A45. It bypasses Naples straight into Rome, away from the coast line. The route goes past Caserta, Monte Cassino and Frosinone. The bus driver chose route 6, since even then it was recognized as a faster route to Rome from Naples. Nowadays, there is an autostrada (highway) from Naples to Rome, bypassing both routes 6 and 7.

The bus stopped at Caserta for a lunch break. We brought along eggplant and cheese sandwiches prepared by Francesca. At home, eggplant was our main dish for most of our meals, sustaining us during the worst of times before and after the war. It was prepared in a variety of ways, and it always tasted good. Nonno's farm and our little garden grew a lot of eggplants and zucchini plants. Francesca also prepared jars of tomatoes for all year consumption. Cheese was readily available at reasonable prices from shepherds' families, but most times she made her own cheese at home. When we arrived, it seemed that we traveled forever, although we were only 40 miles from Avella.

The castle at Caserta is similar to the one in Versailles, France, in terms of style and architectural design. Even the paintings in the two castles look similar. The connection between the two places was that the Naples area, including Caserta, was occupied by France during the seventeen and eighteen centuries. Caserta was the main residence of French royalty during the occupation of Naples and vicinity. However, the castle in Caserta was built well before the one in Versailles. It was one thing to read about historical events and French influence in the area of Naples in school books, but it was a totally different experience to see the effects of French influence to the town of Caserta with respect to buildings, art and gardens. During the Allied campaign for Anzio and Cassino, General Clark made his headquarters in the Royal castle of Caserta. We spent a couple of hours in Caserta eating lunch and visiting the parks and the courtyards within the castles.

Once the bus left Caserta, the landscape changed quickly and dramatically. As the bus approached the Volturno River, there were burned out vehicles and scraps of metals spread all over the landscape and small creeks as far as one could see. Unbelievably, there were still remnants of tank parts and spent bomb shells on open fields. The fields on the rolling hills were barren of barns, farmhouses, livestock and farmhands working on the farms. It was surprising to see such beautiful farmlands void of any activities, since it was the spring season when everything comes to life on the farms. Clearly, most farmhands were away and never returned to Italy. Lack of tending or caring for the farms slowed down the return to their full productivity of yesteryear. That was the case when we traveled past those beautiful farmlands.

It felt like being in the aftermath of a tank battle. It was one thing to talk or hear about the War, but it was a totally different matter to see the devastation and brutality of it. To see all the ruins and devastation of farms on the road to Rome made a great impression on the children as well as the adults. We were in shock to the realities of war. Our bus arrived at the town of Cassino in mid-afternoon, but reached the ruins of the Abbey in late afternoon. Unbelievable as it seemed, there were still damaged vehicles and cannons to the left and right of the winding road up the steep hill to Monte Cassino. It is not clear why the Allies chose to attack along such a steep rise. It was pure madness to do so at that time. The bus had a difficult time climbing the hill even in first gear. The road formed a zig-zag construction up the hill in order to avoid direct climb of the hill. It is inconceivable to imagine pushing a cannon or a mule with supplies up that hill! The Polish Army had most casualties in doing so. It was sheer madness.

The Polish cemetery was located at the same site as the Abbey, but slightly on a higher ground. There was not much to see other than the panoramic view at the edge of the Abbey. The Abbey was destroyed to the ground and no one was allowed near it. The Germans had an advantage in holding their positions near the Abbey. As in Avella, German troops could readily hide in caves near the Abbey during bombing. Also, one could see across the Liri Valley and the rivers below. Even a small bird could be tracked! The abbey was totally destroyed by Allied bombing.

We were warned to stay together as a group and to stay away from the Abbey itself. The fear was that there could be some unexploded bombs. The bombing did not help the Allied cause for the Germans never utilized the Abbey as a cover. Abbott Gregorio Diamare [6] claimed the following after the bombing: "I swear there were never any German soldiers in the area of the Monastery". The Abbey of Monte Cassino remains a site of pilgrimage. Veterans come from all over the world, as they did 70 years ago. A monument and a huge cross commemorating the war efforts of the Polish Army at Monte Cassino were placed on the hill near the destroyed Abbey. All combating armies were represented: New Zealanders, British, Americans, Indians, Germans, Italians and the French. All the cemeteries invoke God to glorify the deaths of the young men who lie there.

Whereas most of the Allied troops attacked the town of Cassino and the hill approaching the Abbey, the Gourmier troops attacked from the east toward Monte Cifalco and Atira, located behind enemy lines. It was the latter approach or attack that turned the tide at the battle of Monte Cassino, not the direct approach uphill to Monte Cassino. The Germans had no choice but to jump on the Via Casilina toward Rome after the breakthrough by the Gourmiers on May 17, 1944. The chase was on, as the Germans escaped North up route 6 toward Rome, the same road that we were on to Rome. The trap was set at Valmontone (eight miles from Rome) on route 6 for General Clark to stop the German retreat there. However, the lure of Rome was too great for General Clark. He dashed from Anzio to Rome using the old Via Appia (route 7). The word "old" implied that there were still lava stones paving the road. Romans built the original road using stones of lava from Vesuvius. The lava stones were later replaced with regular stones, as modern day traffic could not travel on the big lava stones.

Yes, General Clark got the credit for conquering Rome from the South for the first time. It never occurred to General Clark that the reason there were no other Generals before him was because they thought it was not a judicious route to approach Rome. In the estimation of many critics, military and non-military, General Clark's ambitions only prolonged the war. The prolonging of the war was real, because more soldiers died unnecessarily. At the end of the battle, both sides sustained about 190,000 casualties at Monte Cassino. The road to Rome was then open. The Abbey was rebuilt after the war and Pope Paul VI re-consecrated it in 1964. Cardinal Giuseppe Battista Montini became Pope in 1958 replacing Pius XII who died in 1957.

Finally, we got away from the abysmal town of Cassino and Monte Cassino and headed to Rome, past Frosinone. Although none of us was aware in that bus, Frosinone had a glimpse of hell and survived. The town was literally raped by the Goumiers after the battle of Monte Cassino. The Goumiers came down the mountains making shrieking sounds that terrified everyone within hearing range. The town of Frosinone had a population of 25,000 and sat at the foothills of the Apennine Mountains, much like Avella. Anything in their path was raped, women, men, old and young. All livestock and some women were taken to the mountains. A movie entitled "Two Women" with Sophia Loren, directed by Vittorio De Sica, depicted the story of mother and daughter being gang-raped by the Goumiers. That movie gives a visual presentation of the traumatic experience that the women went through in those days.

From there the Goumiers moved on to Rome. Even in Rome their behavior was far from civilized as attested to by Robert Katz's book "The Battle for Rome" [11]. The Goumiers were not deployed north of Rome and made camp back in Southern Italy before returning to North Africa. When we reached the outskirts of Rome near Frascati, the panoramic view was fantastic. There are little towns atop hills that look like fairy-tale towns, except, that some were completely wiped out. The only thing that we saw of the destroyed towns was a church bell tower, half broken up, and everything else demolished. Frascati was the German headquarters during the battle of Anzio. Frascati was leveled by the Allied bombing, but, somehow, Kesselring was uninjured. Clearly, unprovoked bombing occurred all over the Province of Lazio as well as the Roman district. The same "carpet" bombing was repeated at Monte Cassino, Frascati, Frosinone and many other beautiful towns nearby. Those towns will forever leave an imprint on the passengers of that bus.

Finally, we arrived in Rome and drove past the Colosseum toward the Lungotevere road along the Tiber River. Of course, all of us in the bus were excited and intently soaking in all those magnificent monuments. From the Lungotevere it was a short distance to Via della Conciliazione which stared right into Saint Peter Square and the church of Saint Peter. We arrived in the early evening hours, still daylight. Frankly, Sebastiano and I were not that impressed with all those monuments. We have seen them before in Avella. Every palazzo in

Avella is decorated with a number of Roman statues and paintings and we were aware of the Roman aqueduct, for example. However, we were impressed with the city traffic in Rome. It was bustling with buses, cars, taxis, motorcycles and caccavelle (Fiat 500) all over the city. In Avella, if we saw one car in town, it was a big event for that month.

Saint Peter Church, the Square, the Colonnades and the surrounding buildings looked so huge that we were in awe. Churches in Avella were thought to be big according to the standards of the locals, but they did not compare with what we saw. It is interesting to note that when Michelangelo [85] built Saint Peter Church, he was inspired by Brunelleschi's work of the Duomo in Florence. Brunelleschi [86] solved the problem of supporting large weights of big Cupolas. Apparently, this problem was solved earlier by the Romans, when they built the Pantheon, and Brunelleschi adopted the Roman design at the base of the building to build the Duomo. Michelangelo could have saved himself a trip to Florence, if he had visited the Pantheon and examined the building base structure.

At Saint Peter Square, we were perplexed to see a semi-circular white line painted on the street cobble stones connecting the two ends of the colonnades. It served no purpose in directing traffic around the Square. Every car that we saw simply cut across those demarcation white lines. However, it served a purpose in 1944, when Gestapo chief Herbert Kappler, in exasperation, ordered the painting of the white lines. It marked the border between the Vatican State and the city of Rome. German troops were guarding the white line or the "border", much like custom police. The intent of the "border" was to entrap Monsignor Hugh O'Flaherty outside of Vatican territory. He was responsible for aiding the OSS spy network in Rome, under the leadership of Peter Tompkins, who was hiding escaped POW's, Jews and anti-Fascists in safe-houses in Rome. Financial support for the OSS operation was funneled through Monsignor O'Flaherty [21].

When our bus arrived at Saint Peter Square, there was utter confusion. Nuns, Priests, children and traffic policemen running around the Square and no place to Park. After, a couple of times circling around the Square, the bus parked in the street where a number of Cafes were open. When we got out of the bus, we had no idea where we were relative to where

Zio could possibly be. It was all so overwhelming with all those people that appeared to be lost. The trip was tiring and our minds were taxed to the limit with all that confusion. We didn't panic, but we needed to take a break. The smell of espresso coffee was too much for Sebastiano and me for we accommodated ourselves in the Café next to the bus and ordered one "sfogliatella" (Neapolitan pastry) and two espressos. We were surprised that the Cafe featured a Neapolitan pastry in Rome. Our curiosity got the best of us for we had to try the pastry. It was better than what we expected and it appeared most of the customers in the Cafe spoke in a Neapolitan dialect.

Upon further straining of our necks to see who was around, we discovered "Zio di Roma", Zio Renato, sitting two tables from us. He wore a rumpled, tan colored, linen suit typical of the wear in Rome and a dark tie and wore glasses. The probability that we should randomly enter the same Cafe where Zio was rather small. However, our love of the sfogliatella pastry brought all of us together in that Neapolitan Cafe. He had the appearance of the famous Italian actor Vittorio De Sica. His daughter was sitting with him and were staring at us. They flashed their placards at us with our names on them. They were the people who were related to Serafina and were our guardians in Rome. They waited for more than two hours and walked up and down the streets near the Square looking for us. Exhausted, they took a break in this Neapolitan Cafe, where we walked in. The distinguished looking man was Dr. Renato Mezzano and the daughter's name was Angelina.

That explained the distinct dialect that we heard in the Cafe. After exchanging pleasantries, we got down to details. Zio Renato said to think of him as our own father and he had the responsibility of taking care of us just as with his daughter. He also said that our father would wanted to be this way. Also, he was responsible for bringing us into this world by arranging the marriage of our parents. What a small world! We were too embarrassed to call him Papa for it hurt too much to do so. So, we called him fondly, Zio (uncle). We were relieved and immediately made plans to stay at his house. Sebastiano then informed our local priest that we had made those arrangements in Rome, but planned to return to Avella on the same bus as pre-arranged. However, the priest insisted on meeting Zio. Had we stayed at the Vatican, sleeping quarters would have been provided for all the traveling pilgrims. In addition, breakfast and dinner were served by staffs at the Vatican.

We headed toward Zio's car which was parked behind Saint Peter church. The car was a Fiat 500 which was fondly referred to as the "caccavella" (little heating pan). It barely fit four people. When you were inside the car, it felt like being inside a sardine can. It appeared to be that small. We circled around Saint Peter church and got back to the Lungotevere road along the Tiber River district. As we headed toward Zio's house we passed by the "Carcere Regina Coeli" (Rome jail building). It literally translates roughly as the queen's sky jail. Another translation is Queen of Heaven, with no mention of jail.

Zio made a curious statement as we passed by the jail that I did not quite understand then, but have never forgotten: "That jail brought a lot of misery to a lot of Romans, including me, during the war". My first reaction was: How could a medical doctor have anything to do with a jail. I chose not to pursue what he meant. After all, I was still a guest and wished to be on good behavior. After a five to ten minutes ride we arrived at Zio's house. The car was parked on the curb and we went up one set of stairs. The apartment consisted of three to four rooms. We learned where we were going to sleep and were then introduced to Zio's wife, Sarah, who was Jewish.

Her immediate relatives lived across the Tiber River and it is often referred to as the "Jewish" Ghetto. Jews of Rome are more representative of traditional Roman [97] ways than modern Romans. The Roman Jews populated ancient Rome near the Tiber River for over two thousand years, even before the time of Saint Peter in Rome. They were free citizens under Julius Caesar, but enslaved by Emperor Titus. In medieval times Pope Paul IV built a wall around the district where Jews resided and referred to that area as a Ghetto. However, about 300 years later the wall was taken down and never built again.

During the Nazi occupation the ghetto was raided by German soldiers on October 16, 1943 at six in the morning. The German soldiers came in with trucks and surrounded the area. Going from house to house, 1023 Roman Jews were rounded up and, two days later, were shipped from Tiburtina railroad station to Auschwitz [71]. Not a single mention or denunciation of the deportation was heard then from Pius XII. Relatives of Sarah were deported in that fateful day. In fact some of the trucks that carried these unfortunate people to camp passed right in front of the Pope's window which is exposed to Saint Peter Square. Trucks stopped in front of Saint Peter

Square so that soldiers could take pictures. How macabre that they should stop outside the "border"! In the fall of 1945 only sixteen returned from Auschwitz to Rome. Some of Sarah's relatives never made it back to Rome.

That evening we had a sumptuous dinner: Pasta dish, roasted rooster, salad and sfogliatella for dessert. Zio wanted to hear news from Avella and, in particular, about Serafina. Also, he wanted to know whether I was going to become a priest, since I had served as an altar boy. I put him at ease with his apprehensions about priesthood and explained that I viewed the duties as a job and business proposition by the priest. As I explained to Zio, it didn't work out because the priest kept changing the financial arrangements at his convenience. Sebastiano had no such concerns for he was cared for financially by our seamstress aunts.

Zio then made arrangements for the next day's pilgrimage to Saint Peter Square. He had to leave early in the morning and drive us to the bus station where we would pick up bus # 64. Bus # 64 route in Rome still originates at the Termini train station. The bus would transport us directly to Saint Peter Square. Coming back we would walk through the ghetto and cross the river, over the bridge "Ponte Sisto", into Via Garibaldi; they lived two blocks from the bridge. He handed us a local map so that we would not get lost and drew a path for us to follow. However, after going over in minute deta how to navigate through Rome, he said: If you have any money put it next to your balls, when you board bus # 64. The bus was full of pick-pocket thieves. After sixty years bus # 64 still has the same reputation. My wife and I have visited Rome many times and often take bus # 64. We have never had a bad incident doing so. It would have been embarrassing for a Neapolitan like me to be pick-pocketed by a Roman! In Naples all the scugnizzi and their relatives were pick-pockets thieves and I was very familiar with their routine and distractions, even as a child. In the bus, Sebastiano and I stood up shoulder to shoulder so that our back pockets were not exposed to anyone.

In the morning when we boarded bus # 64, we were so excited that we forgot to pay for the transportation ticket. Interestingly, as we were about to pay for the bus ticket, passengers on the bus waived us off and told us not to pay. We were informed that nobody pays in Rome. So, we adopted the Roman axiom: "When in Rome, do as the Romans do". We did not pay. These days, we take the time to pay on buses and trains in Rome to make up for past indiscretions.

When we got to Saint Peter Square we registered with our local priest and he informed us which group of children we were supposed to follow in line. That was about 8-9 in the morning. In two hours we advanced only about 50 feet under the Saint Peter circular cupolas, and it was hot. We had to wear the usual white uniform used by altar boys and it made us even hotter. We inquired with other boys where they were from and whether or not they were altar boys. They came from Campania and Abruzzi area and there must have been at least 5,000 altar boys.

Finally, we were ushered into a large auditorium and placed about 100 feet from the stage. Precisely at noon, the Pope showed up in a white robe and the choir started singing. He was about six feet tall and skinny. As Francesca would say, he looked "sciupato", pale and sickly. There was a blessing and a prayer in Latin from the Pope. Then he began to speak for 40-50 minutes about what it was to be a pilgrim and altar boy. For me it was a bunch of bull shit. As far as I was concerned it was a free ride to Rome and to see Rome in its splendor. If that was what was meant as a pilgrim, I had no problem with that. In an adjacent building, lunch was served and were told that the Pope would come around and talk to the altar boys individually. He never showed up. Probably, he was not about to eat the same food as us.

In early afternoon, we had a choice of either joining the group of altar boys and attending the afternoon mass in Saint Peter church or getting on the bus on our own and going sightseeing in Rome. The afternoon mass was "advertised" very strongly by the priests. For us, it was a no brainer. We decided to hit the road with bus #64. My first choice was to see the bridge where General Scipio of the Roman army held back the invasion from Carthage. Sebastiano, who was well versed in Latin and, therefore, in ancient Roman history said that there was no such bridge. Perhaps, "Ponte Palatino" may have been it, he thought. So, we decided to just get on the bus and circle around the whole city. We didn't pay for the bus tickets throughout our tour of Rome. Nowadays, in order to reduce fare cheating on Roman transportation systems, tickets may be purchased on vending machines.

It was a truly relaxing afternoon for us taking in the panoramic view of most important monuments of Rome. We got off a couple of times at the Colosseum and the Forum Romano, but we didn't stay long. The

Colosseum in Rome was about two to three time times bigger than the Colosseum in Avella in terms of spectators' attendance. In 1949, the colosseum in Avella was still a well-kept secret of the farmer. We spent most of our time at Villa Borghese where we went to the Zoo. The most fascinating wild animal there was the black panther. I was enchanted with the ferocity of this animal, as it was shown in a documentary movie at the Cinema in Avella. In America, the Black Panther is rarely featured in Zoos.

Getting back home to Zio's house was no problem. The bus stop was only about five blocks from Zio's house and, besides, heading toward the river was trivial from the bus stop. We returned to the Via Garibaldi home in the evening hours and were starving and had no Lira (no money). Sarah and Zio wanted to know all about the Pope's reception and whether or not we got to see the Pope. Most Romans don't come in close proximity to any Pope at any time and I guess it was a big deal to them for us. We downplayed the encounter as a ritual by the Pope and told them that we spent time at the Zoo in the afternoon rather than in the church of Saint Peter. Sarah and Zio were dismayed.

Again the dinner was first class and afterward we had a chance to talk. First, Zio wanted us to hand carry a letter to our neighbor, Serafina. We talked about the war and how things were in Avella and in Rome. We told them about our experiences with the Germans, British and Goumiers. Zio said that they were lucky in Rome in that he had heard of only one bad incident with the Goumiers in Rome. A Cafe and Bar on Via Veneto (near the American Embassy) was visited by Goumiers and they ordered espressos. They complained that the coffee was too weak and demanded to see the manager. When the manager showed up, an argument ensued and the Goumiers proceeded to rape the manager behind the counter, as well as the waiter and customers. Once the story appeared in the local papers there was not a single Goumier to be found in Rome. They were sent south to Campania- Sicily and eventually back home to North Africa.

As for Renato, without warning or provocation he was picked up on March 24, 1944, about 6:30 pm by a German truck full of soldiers and civilians, and driven to the Saint Peter Junction on Via Ardeatina. The junction is the intersection of roads where Via Appia Antica (old Via Appia) [93] meets Via Ardeatina. It was also the junction where Saint Peter asked for directions to Rome 2000 years ago. Zio claimed that he was not a partisan or involved with the resistance. He was just taking a break smoking a cigarette by the Tiber River before curfew would be in effect. He thought that the whole incident was strange, because there was no provocation by the populace to warrant apprehension of him without a warning. A truck drove by and parked on the sidewalk blocking his path to cross the street to the other side. He was picked up by two soldiers with pointed rifles and ordered him to get in the back of the truck.

View of old Via Appia toward Via Ardeatina at bottom of the street. The stones are lava stones from original construction. Photo courtesy of Anmarie Vittoria, 1981.

After about 20-30 minutes, the truck stopped at the Saint Peter junction until approximately 11 pm and, then, driven back to the Regina Coeli Carcere (jail) overnight. The next morning the jail warden released him and apologized for the inconvenience. There was no explanation for the detention and Zio never found out why he was detained.

We left Zio's place early in the morning to take bus # 64 to Saint Peter to meet our party of altar boys and priests. By now we were "veterans" of getting around Rome and we got there rather quickly. We were not worried about thieves on bus # 64 anymore. We had no money. We were ready for the long trip home as Zia Sarah fixed nice sandwiches of "carciofola Ebrea" (Jewish artichoke) and cheese. I suppose that when Zio said he would take care of us, he meant it. He was strict, but we got a glimpse of what our Papa would have been like if he were alive. We thank God for that short special moment with our Zio di Roma.

The bus departed at exactly 8 am taking route 7 (Via Appia) instead of route 6 (Via Casilina). Route 6 is along the interior of Italy from Caserta to Rome. Via Appia was the route built in ancient Roman times and was along the coastline all the way to Sicily. The bus drove past Anzio and Nettuno all the way to Gaeta. Once past the mountain chains of the Apennine Mountains the bus detoured to Caserta in order to take a lunch break. We took time out to eat Zia Sarah's special lunch prepared for us. The pilgrimage was over and we were finally home in the afternoon.

In our trip to Rome I could not possibly relate to or understand why Zio was apprehended by the Germans. Nothing of what he said to us registered or made sense to me then. Compared to the occupation of Avella by the Goumiers, Zio's small infraction due to the occupation of Rome was a relatively minor incident. However, years later when I became interested in the history of WW II as related to the occupation of Rome, I came across two books by Robert Katz: "Death in Rome" and "Black Sabbath". Then, everything that Zio related to me during that pilgrimage registered very clearly.

The books by Katz were written in the late sixties, more than twenty years after the war. They triggered in me a passionate desire to address and try to understand the events of those days in Rome. I tried to relate those events to Zio Renato and people around him at that time. Zio returned to Avella in late-seventies and retired there with his family.

I visited Italy in 1976 in order to attend an international Conference in Magnetic Materials in Florence. I was employed at the Naval Research Laboratory as a research physicist in microwave magnetic materials and was invited by the IEEE organizing committee to give an invited talk. I remember the conference well, because it was the first year that a Chinese delegation of scientists ventured outside China to attend a conference in the Western world. On the way to Florence by train I met many Chinese scientists going to the conference. They were so happy and behaved like little kids out for a joy ride. I was peppered with a lot questions about America and most trivial things, not about anything scientific. On the way back from the conference we stopped in Rome to look up Zio's family on Via Garibaldi.

Surprisingly, Zio and Sarah were no longer there and the occupant never heard of Zio. I decided to take my wife to the Jewish Ghetto and taste the "Carciofola Ebrea". She enjoyed it as much as I. Finally, we took the opportunity to visit the town of Avella. I asked Serafina the whereabouts of Zio; smiling, she told me that he retired and lived in the other side of town with his family.

Immediately, arrangements were made to see him the next day for dinner. I warned him that I had a lot of questions about the war years in Rome. I knew exactly what I was going to ask him as a first question: why were you put in jail at Regina Coeli? In all those years I never forgot what made me so curious about his statement about that jail. The next day, my wife, Serafina, her two sisters, and I went to visit Zio. Again, he looked immaculate with his linen suit and blue tie, but now he had grey-white hair.

He was deeply moved and embraced me. After everybody was introduced Zio and I disappeared into his private study room. I asked him if he was a partisan during the Nazi occupation of Rome. With tongue and cheek he answered as follow: "Yes and no. Capitaniello, as far as I knew, some of my aides were potting flower plants in vases". However, he was not a member of any partisan cell in Rome, but they, at the clinic, were on the lookout for German tanks on Via Appia near his clinic on the way to Anzio. They potted yellow flowers in a vase on window sills to indicate how many tanks passed by on a particular day. The number of flowers planted followed a code system of numbers. For example, if the vase on the first window had two flowers planted and the second vase on another window three flowers, it meant 23 tanks had passed on the road below the window. Someone not known to them would gather the information and pass it on to the OSS (Office of Strategic Service). Eventually, the information was radio transmitted by some unknown OSS spy to the Allied Army at Anzio.

He then went on to say that the reason that he was put in jail at Regina Coeli was mysterious to him. It had nothing to do with the potting of flowers. He then related to me the circumstances under which he was picked up by the Gestapo truck. After dinner, he went out to smoke, toward the Tiber River, which was only a block away. That was his usual outing after dinner. I interrupted him to ask: "Did you notice a beat up boat with green canvas on the boat moored on the banks of the river?" His reaction was total disbelief as if to say, "How did you know about the boat? You weren't there".

Indeed, he confirmed that there was a small boat moored there forever, but he never saw anybody approach the boat in all the times that he was out smoking or, for that matter, at any other times. I explained to him that according to Katz' book the OSS operated a transmitter radio out of that boat, and the operator was a former Lieutenant of the Fascist Army stationed in Rome. His name was Giglio Maurizio and his code name in the resistance was "cervo". The chief spy in Rome for the OSS was Peter Tompkins who was a former student at Harvard University and was very fluent in Italian. He spent most of his childhood in Italy with his parents who were financiers. When he went back to school he majored in botany and wrote a book on the subject matter as well as a book entitled "Italy Betrayed".

I stated, "mio caro Zio, the information that you gathered about German tanks was eventually passed on to Giglio" [11, 97]. Unfortunately, he was apprehended by the Gestapo in Rome and betrayed by a double agent. To this day no one knows who the double agent was. The fate of Giglio was death at the Ardeatine Caves. Zio was stunned to hear about the boat and the clandestine activities associated with it.

After my explanation of the significance of the boat, Zio resumed his story. As he was smoking a cigarette a German truck came straight at him, driving onto the sidewalk, and two to three soldiers pointed rifles at him. They ordered him onto the back of the truck and there were five other civilians in the truck. The truck then proceeded along the Lungotevere, road along the river, randomly picking up civilians and loading them onto the truck until there were seven to eight civilians. He thought that they were going to be shipped to Germany for forced labor, since there were so many inducements plastered on walls about what a great place it was to work in Germany. The truck headed toward the old Via Appia until it reached a fork on the road. To the right of the fork was Via Ardeatina and, to the left, Via Appia Antica. The truck was parked for at least four hours until a German officer on a motor cycle came by and ordered the truck to take the prisoners to Regina Coeli jail. The truck arrived at the jail just before midnight. Zio stayed there overnight and in the morning he was released. After writing a character reference letter on behalf of the warden, Pietro Caruso, he was released. In the letter, he was told to state that the Germans picked him up, but it was the "good" warden who released Zio. In those days a lot of important Fascists tried to cover their asses knowing the war was going to be over soon, and they wanted to be in the good grace of whatever new administration. It was just a matter of time that the war was going to be over and the Allies would win.

Over the years the Via Rasella and the Ardeatine massacre has been retold by many writers with new facts and revelations. This book debunks the notion that the extra five civilians executed at Via Ardeatina were victims of a clerical mistake by the Gestapo. The Gestapo executed 335 civilians instead of 330. It was a calculated and organized undertaking by the Gestapo to "insure" the execution of 330 civilians at the Ardeatine caves. Since the extra civilians were witness to the massacre, the Gestapo murdered them. Thus, it was murder. The extra five murdered at Via Ardeatina could have easily been Zio Renato, if the number of prisoners fell below 330 at the caves of Via Ardeatina. It turned out that another truck was sent out earlier with the same mission of picking up innocent victims in order to meet the quota of 330. In addition, this truck was sent out to make up for the two prisoners who escaped from the Ardeatine caves in late afternoon of the 24th of March, 1944.

By 3:30pm of the 24th the execution began and continued until 10:30 pm in the Ardeatine Caves. At approximately 5:00-6:00 pm the Germans decided to indiscriminately round up people in the street and load them on trucks, since two prisoners escaped from the Ardeatina caves. Zio was one of the civilians picked up in the street, 6:00-7:00 pm. Zio was lucky for an earlier truck apparently must have picked up sufficient number of people off the streets to meet that quota of 330 plus five extra prisoners. Obviously, he never connected himself to the Ardeatine massacre, although he was within a few steps from being massacred.

I was happy to hear from Zio that although he indirectly participated in gathering intelligence information for the partisans during the Nazi occupation of Rome, he was not enamored then of Communist ideas of farm communes in Russia. His family owned farms and properties all over Avella and it made sense financially to return to Avella to manage the properties. We stayed in Avella for a couple of days, long enough to visit the cemetery where Nonno was buried. He died in 1965 and his last words, according to Aunt Candida, were: Caro capitaniello mio (my dear little captain). Then again, Candida was always so dramatic. It was her artistic nature in her. Ten years after our visit to Avella Zio Renato died.

In 1988, the corporal returned to Avella to rest with his Papa in the cemetery. Francesca, who died in 1990, will soon join her corporal. Francesca went back to Avella in 1989 after a violent earthquake demolished our house and sold the house and the garden to our beloved neighbor, Serafina. Uncle Joe went back to Avella to visit Mastro Nicola for the last time to re-live past memories. He died on that memorable visit. My cousin Giuseppe who was the son of aunt Candida, the seamstress, went into the business of antique porcelains from archaeological diggings in Avella and legally selling them, as well as paintings, to museums throughout the world. Giuseppe's younger brother was Michele in honor of my father. He served in the Italian mountain army division and was camped near the Alps. After the Army tour he became a singer and competed in the San Remo festivals. He died at a young age of cancer.

EIGHT
SHADES OF ANARCHY AND CHAOS

June, 1944 was a beautiful month in Avella. It was sunny and spring flowers were fading. Although the sun was unforgiving, large numbers of people were out and about in the main piazza. They wanted to vent their ordeal of the past winter and spring. Also, they had just heard the good news about the Americans being in Rome. There was a certain amount of euphoria evident for the first time in a long time. People were looking forward to better times and going to the piazza for any occasion in order to find out the latest news. News spread by word of mouth and by newspapers. Not many people had a radio. Main Street cut through the piazza about four blocks from Nonno's house. On the left, or south side, of the piazza there was a large circular water fountain with water gushing from the center of the fountain, much like the Piazza Navona fountain in Rome. The water was turned off only when a staging for an Opera or a podium for a speaker was placed on the fountain.

Opposite the palazzo, City Hall, post office, coffee house, doctor's office and convenient stores were spread around the piazza. The tax collector's office was closed, as he left town with other Fascists. North of the piazza was a street that led to Saint John's church. My favorite spot, as a child, was to sit on the sidewalk basking in the sun, like a lizard, to watch the spectacle of people in the piazza. It was truly like watching a theater performance, where the people were the actors and the piazza the staging. There was usually a large gathering during national events as in the year before, with the incarceration of Mussolini, and in 1944 with the liberation of Rome. In between times, we experienced hell on earth. Then, it was time for venting good feelings by all.

On that June day there was electricity in the air. People went out in the piazza and expressed their political aspirations without being intimidated by Fascist thugs. People were shouting obscenities and gesturing to each other about Mussolini, with all taking center court in the middle of the piazza. Then again, Italians love the theater and the drama associated with it. It was nice, for a change, to see happy, smiling faces instead of gloomy ones of the past years.

Main Street cut right through the piazza all the way to the bridge and O' Vicolo district. The bridge was blown up by the Americans with the help of Don Camillo the year before. Don Camillo and the Communists lived in the O' Vicolo district which was inhabited mostly by shepherds and other poor people. The O' Vicolo district was equivalent to what we refer to in America as a district on the wrong side of the tracks, except that, in Avella, the tracks referred to the Clanio creek. We all thought that the nightmare was over, no more soldiers camping in farms and drunk soldiers in town. The people were starving, but hopes were high. Things were corrupt all over town, but we were totally blissful and not aware of corruption anywhere. There were spontaneous celebrations, mostly by partisans or Communists groups, but, to me, it meant that I didn't have to hide in the toilet cesspool or in the pigsty anymore.

On this special day when everybody seemed to be happy to be alive, Francesca visited a friend who owned an all-purpose store located in the main piazza more for the purpose of gossiping than to buy anything. We simply did not have any money. The store was located across the piazza from City Hall, and it was a combination of novelty store, toy shop, hardware, or anything to derive business. I never figured out whether or not the owners were relatives or friends, because conversations always started out very friendly with hugging and family gossip. Those chit-chats were nothing more or less than a prelude to negotiations about the purchase of something in the store. Even as a child I knew that it would lead to negotiations and I detested that with a passion. The haggling bored me within minutes.

I was beginning to get around town on my own and curiosity always got the best of me. I was spending more time at home with Francesca, but, come dinner time, I would walk to Nonno's house to see what was cooking. Depending on the food availability I would either stay with Nonno or walk back home. Sebastiano did the same. After finishing up homework, he sometimes would walk with me to Nonno. On returning home from Nonno, I would walk past the Nuns' private school, cousin

Carmine's house (Uncle Joe in hiding), a farmhand whose farm was taken over by the Goumiers, wine making shop, horse barn, palazzo of a music Maestro (in hiding), barbershop formerly owned by Papa, Fascist home, Saint Peter Church, two bakeries, bird catcher, soccer friends, and shepherd neighbors. This pretty much constituted the Saint Peter district. The O'Vicolo and the Saint Peter districts couldn't have been more different in character. Whereas the O'Vicolo district was proud of their fire-brand revolutionary in Don Camillo, the other district was equally proud of their Figaro when he was alive. Our district was ready for the next Figaro.

Most often, people in the district would ask me where I lived and the name of my mother. They were not used to seeing a four or five year old child walking in the streets without being escorted by an adult. I would give them Francesca's nickname as "Cicchella". That was the name that I learned in calling for Francesca. The shepherd families immediately recognized that name for it was the nickname they gave to Francesca, when she was a child. It is the name of a bird which is constantly chirping. It didn't take long for the district to associate us with Figaro, Papa. In unison, they started to call me "capitaniello" and my brother "capitano". Those names stuck until we emigrated to America. Sebastiano would have filled the role of Figaro capably, if he didn't emigrate to America. When Francesca and I visited the multi-purpose store in the piazza, I sneaked out for I could not stand all that haggling. As I exited, I crossed paths with a group of shepherd teenagers coming from the O' Vicolo district carrying a large red flag. The flag was emblazened with the hammer and sickle symbols representing the international Communist flag. They recognized me and left me alone wandering in the piazza. They were advocating the overthrow of the present government of Badoglio and the King of Italy.

The Communist group started to sing Communist songs right in the middle of the piazza, inciting a workers' revolution to overthrow the government. The songs were easy to sing along with or to hum and, to this day, I still hum those songs. "Avanti popolo, chi non lavoro non mangera…bandiera rossa di liberta", "forward people, whoever doesn't want to work will not eat…..red flag of liberty". While I was away from the store I visited the headquarters of the Communist Party in Avella where Don Camillo recognized me and took me to the headquarters. He showed me pictures of Palmiro Togliatti, leader of the Italian Communist

Party, and other pictures of cities in "mother" Russia. I did not have a clue as to what he was talking about. I suppose that was the early stage of indoctrination to Communism. I was too small and all I wanted to do was to get away from Francesca in the store and look around the piazza.

Just about this time there was a commotion, when people were running after a caravan of cars heading to Main Street toward the Palazzo next to the fountain. It was the first time that many civilian cars drove through the town. That represented a big event. I don't recall anyone owning a car in Avella at that time. I followed the caravan all the way to the Palazzo and sneaked past the concierge at the portone. It was like entering a different world, but I had no idea where I was and who the person was in the caravan. Again, curiosity got the best of me as people in the piazza gathered around the cars to peek into them. One of the cars was transporting the only royalty that resided in Avella and that was the Count. Inside, the palazzo reminds me now so much of places like the palaces in Caserta or Versailles. The farm within the palazzo was mind boggling and in the middle of town. It was at least 100 acres. The concierge finally escorted me out of the palazzo. I didn't know people could live like that. I could not even afford a pair of shoes.

The O'Vicolo district is on the right side of the palazzo Main piazza and the royal palazzo. The water fountain is in front of the palazzo.

Main Street runs from left to right.

The royal palazzo was across the street from the store, and I made my way through the crowd and back to the store. I thought that I would be scolded by Francesca, but, to my surprise, she never discovered that I left. She was still haggling or gossiping with the store owner. To hear that was painful. Years later, when I was on the Board of Directors of a microwave Company in the suburb of Boston, Mass. dealing with radars, a colleague on the Board suggested that I "try my hand" as a negotiator. He felt that I had natural skills for it. To think that

Francesca had such influence on me, after spending those hated hours watching her haggle over little money, was disconcerting to me.

There were a lot of unprintable words spoken by many people about Mussolini in the piazza that day. By then, Mussolini was history and did not affect people's lives anymore. The name Mussolini invoked heartfelt invectives in our household and a lot people felt the same way. Hence, knowing that there would not be any more retribution, people were simply venting for everyone to hear. In retrospect, I believe now that these demonstrations throughout the south of Italy, including Avella, were inspired and organized by the Communist party or the partigiani (partisans) who were mostly Communist.

The Communist Party became very active with the return from Russia of the Communist party leader, Palmiro Togliatti. They became active within the partisans' sabotage activities against the Germans and politically against the Badoglio's government. Their aim was to topple any stable government on their way to power (according to the Communist Manifesto). They liked the idea of no government and creating a political vacuum in which they could take over the role of government. In some sense, it was a form of controlled anarchy. In Roman times the winning general in a civil war would make up a "hit" list to eliminate opposition. The "hit" list of the Communist party included all opposition parties that were in their way to power, and assassination of opposition leaders like Leon Trotsky. He was assassinated on August 21, 1940, in Mexico.

In short, people did not want to go back to Fascism or Monarchy, but their views of what they wanted in the next government differed. One view, Communist party, was to re-distribute the resources and wealth of the country, especially the redistribution of the large farms belonging to the church. Since the churches owned most of the farms in Avella, the clergy took exception to the programs outlined by the Communist party. Basically, the Communists were aspiring to another revolution in Italy.

Another view, advocated by the Christian Democrats, wanted nothing to do with an anti-Christ political party like the Communist party, but restore a democratic party under a new constitution. It was no surprise that this view was supported by the Catholic Church. In addition to these two parties, there were 30-40 other parties whose views vacillated between the two extreme points of view. For example, one party advocated one loaf of bread a day to everyone. However, believe it or not, there was one party, MSI, advocating the return to the Fascist government and another a return to the Monarchy. The latter two parties were in the minority. In effect, we had a political vacuum in leadership.

Prominent people in Avella usually shied away from politics, but delved strongly into business ventures. New faces began to show up in town. For example, a relative of mother came from Benevento. His aunt who lived next door died from a simple case of influenza, since there was no medicine during the war to cure her. The suspicion in town was that the nephew was a former Fascist, but no one was certain. However, the suspicion did not draw any attention from the local partisans or Communists. There were many cases where Communists took law in their own hands [98] and it was not a pleasant situation. In Baiano a former Fascist jail warden was lynched by the Communists right after a trial without due process. The warden was accused of false imprisonment of a partisan.

In a nearby town of Cicciano, people stormed the courtroom while a former Fascist official was on trial for past transgressions. The people dragged the Fascist defendant outside the courtroom and hung him from a tree. The sad thing about this person was that, in fact, he actually was responsible for hiding Allied soldiers in Cicciano after the infamous landing of the 509th parachute battalion in Avellino. The rationale for the lynching was that the Fascist on trial was going to be killed anyway! Yes, it was that crazy world in 1944-45. Could that happen again? Yes, if we forget our past history. We will be doomed to re-live it. No one was held responsible for the lynching.

Civilian Partisans and Communists rounding up former Fascists in Southern Italy [108].

In Avella, the Fascist Mayor left town. To this day no one knows where he went. There was no one running City Hall. Fortunately, in Italy Mayors do not "run" the town; the bureaucracy runs a town. Whereas local Fascists were leaving town, royal families were returning to Avella.

Former Italian soldier joining the Partisan movement [108].

However, there was a happy ending for one local Fascist residing in the Saint Peter district. Although many Fascists left Avella after the downfall of Rome to the Allies, one Fascist, with whom my family was very friendly, was a shoe repairman. The shop of the shoe repairman was located below the apartment where the priest of San Pietro lived, a block from my house. The family of the shoe repairman adored Benito Mussolini and they were members of the Fascist party. My mother knew the family well, because one of their sons named Vittorio, was stationed in North Africa with my father and died about the same time as my father. Before the war my father had his shoes made at the shop by the father, and reciprocated by giving free shaves and haircuts to the shoe repairman and his sons. Like my father, Vittorio's remains were still in North Africa. All his children were named after Mussolini's children: Bruno, Benito, Vittorio and Romano.

The "black sheep" of the family was son Pasquale who was not named for any of the Mussolini's. The wife won out in naming this son Pasquale, which means "peace" in English, but there was nothing peaceful about Pasquale. He quarreled with any one in town about the family's identity with the infamous Mussolini names. He wanted to distance himself from those infamous names.

With names like Benito, it was inconceivable that people in the town could not have known that they were Fascists. I believe that the whole town knew, but they kept it a secret. The neighborhood liked the family. Inside their house, pictures of Mussolini and Mussolini's sons were prominently displayed. Romano and Benito, the shoe repairman's sons, were the oldest ones and were excellent trumpeters. Their music was South American style. Sometimes I would sit down on the steps of San Pietro church across from their bedroom window and listen to them play. It was so beautiful and mesmerizing. I loved the special beat of South American music: tango, samba, and basa nova. Once I heard one note I was trapped there until they stopped playing. They usually practiced their music in early afternoons until dark sometimes. I was so sad, when they left town soon after the war and emigrated to South America. There is no doubt in my mind that they were great musicians and would have had great careers anyplace in the world. For what I remember of the music played I can say now that they were great talent. Every year I would ask their father, when are they coming back? He would say to me: "Next year, capitaniello, for sure". The word "capitaniello" was in reference to my father showing respect in calling me little captain. They never came back. Like many other Fascists, the trumpeters were escaping to South America to avoid the wrath of the Communists in town. It was just a matter of time before Communists would be knocking on the door. They adapted their style of music to South American style knowing full well that they intended to go there.

City Hall operated without a mayor and council. Favors from the bureaucracy went to the highest bidder or bribe. Political anarchy was rampant and City Hall was totally corrupt. No one paid taxes for there was no one collecting taxes. As such, tax records disappeared from City Hall. The police department consisting of a Maresciallo (chief of Police) and two Carabinieri, were not paid for a long time. The police itself were involved in a lot of shenanigans to raise money. It was a wonder how police were ever paid, since the new government of Badoglio was not in Rome printing new money. Fascist money was worthless at that time. Thus, the Carabinieri, local police, were in the same predicament as the City Hall workers. That must have created quite a dilemma. The new guardians of the state were castigating or replacing the old system, but somehow money, directly or indirectly, reached the bureaucrats illegally. The new system was mostly based on bribes. In some sense nothing has changed to this day.

For the year 1944-45, things in Avella were dire. There was no food other than what one could scavenge from the hills and farms. There were not many farmers on the farms. Foreign soldiers took every single livestock in the farms and more. When Nonno and I returned to Nonno's farm in the summer of 1944 to scavenge for food, all of the fruit trees were cut including hazelnut and grape trees. The parsonale's (farmhand) living quarters were razed to the ground and loose tapestries, wood planks, bricks and kitchen items were strewn all over the farm. The caves, where we went for cover during air raids, were filled with debris and dirt. In short, the farm was a total mess and no food was to be had anywhere in the farm. The British did not compensate a single cent for the use of the farm. They just made life miserable for the parsonale, especially.

It took a couple of years for fruit trees to grow, grape trees three to four years, hazelnut trees five or more years and on and on. The farms were decimated and out of business. It took at least five years for the farms to again be as productive as before the war.

By the end of summer and into fall, 1944, farm laborers were in great demand, but many capable workers were simply not around. They were in some strange lands far away from home, and many were casualties of war. Most of them never made it back. So, town people helped themselves to the summer and fall harvests of 1944. They simply went out into the farms and picked fruits and vegetables for themselves and were able to make preserves to last for the winter season. The shepherds were immune to all of these farm worries. Life for the shepherds was the same with or without foreign visitors.

Grandfather Carmine left two small plots of land near the foothills of the mountains, near the dry creek, full of fruit trees. In all the years, during the war, that we lived in Avella we were never able to pick one single fruit from those trees. Other people just beat us to the ripe fruits, since they lived closer to the garden. Reporting this to the Carabinieri would have signaled for the police to be first in line to pick these fruits. Security of farms was non-existent, since the local police, carabinieri, had their hands full in trying to survive without pay and keeping the partisans or the Communists apart from the Badogliani, the King's government, Fascists and Christian Democrats. Civil war was brewing all over southern Italy in late 1944.

How we survived that period of time is beyond my comprehension today. I have asked myself many times, how did we manage to survive? I can come up with only one simple answer: the mountains. Remarkably, the people showed no signs of desperation. There was a special spirit to managing things on their own to survive, since a monkey (Mussolini) was off their backs. I believe now that special spirit was derived from people's belief that the mountains and the farms somehow would provide whatever was needed in food or otherwise. It certainly served the shepherds well.

Beyond chicory and tomatoes picked in the farms there was no other food. People were scavenging all over the foothills and searching for anything: wild roots, green vegetables, chicory, dandelions, wild edible weeds, fruits, chestnuts, mushrooms, snails, etc. Shepherds did very well in this period of time, because the mountains were their "home away from home". Besides, they still had their sheep. I spent a lot of time near Nonno's farm looking for snails with other kids. The only danger in this endeavor was snakes hiding between rocks where snails often resided. We kids learned to use sticks to probe for snakes. Sometimes we took dead snakes home to eat. Eggs, meats, dairy products, white flour were things people would barter for and dream about. Whatever little food there was, people were willing to share or barter. Nonno taught Francesca to make pasta by "hand" so that we had spaghetti dishes more often at home and at Nonno's house on Sunday. Shepherds managed to save some sheep and do some business. Francesca was put to work making cheese from sheep's milk. A shepherd's family who had close ties to my grandfather, who was in the USA, did Francesca a favor in hiring her. They were using grandfather Carmine's fields on the mountains and paying nothing. It was not really a job for it didn't pay much money, but, at least, it put some cheese on the table. Bread was still a big item to obtain. Since the British left, there was not much bread to share.

The process of making cheese was the same as the so-called Romano cheese produced then and now. The only difference between the commercial grade and the one produced by Francesca was the length of time the cheese was cured or aged. Typically, in the morning we would eat ricotta or other cheese with bread provided by Nonno, bread and tomatoes at lunch, fried zucchini or eggplants for dinner. Chicory salad complemented the meals. There was very little milk for it was used to make cheese and ricotta, but sometimes we had hot milk in the morning. Sunday was special. Nonno cooked for the whole family and I loved to watch him. I would sit on the staircase above the kitchen and observe every move Nonno made while cooking, just like Topolino, little mouse. Typically, in those days, he would prepare a spaghetti or macaroni dish with tomato sauce. At least, we graduated from polenta for the morning meal, lunch and dinner. Polenta most often replaced bread in our meals. Meat in the tomato sauce was a rarity. Coffee made from dried chicory was consumed almost in every household. Coffee from dried chicory was too bitter for me to drink. I believe adults drank chicory coffee just to dream about the "real" roasted coffee of the past and the hope that one day soon they would be getting ready to taste real coffee or espresso. Once in a while vendors from Naples would arrive with a mule-driven wagon full of sardines or fish products that smelled up the whole street or other vendors would bring fresh vegetables. Although there was a scarcity of basic foods, the will to make do and manage to eat and survive was great among all of the people in Avella. Also, there was a spirit of co-operation and helping out people with no means at all or were sick. There was a spirit to survive and go beyond this calamity.

For the first time ever, Christmas of 1944 was celebrated in the full traditional way. I don't recall how earlier Christmases were celebrated, but this one was memorable. Bagpipers visited people's houses and played traditional Christmas tunes. Usually, bagpipers visited homes where the "presepio" was prepared in the corner of a room. A "presepio" was a miniature nativity scene that included the scene of the manger with baby Jesus, Mother Mary and Joseph. Ceramic mules or donkeys served as background. In addition, the scenery was embellished with miniature mountain scenes of sheep and shepherds, "Osteria" restaurant, Roman soldiers, shepherds on hills and houses. It was supposed to mimic the scenery as it may have been at the birth of Jesus. However, the miniature statuettes and various complementary scenes always reflected the local scenery and the people, not reflective of the actual birth in Bethlehem. This contradiction, of course, was glossed over when I was there and still is to this day.

Francesca allowed me to follow the bagpipers all over town, but not to enter people's houses. I would stand outside the homes and listen to the bagpipers inside. For the first time I was allowed to celebrate Christmas mass at midnight with the family. It seemed like the whole town was doing the same. The scene was surreal as if the whole town was thanking God for this nightmare to be over. The people sang Christmas songs at the top of their lungs. Never again in all the years thereafter did I hear the people sing those beautiful songs of Christmas as loud as on that Christmas night of 1944. I believe now that the people of Avella wanted God to hear their thank you for ending the nightmare of the past four years.

Christmas day of 1944 will always be remembered as that magical night, when the people of Avella turned out in droves to thank God for ending the catastrophe. It was a special occasion in time that had nothing to do with the Holiday itself.

Besides the festive mood as reflected by the bagpipers, people bought small cherry bombs that they would toss up in the air and that exploded on the ground or on the walls of houses. I remember being warned by my aunts to keep away from the explosions for sometimes little rocks may splatter. Besides cherry bombs, firecrackers and hand held fireworks on wooden sticks were the favorite items for small children like me.

Many years later, my cousin Carmine and I would place the fireworks with the stick inside an empty soda bottle and fire them across a large garden. We learned that by twisting the paperwork around the powdered end of the explosives, we could launch the fireworks at a longer distance. We then graduated into making launching pads in order to increase the delivery distance even more. I guess that was our venture into rocketry. Fortunately, the fireworks never reached the other side of the garden where other families lived, about three football fields away. However, I followed up with the delivery of little explosives into making little bombs. Years later, I refined the technique to be able to control the loudness of the explosion or the potential damage to a wall. For example, I would collect small amounts of powder used for cherry bombs into wrapping paper. The wrapping paper was extended sufficiently to allow for lighting it with a match. The bombs were powerful enough to blow up a stone wall two feet wide.

Besides fireworks testing, toys were exchanged for the first time. Cousins Carmine and Giannina often invited me to share the latest toys bought by Uncle Joe. In particular, Uncle Joe bought a toy car whereby one had to paddle to get it moving. It lasted about a week before it was a total wreck. We would ram the car into a closed door separating the inside courtyard where the cousins lived with relatives. In the middle of the courtyard there was a huge fig tree that was more than two stories high. The tree branches extended all the way to the second floor balconies. That was great for figs could be picked easily from the balconies, and we all indulged in the picking.

We played a game of seeing who could break the door down with the toy car. However, one day the separating door opened just as one of us was ramming the car into the door. The toy car ended up in the middle of the street under a parked delivery truck. Fortunately, the truck driver was parked in the street on an errand. After that incident there was no more ramming of the door. For us kids it was an outlet for it allowed us to dream about the outside world as depicted in movies at the Cinema. For example, cousin Giannina imagined herself to be driving a Ferrari at the Grand Prix. I was just happy driving anything.

When I was 8-9 years old, I placed a miniature bomb wrapper made by me in a side wall that separated the monastery of Saint Anthony from the town. The other side of the wall was a garden where the monks worked almost every day on the fruit trees. The purpose of the wall was to prevent looters from raiding the garden. My fascination was in the capture of small lizards which had their nests within the wall. The wall was about two feet wide and full of small holes where lizards would poke their heads out. I developed a technique for capturing the lizards. I would bang on the wall and simultaneously place a grass weed circular nook around the hole in the wall. As the lizard would poke his head out of the hole, I pulled on the grass weed and captured the lizard about 50% of the time. Somehow, I was fascinated with lizards, since watching movies about dinosaurs at the local Cinema. However, with the placement of a miniature bomb in the hole of the wall, I rationalized that by placing more than one hook over the holes on the wall I could catch more lizards with one bang. Besides, I didn't have to bang on the wall.

The traps or hooks were put in place and lit the fuse. After about 10 seconds there was a very loud explosion, but no lizards were captured.

All the hooks fell to the ground and the lizards were running around outside the wall. That was not the only repercussion that came out of the explosion. Within 5-10 minutes monks came out in the street wondering what the hell happened. They examined the big cracks on the outside wall where the bomb was placed. I calmly came out of Nonno's house and inquired as to what happened. The monks asked Nonno, if he saw anyone near the wall. Nonno said that he was asleep during the afternoon siesta. There is no doubt in my mind now that Nonno knew who did it. He kept looking at me and asking me what happened a number of times. I said perhaps that it was the curse of San Gennaro, when lightning hit the wall. It was an obvious lie, since it was a sunny day. San Gennaro is the patron Saint of Naples and the Saint is blamed for good or bad omens. I adopted San Gennaro for one day as the patron Saint of Avella. The permanent patron of Avella was and is San Michele, the Archangel Saint. Of course, that was an admission to Nonno. Thereafter, I went back to the old technique for catching lizards.

New Year, 1945, was celebrated in a strange way to me at that time. On New Year's Eve, people would toss all old dish wares, glasses, and anything old out the window to bring in the New Year. When I first saw that as a child, I was totally confused, for all the while, I was told by everybody in the household to be careful about this or that as it may break. Everything that we had was old and chipped. If we threw all the broken or damaged plates out the window, we would have nothing left, and that would be silly. That tradition is still in place today.

There were no gifts on Christmas morning or at New Year's Eve. However, on January the fifth of 1945 Francesca told Sebastiano and me to put up a clean sock to hang from the bedside in order to prepare for "Befania". "Befania" celebrates the occasion of the three Magi bringing gifts to baby Jesus, and this occasion did not occur on Christmas day. Befania represents an old witch floating on a broom to bring gifts. It occurred on January 6, according to religious beliefs. I got a couple of dry figs and a couple of hard candies. Sebastiano got extra candies that we shared. That was the beginning of normalcy! We transitioned from hell six months ago to blissful, peaceful times.

Nonno and I returned to his farm in the summer of 1945. His beloved cherry tree was growing beautifully and it looked like it was about to be productive. In late spring of 1945 it did produce white flowers and in May-June big red/white cherries. The parsonale brought a basket full of cherries. They tasted so good. For a year, the parsonale was busy rebuilding his dwelling on the farm, raising the livestock and planting trees. The farm was ready to be productive.

We could no longer trespass into the neighbor's farm below, since farmhands began to show up in that farm where the colosseum was located. Their hazelnut and olive trees were left intact and it was time to cultivate the fruits on the trees. Hence, we had to take the longer route home. Soon after the war, a tall fence was placed alongside the fault line and the dirt road separating the two farms. I suspect then that the owners did not want to reveal the location of the colosseum in his farm. Unfortunately for them, the colosseum was too big to hide.

The access to the pool by the people of Avella started about the summer of 1945. We all heard about the existence of the pool, when soldiers were in camp. Some of the soldiers ran in the nude at times near our house. No one from Avella was allowed near the pool then. The pool was popular among the young people of Avella and vicinity and there was a mad rush to the pool that summer. Sebastiano, friends and I visited the pool and it was unbelievably crowded. Even people from Sperone and Baiano came. There was no entrance fee and no lifeguard. Sebastiano was there trying to learn to swim. His friends were really good swimmers and taught Sebastiano how to swim.

For the next couple of weeks Sebastiano would take me to the pool trying to teach me how to swim. The only unfortunate incident was that one kid was bitten by a viper snake. We soon realized that these snakes were poisonous vipers and were all over the place. It did not take long for teenagers to wipe out most of the population of snakes near the pool. They used sticks and metal rods to kill most of the snakes in the cabana housing.

Sebastiano learned to swim within a week; I was still struggling. Sebastiano tried to teach me for a long time, but no success. I was simply scared of the water and still am. In frustration, Sebastiano threw me in the water and "ordered" me to swim, but I didn't drown.

As all good things come to an end, a couple of years later an entrance fee to the pool was charged. We thought the idea of charging a fee was farcical, since there was no mayor in town, no police chief and not even city bureaucrats. So, no one paid the entrance fee. Besides the water was free, since it was drained from the Roman aqueducts carrying water nearby. I believe now that the people charging the fees were part of the local camorra (thugs), as the people charging for the entrance did not represent the commune of Avella. There was no local government. However, we were about to enter another shade of catastrophe, lawlessness and anarchy.

The problem was exacerbated even more once the USA Navy established a major military base in Naples in 1945. The black market was rampant in Naples and towns nearby. The local Mafia, or Camorra, was dealing in contrabands of American products and cigarettes as they were sold all over the area and shipped to all corners of Italy. Prostitution was also flourishing in Naples, where scugnizzi would pimp even their mothers. The Allied Military Commission (AMC) placed known Camorristi as mayors in the Naples area as well in Naples, replacing the Podestas (mayors) of the Fascist regime.

The man in charge of assigning mayors all over the area was none other than Vito Genovese, reputed Mafia boss in New York City. The Camorra grew from a local crime outfit to a national syndicate in Italy. Nowadays, it rivals other international crime syndicates. As a result Naples gained a bad reputation. Only the Camorra provided public security and safety. The Camorristi Mayors were in charge of the local police! As such, total chaos reigned in Naples. Towns in the Naples area were also controlled by the Camorra in coordination with the Camorra in Naples.

In Sicily things were a little different. Before the war Mussolini exiled a lot of "capo" Mafiosi to isolated islands in the Mediterranean and was given credit for having eradicated the Mafia in Sicily. During the allied invasion of Sicily, the US Navy "employed" special consultants to help the Allied Army in the invasion of Sicily, and the likes of Vito Genovese and Salvatore "Lucky" Luciano were employed. The motives of both Mafia bosses was to return to the USA as they had been deported to Italy by the US Immigration Office as undesirables. The Allied public administration allowed the exiles to return to Sicily to assist the local administration in running the towns. This was like having the wolves guard the sheep. The only benefit, if one were to stretch it a bit, was that no bandits were running loose around the hills of Sicily, as they were in the Naples area. The Mafia [99] was not in the business of fostering competition with bandits not associated with the Mafia. As a result, the Mafia returned to its former power it had before the Fascist government came to govern Italy.

A friend who was born in Sicily just before the war, was lamenting to me the loss of his father at the time of the Allied invasion in Sicily. He told me that his father died during the invasion. I assumed that his father was in the Italian Army and I inquired whether he had been in the black shirt division, like my Uncle Joe. No sooner that I asked this innocent question, I was harshly rebuked for asking such a question. His answer was "Of course not". As a result of the father's death his mother and he had no choice but to leave Sicily and immigrate to America. The point here was that things in Sicily were in such tight control by the Mafia in those days that even elimination of some people was "routine" and not punishable by law. Whoever put away his father could not afford to have the son take a vendetta later. They had no choice but to immigrate.

It was just a matter of time for street thugs, or simply bandits, taking over the hills, the farms and the streets of Avella, since the Fascist mayor left town and there was no one else taking over City Hall. The political vacuum was taken over by bandits. At the beginning of 1945 a new fear factor and anarchy entered people's minds. Different shades of anarchy existed in the Naples area as well as south of it.

There were bandits who terrorized local towns. They were local young thugs who were out of work and allied themselves with others from nearby towns. They hid in the hills and knew the area and people well. I suspect that the local ones provided necessary intelligence for out-of-towners and vice versa. The appearance to any town was that out-of-towners were doing the bad deeds, when in fact there was complicity between all the thugs. The glue that bound the thugs in those days was none other than the Camorra headquartered in Naples. Moderate to large scale planning by thugs had to be approved by the Camorra. In effect, the Camorra replaced the central government which did not exist at that time and it bankrolled the police departments in the area and the bureaucrats. Thus, the Camorra was part "Robin Hood", part of the establishment and part a Machiavellian organization. The few thugs that were caught by police were not part of the Camorra organization for those thugs interfered with the business as usual by the Camorra.

NINE
END OF FASCISM IN ITALY

The concentration of Allied troops was shifting toward northern Europe by the fall of 1944 and by the winter of 1945 the Battle of the Bulge was over. It was just a matter of time when the war was going to be over. Finally, Stalin, Soviet President and Communist Party Secretary, got his wish of a second front in Western Europe. The race to Berlin was on between Allied and Soviet Union troops. Elite Allied troops in the Italian campaign were siphoned off to Northern Europe to participate in the Normandy invasion and thereafter. Similarly, German troops were withdrawn from Northern Italy and the Balkans to defend their homeland in Germany. However, there were remnant German troops stationed from Florence to the Alps for the sole purpose of tying down as many Allied troops in Italy as possible. Two to three German divisions were stationed in North Italy. At the peak of battle in Southern Italy there may have been as many as twenty-five or more German Divisions. As for engaging in major battles in Italy, it was not a desirable thing to do from the Allied and the German military point of view. It was a stalemate by an unwritten consent.

Mussolini's new Fascist government, with its capital at Salo on the Garda Lake, was made up of former Fascist members of the party council. This council voted on July 25, 1943 for a vote of no-confidence (19-6) in the Fascist government under Mussolini. The remaining members who went with Mussolini to form the government at Salo were arch-fascists who still had confidence in Mussolini's ability to regain his power. They were simply fanatics or flawed people. There was only one fate awaiting these people, and they knew it. One member of the council who voted for no-vote was Mussolini's son in-law, Count Galeazzo Ciano. Ciano married Mussolini's daughter, Edda, and had three children. Ciano was pursued relentlessly all over northern Italy as a traitor by none other than Hitler. As long as there was no intent by the Allies to advance any further in North Italy, the few remaining die-hard Fascists in Salo lived in a blissful and delusional world. I am sure as the sky is blue and the ocean is deep that all of them thought of an escape route, but where to and who would want them?

The Swiss government let it be known that these Fascist fanatics and Mussolini's family were not welcome in Switzerland. By now, Spain was desperately trying to be neutral and wash their hands of their Fascist past. North of the Alps the war was still raging. As is well known now, the escape route was to South America via the Vatican. Exactly, how this escape route was exercised then is beyond the scope of this book. However, in the winter and spring of 1945 this escape route was well known to Nazis and Fascists. The rationale for this policy in the Vatican was the following. The Church was there to help people in need and distress, regardless of affiliations! The church was not there to judge. The claim by the Vatican was that they helped both sides to escape: Jews, Americans, English, Italian, German, Russians, Gypsies, Serbs, etc. On paper this policy sounded good, but it was a hollow gesture. There was a major difference between escaping Jews or civilians and Fascists or Nazis. Escaping Nazis and Fascists were criminals and the others were not. Thus, the church was abetting criminals.

The retreating German Army in Italy was not overly concerned about being attacked in force by the Allied Army stationed in Italy, since both armies were depleted of manpower and the skirmishes in north Italy were irrelevant to the overall outcome of the war. As a matter of fact, even General Kesselring was transferred to the Western front in March, 1945. He was lucky, as most German soldiers stationed in Italy were transferred to the Russian front. The main concern was partisan activities against the German Army in North Italy, survival, and keeping the Fascist government at Salo solvent and viable. Partisans consisted of Communists, Russian Army deserters, American and British POWs, Italian anti-fascists, and Italian Army deserters. Their goal was to disrupt the German war machinery anyway possible: sabotage, explosions of bridges, capture and killing of German troops, spying, and radio communications among Partisans.

The reprisals by the German Army on the capture of Partisans was brutal. If captured by Germans, one would not expect to come out alive.

Even when Partisans were not captured, the reprisal on civilians was brutal. Reprisals on civilians were justified only by the German Army on the basis of international law, such as the Hague Convention of 1907, whereby the Allies and Germany were signatories. For example, in June 1944 in Val di Chiana (Arezzo) and in September at Marzabotto (Bologna), Germans slaughtered 971 civilians, male and female, in response to Partisan attacks. I never understood the justification, since these civilians had nothing to do with the attacks.

As mentioned, part of the goal of the German Army was to maintain the Fascist government at Salo. They did this by spying on the populace to seek out potential saboteurs and traitors to the Fascist regime. The Germans, in particular Hitler, regarded Galeazzo Ciano a potential threat to the stability of the Fascist regime. He was regarded more as a traitor than a threat. This was due to the fact that Ciano was one of the members of the Fascist council who voted against Mussolini in July 25, 1943. Also, Ciano had in his possession a diary dating back to the mid-thirties which gave details of Germany's relationships and betrayals with Mussolini and Ciano himself. The diary was critical of Mussolini and Nazism in particular. The publication of such a diary would have been detrimental to the Fascist and Nazi regimes. The Germans desperately wanted to get hold of it. Another reason to get the diary was a question of survival. By December 1944 different factions of the Nazi government competed against each other to gain gossip information against a potential foe in government. The stakes were high in all respects.

After Mussolini was arrested on July 25, 1943 most of the Fascist government functionaries, including Galeazzo Ciano, went into hiding all over Rome. The fear of the Fascists was that they also would be arrested irrespective of how they voted on that fateful day. King Victor Emmanuel III and General Badoglio did draw up a list of Fascists to arrest. As such, the Fascists had plenty of time to hide and sort out things. Time was on their side, but they never realized that. In particular, Edda and Galeazzo Ciano panicked and decided to immigrate to Spain on a false passport, as soon as possible. At this point, it is incomprehensible why the couple went to the German officials in Rome to request a plane ride to Spain. First, it was well known that Ciano opposed the alliance between Italy and Germany. Second, Ciano was not on particularly good terms with some Nazi officials. Third, Ciano voted in the council's meeting on July 25 in favor of no confidence in Mussolini's government.

The plan to go to Spain was not Ciano's idea, but Edda's. She was the oldest child of Mussolini and his favorite child. Also, she was in a good personal relationship with Hitler. She simply miscalculated her power to "influence" people at the top of both governments. Under the pretense of flying directly to Spain, Colonel Otto Skorzeny of the German Air Force flew the plane to Munich, and the whole family was put under house arrest. Hitler's attitude is best described in a conversation he had with Mussolini: "I don't doubt that you will agree with me in believing that one of the first acts of the new (Fascist) government will have to be to sentence to death the traitors of the Grand Council. I judge Count Ciano four times a traitor; traitor to his country, traitor to Fascism, traitor to the alliance with Germany, traitor to his family. But I advise you, it is preferable that the death sentence be carried out in Italy".

Indeed, that is exactly what happened. Ciano was deported to Verona jail. Mussolini set up a kangaroo court that found Count Ciano guilty of treason and condemned him to death by the firing squad, together with other Fascists. Ciano was dead on January 12, 1944. While the intrigue of the incarceration and the trial was happening his wife and three children escaped to Switzerland, by car to the border, and then by foot into Switzerland. Edda wrapped Ciano's diary around her waist, as she crossed the border. She tried to swap the diary for the freedom of Count Ciano, to no avail. Ultimately, she concluded that she could not trust the Nazi officials. What a surprise! Before she left for Switzerland she told her father that the war was lost and that she could not believe that her father was going to put to death the father of his grand-children. That miserable and delusional person did exactly that.

Like Count Ciano, Mussolini was trapped in Northern Italy by the Partisans. North of the Alps there was major warfare between the Allies in the West and the Russians on the East marching toward Berlin. South of the Po valley there was a stalemate by consent whereby Allied troops were facing enough German troops to force a stalemate. Partisans were getting more brazen and were roaming the hills surrounding main cities like Milan. A meeting on April 24, 1945 was arranged by Cardinal Schuster, of the Milan diocese, between Mussolini, his associates, partisans and aspirants to future governments.

Discussions pertained to terms and conditions for surrender by the Fascists. The meeting broke up with Mussolini promising to respond to the terms of surrender offered by the partisans. the next day he left for the city of Como on Lake Como with a caravan of 20-30 Fascists. Arrangements were made to re-inforce the Mussolini group with 5,000 more Fascists. However, reinforcements never arrived, since they were tied down by the partisans on the way to Como. Thus, Mussolini was one to two miles from the Swiss border, but he never crossed it.

For years people have been speculating about whether or not Mussolini was contemplating escape to Switzerland, especially when he was only 20 minutes from the border at a steady walk. The answer is an unequivocal yes. It made no military sense to be so close to the border without the means to do anything militarily, since the concentration of Fascist troops was located 30-50 miles to the East of Como, toward Milan. When he arrived in the city of Como, with a group of Fascist officials, there were no partisans in sight, and the border was an open field, one mile away. The closest custom police station was at Porlezza, fifteen miles north of Como. Given these circumstances Mussolini had the intent to cross the border. As Francesca said years before the war: "No balls". He decided to stay put. In fact, he ordered the Fascist interior minister Guido Buffarini to Porlezza to investigate the border. When Buffarini was turned back at the border by the Italian and Swiss guards, Mussolini must have decided that the ruse was up. He then headed north to the Brenner Pass to cross another border area into Austria. The point is that Mussolini wanted to escape by any means. He was caught by the partisans at Dongo, 25 miles north of Como, dressed as a regular German soldier. He and his mistress Clara Petacci were shot to death by a special Communist agent Walter Audisio [37] on April 28, 1945 with the explicit order from the Communist leadership to kill Mussolini.

On that historic day, it was a beautiful sunny spring day in 1945. I could see from the bedroom window that people were streaming toward the piazza. I knew immediately that something important must have just occurred. I quickly got dressed and followed the crowd to the piazza. There was an enthusiastic celebration with the news that Mussolini was dead. Again, I observed the spectacle from the usual spot opposite the water fountain in the piazza basking in the sun. People were very happy. There was no remorse from what I could see. The same group of people, partisans and Communists that I saw the year before, were carrying their red flags all over the piazza, and this time they had a radio blaring the news of Mussolini's death. Also, they had a two- men band playing a tambourine and   trumpet and singing the famous Communist revolutionary songs. The mood was jubilant and engaging. By this time a coffee shop/bar had opened up at one corner of the piazza. I smelled the beautiful aroma of sweet espresso for the first time. I knew right way that this was not coffee made from dry chicory. People were waiting in line for an espresso and sat outside and took in the atmosphere and all the commotions around them. The people sensed a truly historic moment. Everyone just wanted to turn the page over and enter a new chapter. In our house I must have heard the name Mussolini a million times. As a child at that time what was important to me was what was for dinner for that night or was there any food. Yes, food was the main preoccupation. I had no idea why these people were celebrating and why the commotion, but I knew enough to know that they were happy for a change.

In retrospect and in talking to my family and friends after the War, the consensus was that Count Ciano was the villain of his family. He profited most financially and, therefore, it was no big loss, when he was murdered. Uncle Joe told me that when he was stationed in Sicily, Italian soldiers would scurry around town for food, whereas German soldiers were well supplied. Imagine, he told me, they had marmalade for breakfast! After two days, his battalion ran out of ammunition and food. Ciano was the point of contact, together with companies that he did business with, for the acquisition and distribution of war materiel. To this day people are still discussing whose fault it was for entering a war so unprepared. As for me, there should never have been a war under any circumstances, but in this case only one man was responsible and we know who that was, Mussolini.

THE TRANSITION PERIOD, 1944-46

TEN
FEW RETURNED HOME

After the Germans occupied Rome on September 10, 1943, up to 725,000 Italian military personnel became prisoners of the German army. Some were inserted into the new Fascist army in Salo, but most of the prisoners were transported to Germany and worked for the Nazi war machine. In the African campaign, more than 600,000 Italian prisoners came under Allied control and were returned to Italy slowly. As many as one million Italian soldiers died or were stranded in Russia and the Balkans. About 10,000 prisoners returned to Italy after the War.

Before the War, there were 40,000 Jews living in Italy, but 8,000 were deported from Italy and executed by the Nazis. It is no consolation to know that Italy had the lowest percentage, besides Denmark, of Jews killed in WW II. I believe that if Pope Pius XI (not XII) were alive during German occupation of Italy, not a single Italian Jew would have died. According to Pius XI, the killing of anyone for political or religious belief was against any religious credo that the church tried to promulgate for centuries [18]. Contrary to Pius XII, who became Pope in March of 1939, 8,000, Italian Jews died at his "watch."

After the deportation of Jews from Rome on October 18, 1943, Pope Pius XII instructed Cardinal Luigi Maglione to ask the German Ambassador, Ernst Von Weizsacker [71], how the Pope should proceed with this terrible event. In particular, should the Pope register a formal protest? The German ambassador suggested that the Pope be "silent" and he would look into it. This was absurd. It is like having a "good shepherd" asking a diabolical "wolf" how to best protect his sheep! Yes, they were his sheep, because Jews were Roman citizens long before anyone else in Rome.

People who defended the Pope's decision have claimed that Pius XII was silent for the greater good, so that a lot more Jews in Rome could be saved. According to Vatican officials, German Police were needed then to protect the Vatican from the Communists and partisans in Rome. Again, this is absurd, since the Communists were no threat then and now. Secondly, there were a lot more Jews in Europe who were still in danger besides the Jews of Rome. Robert Katz summarized it best, when he stated in his book: "There would be a Saint of Silence, but the divine grace that is supposed to shine in such a servant of God would light nothing in its path". I ask myself: what would a Saint do in such a situation. Pope Pius' XII behavior at that time cannot possibly be condoned as Saintly. I believe that a Saint would then have demanded to be transported on October 18, with the Jews of Rome, to Auschwitz.

The winter of 1945 was bitterly cold in Avella. It snowed in downtown Avella for the first time in fifty years, according to Francesca. However, in town, the snow only lasted 10 seconds, but it was exciting to see it for the first time. Mount Avella was covered with snow from the peak to the foothills. Usually, it was only the peak that was covered with snow. New faces were showing up in town. Approximately 20-30 men who served in the Army, Navy and Air Force during the war returned to Avella. Of which, 10-15 returned from North Africa. However, there were instances where entire families returned to town whom I had never seen before. One Jewish family was abducted by the Germans during the occupation of Avella. No one knew why they were picked up, until one neighbor moved into the vacated apartment. One of our neighbors invited Francesca for the purpose of strategizing in securing a scholarship from the nuns' private school. The neighbor's daughter attended the same school as me. Her name was Santina (little Saint) and her father died in Libya in the war. Like me, she attended the nuns' school on a scholarship based on her father's death in Libya. I am certain that Francesca and her mother compared notes when negotiating with nuns about entrance fees to the school. She was a bundle of energy running all over the building where she lived. Her brothers were classmates of Sebastiano and were a good influence on Sebastiano, when it came to schoolwork.

One day Santina told me that the apartment next to her apartment had been empty for a long time. In fact, people had raided the apartment quite often, but her family has stayed away from it. I, innocently, asked her when the family was coming back. Santina said that they will never come back. Mother, son and two young girls emigrated to Poland by train and settled there. Again, I, innocently, asked whether the family had contacted her family about their furniture and paintings, etc. or has anyone told them what is happening to their apartment. Her response was: "No one has ever heard from them or contacted them". We know now what happened to them. The rest of the story can now be told. The son was the same teen ager who was abducted by the Gestapo in Avella near Francesca's house.

Two doors away from Francesca's house lived a grandmother, her daughter and two boys. I knew the boys very well, Stefano and Paolo. Stefano and his Uncle, who lived about a block away, raised birds and sold them. They specialized in raising canaries which were caught by setting up a special trap in the foothills. I noticed one day that a funeral was taking place at their house, although when Francesca and I visited their home for the funeral reception, the casket was closed. Francesca explained to me that the boys' father died in Greece, and his bones were returned home. It seemed as though the whole town turned up for the funeral. Long after the funeral, our friendship grew stronger for we had something in common. Stefano and his Uncle would sometimes take me along to lay down traps for the birds. Soon after, I would venture on my own to set traps and catch birds.

In fact, I tried to go into business, much like Stefano, selling the birds to other kids. The favorite bird of most children was the yellow canary. Most of the birds caught or trapped by me were sparrows and ravens. They didn't mind me setting up business for I was no competition to their business, and must have sensed as much. Also, both Stefano and his Uncle never revealed where to catch yellow canaries. They pointed to an area where I could catch only sparrows. Later, I tried to sell kites and again it competed with Stefano. This business also failed.

Stefano was destined to follow in his Uncle's footsteps which was to be in the business of selling birds. He attended elementary public school for five years. He qualified for a scholarship to the nuns' school, but chose to attend public school. His younger brother Nicola, on the other hand, did choose private school with the nuns. He went on to the University of Naples and majored in electrical engineering. He moved on to Germany to gain employment. Stefano had no patience for schooling. He liked to use his hands on anything, especially on things that had potential to make money. He started a business selling kites and did very well, although he was competing against specialty stores featuring large and fancy kites. His love was trapping canaries in a net and selling them, and, basically, he was running a monopoly in the business. There was no one else in town competing with him, and demand for canaries then and now remains big business in Italy.

The dirt road leading to Nonno's farm. Notice on the right side of the dirt road there is a drop in ground level of six feet, indicating an earthquake fault line. This area was a typical setting for trapping birds. Photo courtesy of Anmarie Vittoria, 1981

Next to his house, there was a palazzo that belonged to a royal family. In all the years that I lived in Avella, and to this day, the royal family has never returned to lay claim to the Palazzo. Stefano's family was the guardian of the property, which included a small garden across the street from the palazzo. The garden was full of orange trees whose branches extended over the fence to the street. Sometimes, Stefano allowed me to pick oranges. The more interesting site was the courtyard inside the palazzo. It was adorned with antique Roman statuettes with heads chopped off. In the center of the courtyard there was a fountain which no longer sprayed water. On the walls, bordering the steps to higher floors, there were graffiti signs in Arabic.

It made no sense to me, since the royal family was not of Arabic origin. The reader should recall that the day the Goumiers visited our house they climbed over the roof of our house and jumped over to the neighbor's (Stefano's family) loggia, balcony. We surmised that something terrible must have happened. The Goumiers were capable of atrocities. We never found out what else occurred in the raid by the Goumiers, but could only imagine.

Stefano told me that the Goumiers did not stop by their apartment. I found it hard to believe then, since the only way to the streets from the roofs was through their apartment or jumping from their roof onto another roof. The Goumiers certainly did not return to our apartment to get to the street. I now believe that those graffiti signs were inscribed by those Goumiers who invaded our house. Apparently, after invading our house, the Goumier soldiers went from roof to roof and eventually came down to the courtyard of the Royal palazzo. That was the way out for the Goumiers to the street, through the large portone entrance. This implied that Stefano's family never encountered the Goumiers at the time they invaded our house.

Near Stefano's house there was another family consisting of mother, father and two boys. One of the boys was crippled with polio. These two boys were outright mean. Kids can be the cruelest people, especially to each other. They would say to me: Our father returned to Avella from Libya, and your father died because he didn't want to dirty up his clothes diving into a ditch and avoid the bombing". They would further say that in order for their father to survive thirst and hunger in Libya he was willing to drink piss water from a camel. Yuk. After these exchanges, I never wanted to socialize with these people, and totally avoided them like the plague.

After the war Francesca suggested that I work as an apprentice in the wood shop owned by their father. I told Francesca that there was no way that I would ever enter that shop even if they paid me, though we desperately needed money. I never relayed the conversations to anyone that I had with those nasty boys. In addition to the wood shop, my mother sent me to a tailor shop to learn the skills as an apprentice. Again, I tried at this new skill but failed. I couldn't sew even if my life depended on it. I kept jamming the needle into my fingers. Finally, I was sent to a barber shop to learn to be a barber. It turned out that the shop was the same one that my father rented and worked in before the war. The barber, before the war, served as an apprentice to my father. The barber would recount a lot of stories about a lot of stories about Papa, but those memories have dimmed. The gist of the stories was that Papa knew a lot of people and was generous with his time, but a poor businessman. I was never taught to cut hair and was assigned to clean the shop daily for six months. I wanted to follow in the footsteps of Papa. I thought that I was destined to follow in his footsteps. However, at this rate, I would have to wait for the barber to retire or die before I could practice to be a barber. So, I quit.

Clearly, Francesca wanted for me to learn a skill and follow in the footsteps of Papa, since she had little understanding of educational opportunities in Italy. The truth of the matter was that there were no opportunities and she must have sensed as much. Also, at that time there were no academic opportunities to look forward to, since we were poor. Universities were available only to the affluent. Even attending a University in those days did not ensure a job. There were a lot of "ragionieri" (accountants and/or lawyers) walking the streets in Avella in those days. Sometimes, they would walk to the railroad station with a professional briefcase (probably empty) to give the appearance of holding a job in Naples. Simply put, there were no jobs after the war, period.

After all those failures at apprenticeships, we heard a rumor that money could be mailed from America by relatives, since the war was over. So, my mother wrote to my grandfather pleading for money or anything from America. Actually, the letter was written by Serafina, a neighbor, since my mother was nearly illiterate with only a third grade education. Frankly, we were in a desperate situation. I didn't even have a pair of shoes to go to kindergarten in the fall. The shoes that I had were hand-me downs from Sebastiano, and our friendly shoe repairman (the trumpeters' father) would fix them as much as possible. The only kindergarten school in town was run by nuns, and they had an entrance fee.

Since the war ten families moved to Avella. Three new families moved within a block of Francesca's house, and, at least five more families, moved into other parts of town. I was aware of everything in town for I was becoming a street kid as soon as I started walking. One family, about three doors from my house, has remained a mystery to this day. I suspect that the head of the family was a former Fascist Mayor (Podesta) in some other town in Italy. As a child, I would wander into their courtyard and try to socialize with the children there. There were not many children of my age in town to socialize with.

Rumor was circulating around town that a high ranking Italian officer was returning home. I asked Nonno, if his ranking was higher than Papa's ranking. He thought that it was the highest ranking of anyone in Avella returning home and thought he might be related to Francesca. Francesca confirmed that he was a relative with the rank of Colonel, but she warned me not to bother him. In truth, her tone and language was much harsher than that.

The Colonel returned from Russia after spending time in Siberia. He participated in the battle of Stalingrad and was fortunately taken prisoner by the Soviet Army five miles north of Stalingrad. There were many casualties in the bitter cold of Stalingrad, almost 300,000 Italian soldiers were taken prisoners, and unaccountable number of soldiers died. Many Italian soldiers were shipped to Siberia to start a new life. Most of them died. Cold climate alone does not explain why so many died. A few got married and never returned, and a handful returned with their new wives. This Colonel was one of them.

I was curious to find out about living conditions in Russia. The local Communists were bragging all over town about what a great place Russia was, and people were given parcels of land or farms free. Needless to say, the Colonel brushed me aside, although I knocked on the door of his house. I thought that since we were related, he would not mind my intrusion. He was such an arrogant person that he would not talk to me in the street anytime we crossed paths. Apparently, he was still in the Army bucking to be a general someday. That is the problem with these military people everywhere in the world. After this incident I lost interest in finding out about the rest of the returnees with children. In retrospect, all of the soldiers who returned to Avella were either in a casket or alive. I don't recall seeing a wounded soldier returning.

It got to the point where Francesca sternly warned me that some people just wanted to be left alone and for me to stay away from them. Obviously, I was exhibiting the same trait as Papa, and Francesca wanted no part of that. Finally, another family with maids moved into a large building and they were well-to-do. It turned out that the head of the family was a Judge in Avellino. I served as an altar boy at their daughter's wedding. Their son Paolo and I were very good friends in school and we have remained friends ever since. There was an artistic family in Avella who came out in public. They were in hiding in Avella all this time, since they were Jewish and hiding from the Germans. The father, Don Nicola, was the former artistic director of the San Carlo Opera house in Naples. Their two sons were Nicola and Raffaele. I can't remember the daughter's name. Raffaele was an aspiring tenor and part of the choral group at the Opera house in Naples. In the late forties he immigrated to northern Europe and joined a touring group performing at opera houses of Europe. Eventually, he became the leading tenor in major opera houses.

Soon after the War, the maestro had a lot of patience in putting together a group of novices to perform the opera "Il Barbiere di Siviglia" at Saint Peter church and get decent performance out of them. Indeed, the performance was festive and appreciated by almost the whole town, except for Francesca. My role was that of a handyman for I was an altar boy at that time. There were four altar boys and the priest volunteered our time to help out the staging of the opera. Ever since then I have been hooked on opera music. The maestro was instrumental later in inviting tenor Beniamino Gigli to one of the festivals of Saint Anthony in Avella to sing favorite arias from various operas. Gigli, at that time, was the leading tenor in the world, although he was labeled as being pro-Fascist. During the war he performed in the opera houses in Rome in front of Fascist and Nazi audiences. It would have been a major propaganda coup for the Allies, if he performed in any other place. The Fascists would have never allowed it.

A number of music students came to Avella from Naples and its environs to take piano and singing lessons from the Maestro. I recall one hot summer day in July of 1946, when a young singer, coming out of the building where the Maestro resided, was singing at the top of his lungs. At first impression, I thought that he had gone mad or was hallucinating, since it was so hot. So, I started to look for a side street to run into in order to avoid him, but there was no place to run. As he came closer to me, his singing became more melodious and beautiful. I recall the aria and it was from the first act of the opera "La Boheme" (Puccini), where Rodolfo and Mimi sing in a duet. Over the years my wife and I have heard Boheme numerous times and it always brings back the magic of that hot summer day.

Nicola, the son of the music teacher, was a brilliant artist of the same caliber as painters from the renaissance, but without the recognition. Coming from a small town like Avella, it was difficult to build a reputation as an artist. About February or March of 1945 I began to see both Nicola and Uncle Joe working together on joint projects in the church of Saint Anthony. At that time I was not aware that one of the two artists in the church was my Uncle. It was obvious to me then that Uncle Joe was the apprentice, although he was much older.

In retrospect, that was surprising, because Uncle Joe was trained as a construction bricklayer and I am told that he was a good one. Obviously, Uncle Joe came out of his hiding place in his house and no one bothered to tell me about it. My two cousins, Carmine and Giannina, never gave me a hint even as late as 1945. I was told about Uncle Joe a couple of weeks before Easter, in the church of Saint Anthony. Signore Nicola (henceforth to be called mastro Nicola) and Uncle Joe were commissioned by the monks of Saint Anthony to lay a mosaic painting of Jesus and Mary on the marble floor of the church. The word mastro is derived from the word maestro which translates to teacher. However, in Avella it was used to infer someone who is a master of his art. Only family members were allowed in the church, when the artists were working on the mosaic in the afternoon. I realized then who he was, as my cousins clued me in. I was very proud to have any connection with the only artists in town.

Besides this commission, Mastro Nicola and Uncle Joe received another commission to paint the "Madonna Di Monte Vergine". This painting is now residing in the church of Saint Anthony. I recall spending a lot of time in the afternoon within the studio in the church watching them scaling the drawing and eventually starting the painting. I remember being in Aunt Giovanna's house seeing Uncle Joe starting with a figurine of the Saint on the table. He then scaled the figurine precisely and transported the scaling to a bigger canvas. By changing the size of the scaling he was able to magnify the picture of the figurine.

The same technique was borrowed from his experience as a construction bricklayer. Obviously, Uncle Joe complemented the skills that Mastro Nicola brought to the collaboration. The sketches of the Madonna took so long that I wondered when they were ever going to start the painting. It was worth the wait for it was truly a beautiful painting of the Madonna. The size of the portrait was 12x12 square feet and was placed at the entrance to the church of Saint Anthony. Uncle Joe and Mastro Nicola were in great demand by the local churches after the exhibition of the painting. Churches were the only institutions that had money right after the War.

These two artists received another big commission, this one to restore all the paintings and statuettes in all the churches in Avella: Saint Peter, Saint John, Santa Candida, etc. Besides getting involved with artistic ventures, Uncle Joe was commissioned to build a palazzo with his brother and father. His artistic relationship with Mastro Nicola lasted until Uncle Joe left for the USA with his family. Painting was not Uncle Joe's forte, but he loved sculpting, especially marble sculpting, and he was talented with the chisel. I used to watch his every move with the chisel, when he was sculpturing. I am of the opinion now that people who are involved with construction are most likely good with the chisel and, therefore, good in sculpturing. However, marble from North Italy was not available at that time, but there was enough marble in Avella to work with.

The first Christmas in 1945 with Uncle Joe was memorable. As it is customary in Italy, some people construct a "Presepio" before Christmas. It is usually placed on a table about 6x6 square feet and it is supposed to depict the town scene of Bethlehem, where Jesus was born. However, most Presepios that I had seen in Avella always had the appearance of a local scene, as if Jesus were born in Avella. Then again, no one from Avella had ever been to the nativity site in the Middle East. My cousin, Carmine, invited me to his house to see his father putting together the Presepio for the first time. Of course, Uncle Joe was going to be the main architect and we kids would gather the woodwork all over the foothills of Avella needed for the Presepio. We were in total awe at how Uncle Joe prepared for the tasks on hand. He would sketch the Presepio scenery and put in imaginary figurines. He then looked at the wood that we kids gathered and would say. "This piece of wood will do, but not that one". So, he would come with us to the foothills and help us find the right shape of wood. For allowing us to get involved was a tremendously exciting time. Whatever wood not used for the Presepio was thrown into the fireplace to keep the fire going, and the roasted chestnuts coming. It was truly a magical time. The literal translation of the word "Presepio" is "crib", but it is a misleading translation. It is more like a scenery around a "crib", Nativity scene.

After the wood pieces were put in the right place according to Uncle Joe's sketch, he took us by train to Nola (6 miles from Avella) to buy ceramic figurines and, most importantly, the silver star that guided the three Magi to the manger. The gold star was too expensive.

Nola is a commercial town that dates back to Roman times. The trade route from Sicily to Rome was necessarily passing through Nola. For example, when Roman legions were chasing Spartacus in the Calabria region, Nola was the stopover on the way there. A statue of Caesar is still in the main square in Nola. Cicero was born about 25 miles north of Nola and bought a house there. I never knew that about Nola as an elementary school student. I thought that the statue of Caesar was a fake. Only much later in life did I learn about the importance of Nola to ancient Romans. As a child, I thought Avella was the center of the Universe.

Nola was then big enough to have its own Bishop. It had a lot more stores than Avella including a special store for art supplies and figurines, etc. Nola is located roughly 15 miles North of Salerno. During the Salerno invasion, German supplies passed through there. Nothing has changed in 2000 years. On the way to Salerno one would have to circle around Mount Vesuvius, much like what Uncle Joe did when he escaped from the Germans. On the way to downtown Nola, where all the stores were located, from the train station we passed a coffee house at the corner from which a sweet familiar smell was emanating. I immediately recognized the smell of chicory coffee, but my senses deceived me at that time. I discovered later that it was the sweet smell of real coffee brewed from roasted coffee beans. I felt like floating on air as I got closer to the smell, but we were on a very important mission: Figurines for the Presepio.

Yes, there were a lot of opinions among us kids about how big and shiny the star should be, even how ugly the three Magi should be. Other arguments were about how many and what types of restaurants (Osteria) to include in the Presepio. Finally, the mountain scene should look like Mount Avella, no less! In order to inject some realism into the scenery we concluded that the top of the mountain should be snow-covered, much like Mount Avella in late December. That was realism from kids who had no idea what the original scene was like in Bethlehem, where it never snowed.

Basically, Uncle Joe spoiled us by letting us wander all over the place. Finally, all the parts were bought and assembled in cousins' house. Every evening we children would sit and watch the Uncle working magic on the Presepio. Not a peep was spoken by anyone for our minds were wondering what was coming next. Even a fart was not allowed. After a couple of days it was beginning to take shape or at least I could identify some sceneries. Finally, we were allowed to place the figurines and the North Star on the Presepio. It was the most magical moment of my life at that time. The mind of a child wanders all over the place upon seeing such a scenery and Uncle Joe put his heart and soul into this project. His skills as a construction bricklayer, artistic painter and sculptor came in handy. His chisel work was magnificent for he smoothed out all the rough edges of the wood. The Presepio was completed roughly one week before Christmas.

The bagpipe musicians usually came around to each Presepio two to three days before Christmas, but as soon as I heard the first sound of the bagpipe I followed the musicians all over town. I wanted to steer them to the Presepio built by Uncle Joe for I was very proud of it. The other Presepios at other houses were ok, but the one built by Uncle Joe was, indeed, very special. Finally, the bagpipe players came to Uncle Joe's house to play Christmas music in front of the Presepio and they were most impressed.

Payment to the bagpipers was in the form of money or a glass of "Marsala a L'uovo", vermouth. Traditionally, bagpipers represented shepherds or musicians dressed in shepherd clothes. In Avella, real shepherds were bagpipers and wore clothes that they normally wore. They claimed that it was by far the best Presepio in town. Of course, we were all proud of that recognition. Obviously, this was my Uncle's way of making up for lost time in the war to show off his beautiful skills and to thank God for being alive and able to do this for us. It must have been quite a difficult escapade by food from the hills of Calabria to the hills of Avella, never on flat ground. That is roughly a trip of 150 miles by foot. It must have taken a toll on him physically and mentally.

Of the approximate 250-300 men who left Avella to go to war, about five returned. Other returning soldiers who came to Avella were not born there. Uncle Joe and his colleague returned from Sicily. The carpenter who lived near Francesca's house returned from Libya. Another man who lived near the cemetery with the rank of Colonel returned from Russia. Also, two soldiers returned to the O'Vicolo district whom we did not know very well. I am not aware of any injured soldier returning home.

Finally, one man who was very interesting to me as a child was one who owned small monkeys, and lived next to Uncle Joe's house. The first time that I saw the monkey it was standing on the man's shoulder and was well behaved. However, the monkey went berserk as anyone got near to pat him. I was told by my Uncle that this man was an administrator in Libya dealing mostly with clerical work. There are a lot of monkeys in some regions of Libya, where there is vegetation. The closest that I ever came to the monkey was within an arm's length, enough to get away in case the monkey jumped on me. I was scared for there was nothing loving about that animal. The rest of the soldiers from Avella who served in the Italian Army never made it back home. All who left for the Russian front near Stalingrad never made it back, except for the Colonel.

A lot of the civilians deported or forced to go to Germany to work in factories also never returned to Avella. Thus, the town of Avella was depleted of young and able men, after the war, to restore the town back to normalcy. However, former residents of Avella and new people from out-of-town began to drift into Avella. That included former residents persecuted by Fascists in Avella before the war and, most likely, the out of towners who were Fascists from nearby towns.

One new family moved into the center of town toward spring of 1945. Their g arden w as l ocated n ext t o U ncle J oe's h ouse. Th e ga rden wa s bigger than Nonno's farm of five acres. It is rare to have that much land in the middle of a city, even in Avella. There were two other landlords who had as much land as this person, the Count and the church of Saint Peter. The family consisted of grandparents, parents, two boys, Paolo and Agostino, and daughter Miriam. The family arrived from Rome, where the father was a legal expert for the Royal House of Savoy, the King of Italy, in dealings with the Fascists. He was not a Fascist, but a Monarchist. In the thirties it was difficult to separate the two. While Badoglio was in charge of the government (1943-44), the family had the freedom to move about in Italy. They chose to return home. Eventually, the father became a Judge in Avellino. I got to know Paolo very well. We went to school together from kindergarten until I left for America.

In summary, most of the returning families in Avella were affiliated with the Monarchy and had the protection of Badoglio's government. Also, one Jewish family and a number of families associated with the partisans or Communist party returned to Avella. About 80% of enlisted soldiers from Avella died in war. Soldiers who came back from the Balkans wanted nothing to do with the Communist Party, although they were aware of the partisan movement in the Balkans under Tito, communist leader of Yugoslavia. The Fascist mayor and fanatical Fascists, especially the ones wearing black shirts, left town and most of them never returned. A vacuum in political leadership was created as a result. The first issue to be resolved in Italy soon after the war was whether or not the Monarchy was to be returned to power.

ELEVEN
ANARCHY IN FERMENTATION

In 1946, Italians were finally free from dictatorship, tyranny and occupation by foreign soldiers. Now, they could exercise their free will and aspirations after many years of being harassed by Fascist thugs. It was the pure exhilaration of just letting it go to pursue one's dreams. Unfortunately, crooks and thieves felt the same way, but more so. Not only did they enjoy the same liberty and freedom as everyone else, but they had the freedom to pick and choose whatever illegal activities and choose the victims to their hearts content without consequences. They ran City Hall. There was no law and no public order. Simply put, there was no one running the local government to protect the people. In the Naples area organized crime was run by an organization called Camorra.

The only semblance of government consisted of two old men, General Badoglio and King Victor Emmanuel III, in the region of Italy called Puglia [2, 42]. The government in Puglia was not in communication with any civil administrations in small towns or even in big cities like Naples, and could not possibly administer anything from where they were. Puglia is on the Adriatic Sea and is the poorest province in Italy. There are still Greek settlements there dating at least 2000 years. The modern world hasn't reached there yet to this day. They may as well as been on the moon. In fact, the King and Badoglio were not even in touch with any remnants of the Italian Army, when they left Rome at four in the morning on September 9, 1943. There is no historical record on how the King was able to navigate a caravan of twenty cars through a checkpoint manned by German troops, especially when Hitler wanted the King dead or alive! Thus, after the War, we had the perfect setting for anarchy.

Both the King and the General were "wheeling and dealing" with Allied Generals, royals in other countries and administrators. These two men cared less about who was Mayor of small towns in Southern Italy. They were simply trying to save their asses and be restored to power in a future government. The British royalty desperately wanted to save the Crown in Italy after the war, and Churchill insisted that the King of Italy be part of any future Italian government. This view was not surprising from the British, since Royal houses in Europe were all inter-related. The Americans detested any such suggestions for they have had enough experience with Royalty in the past. Americans suggested a democratic government in the future. While these old people were bickering among themselves, small towns, like Avella, were going to pot or back to hell on earth.

Since the Fascist Mayor left Avella, there was no one in charge of City Hall. Carabinieri (local police) did not report to anyone for there were no one to report to and no Judges to administer Justice, since Fascist Judges themselves were in a vulnerable position for their past indiscretions. Many Fascists were on the run. They were pursued usually by Communist partisans who had scores to settle. Besides the Communist party, there were the Socialist, Democratic, Republican, and assorted other parties, but none of these were about to hang anyone. However, few of these partisans were outright criminals. About 8,000 to 12,000 Fascists in Italy were killed without the benefit of a trial by jury after the War. Nothing has changed since the times of Cicero. History has repeated itself once again. Many more Fascists left their hometowns for South America, Europe and other municipalities in Italy never to return. In effect, the experienced and former bureaucrats who ran the town left for "green pastures". Only a skeleton of previous administrations was in operation to conduct civil service, and they coped as best they could with the chaotic situation. They were not salaried employees. There was no central government to print money. They depended on bribes, much like the police in town.

According to the new tax collector, all tax records were lost during the war. Furthermore, according to the new tax collector, Grandpa Carmine owed taxes from the 20's and 30's. That was not true, but there was no one to complain to. He declared that unless and until the taxes were paid within a short time the land would be confiscated by the State. The new tax collector purchased the land at auction, without our knowledge, soon after we were informed officially of the non-payment of taxes. By the time we left for America the tax collector owned most of the grazing land on the mountains near Avella. Initially, he had no land to speak of. That was a sad episode in our lives. We knew we had been cheated, but the system was too corrupt to correct the injustice. Thus, a handful of families owned all the land, and the peasants who worked in it have always done so in conditions that came very close to slavery. The misery of their conditions has been aggravated by the war and the loss of manpower. Whole towns were out of work in some areas of Naples.

When things were nice and calm in the winter of 1947, there was an ugly rumor circulating all over town. The "brigandi", bandits, from the hills of Avellino were going to take over the town, including the police station. Many other towns were threatened by bandits in the area of Naples. Some towns, in fact, were actually taken over by bandits. That news reverberated in the soul of each person, young and old, in town. People were outright scared. The question in people's minds was: Are we going back to hell? The unthinkable part of it was that hell was going to be created from within. I kept asking family members, if that was possible when we have Carabinieri to protect us. They all said in unison: "They are all a bunch of wimps". At that time, I never saw them out in the street patrolling. To say that the town was vulnerable was truly an understatement.

No one knew, when or where the bandits would show up. One Friday afternoon in the Saint Peter district (closest to the hills), people put up barbed wires across the streets at every block. It looked like the British camp, when Nonno and I visited the camp except, now, the barbed wires were placed in town. It was difficult to understand what good those wires were going to do and to whom! It was frantic and desperate times. Again, there were no Carabinieri around to supervise. Fear came back with a vengeance and it was generated from people like us.

The following night it seemed that all the people in town congregated near Saint Peter church where the concentration of barbed wires was placed. Out of nowhere a little girl about my age, or perhaps slightly older, started to run at full speed toward the barbed wires. The little girl was screaming and was running away from someone in her household. She was not aware of the barbed wires, since it was evening and dark. She ran right into the barbed wires at full speed. Ouch! You could hear grunts all over the square and then quiet all around. It was an anxious moment for those who were there. I was there and I did not want to look at the poor girl.

My body just shivered at the thought of her hurting badly. People were all around her, and slowly and painfully they were separating the little girl from the spikes of the fence. She survived. I kept saying to myself over and over again: How could she not know about the barbed wires? It made no sense for she lived within a stone's throw from the fence. To this day, I have been wondering how it was possible.

The barbed wires were removed immediately after the accident. People didn't care what would happen next. The worst already happened. The vigil for the "brigandi" went on the whole night. No one ever showed up from the mountains. In retrospect, I don't know if the town people could have stopped an invasion of bandits coming from the mountains. That night, again there were no Carabinieri (police) waiting at Saint Peter piazza in Avella. The injury to that poor girl dampened the spirit to fight the bandits. It was not worth getting seriously hurt fighting any one. People were simply tired of tragedies. They simply resigned themselves to whatever happened out of pure exasperation.

The Carabinieri did the best they could under these difficult circumstances and tried to stay neutral and away from troublemakers. The American occupation of the Naples area tried to do something about the unstable situation by deploying military administrators throughout Southern Italy to maintain some form of civility. On the average one Allied Military administrator covered about 10-20 small towns in trying to keep law and order. It helped in some places, but not in the Naples area and Sicily.

In the Naples area corruption was out in the open, in the street, police headquarters, City Hall, restaurants, etc. The counterpart to the Mafia, in Naples, was and is the Camorra and members of the Camorra [100] were called Camorristi. The "headquarters" of the Camorra was in Castellmare di Stabia near Naples. However, the so-called Zona di Camorra (Camorra territory) in 1946 was located about 20 miles North of Naples in the towns of Casoria, Afragola, and Aversa. However, the Camorra was spread all over the Naples area including Avella. Today, it is very difficult to pinpoint the area of concentration of the Camorra. It is like a cancerous virus. Once the virus spreads in a body, it is difficult to track it, even with modern technologies. Camorristi mingle among society much like a virus in a body and are involved in legal and illegal businesses.

New Mayors (Sindacos), who were appointed by the Allied Military Government (AMG) to replace the Fascist Podestas (Mayors), were members of the Camorra organization which was spread over the Naples area. The Camorra Mayors were appointed through the influence of Vito Genovese, the interpreter, who gained tremendous power in the AMG. He was also Capo (boss) Mafioso (Mafia member) from New York City, but was born in a town near Naples. Law and order were in the hands of poorly armed Carabinieri and Publica Sicurezza (security police) consisting of two or three men in each town and were under constant threat of attack by well-armed criminals or brigands. Often Carabinieri walked in town with pistol drawn and cocked. What a nightmare for the local people.

The sale of contraband American cigarettes was a booming business. American cigarettes, shipped to the American base in Naples, disappeared as fast as it arrived on the port of Naples. Obviously, there was inside collusion in order to do business at the scale in which it was conducted. American cigarettes were exported all over Europe from Naples. Certainly, scugnizzi and the local mafia (Camorra) were involved to a large extent, but not a single internal perpetrator in the American base was ever caught!

In addition, there was a black market for American goods normally not available in Italy, such as blankets. Again, the source of these goods was the American base in Naples. Perhaps, the introduction of American cigarettes and goods to Neapolitans may be interpreted as a way of introducing capitalism to Italy? Throughout their 2000 year history, Neapolitans have seen tyrants come and go and in each case they have survived. This philosophy for survival is best characterized by the Neapolitan credo "Ci Arrangiamo", "We adapt to survive". Those times, after WWII, were no different.

The black market flourished as never before. Sixty-five per cent of the per capita income of the Naples area was derived from transactions in stolen Allied supplies and one third of all supplies and equipment imported continued to disappear into the black market. There were 42,000 women in Naples who engaged, either on a regular or occasional basis, in prostitution. The female population was about 150,000, and nine out of ten Italian girls lost their men folk in battles, as prisoners of war, or having disappeared in Europe [13].

The black market operated under the protection of high-placed Allied Military Government (AMG) officials. At the head of the AMG was Charles Polenti and working with him was Vito Genovese who was second in command to the Mafia in New York. The Capo Mafioso was Salvatore ("Lucky") Luciano. He emigrated to the USA, when he was seven years old. Lucky Luciano was deported to Naples at about this time (1947). Thus, we had two "sharks" running the Black market in Naples and the nearby area. The fact that Luciano was "exiled" to Naples implied also that he was unwanted in Sicily. The implications of such a snub in Mafia portends a change in leadership. Indeed there was a change in leadership of the Mafia in New York City in the early 1950's. Genovese became Capo. The fact that Luciano was in Camorra territory, he had very little leverage in the local operation.

The Camorristi went after bigger things, like all the tires from trucks stationed in large storage areas near Naples. An abandoned military tank in a town near Naples shrank to nothing slowly but surely over a span of two months. Buses, and trams came to a standstill, when the departing Germans wrecked the generating station which was carted away in a matter of few days. Telegraph poles, vials of penicillin and even unguarded small ships did not escape the Neapolitan kleptomania. Mastro Nicola's father recounted an incident involving the San Carlo Opera house. The orchestra took a five minute break only to return and discover all its instruments were missing. Nothing was outrageous for this new breed of robbers, scugnizzi and Camorristi.

The Robin Hood tradition was as strong in the Zona di Camorra as it was in the vicinity of Naples. With the help of the AMG, bandits journeyed to the battle area in convoys of stolen cars to collect abandoned small-arms, mortars, and metal scraps. Trains carrying supplies to the battlefront were hijacked and emptied of their contents. Bandits cultivated local sympathy by handing out a handful of thousand lire notes (five dollars) or sack of stolen foods to local peasantry. Tailors in Naples were cutting American military uniforms to pieces, dyeing the material, and turning them into smart civilian wear. Penicillin was then readily available in pharmacies, although these supplies were short at military hospitals.

Many American officers had been chosen to go on the Italian campaign because they were of Italian descent. The Italian-Americans in AMG reigned supreme and knew how to close their ranks when threatened from without. As discussed previously, Camorristi resided mostly around Naples, but bandits were made up of Italians and American army deserters, and drove around in ex-German army Lorries and Allied vehicles stolen from storage. The police in most towns were corrupt and tyrannical and the civil population played a game with flexible rules that changed on a daily basis. The local police were involved in most spoils gathered by the bandits or the Camorra.

This philosophy has been practiced in Naples for so long that their thinking process automatically goes into this mode of living. Clearly, the American base in Naples was a "piece of cake" for them to be able to tap into for survival. That is exactly what was needed at that time in Naples. Everybody was starving before the Americans came. Thus, corruption and civil disobedience prevailed in Naples as well as in towns nearby, but, most importantly, they survived because of the American base.

In Avella it was not as corrupt as in and around Naples, but there were frequent altercations between various factions of the Camorra. In one particular incident, I did witness a violent incident between two brigands. As I was leaving Nonno's house, about a block away, I saw two male adults arguing in a threatening manner until one of them pulled a knife. A violent fight ensued between the two and soon after they were joined by four to five more adults coming out of a wine store. I ran back toward Nonno's house and informed him of what I saw. There was a pool of blood all over the street and into the wine shop, but not a single person involved with the altercation was at the scene. The Carabinieri never showed up.

It was an eerie feeling to know that there was a bloody fight and there were no police around to investigate what happened. To this day I never found out, if anyone died. They all disappeared. The wine vendor at the wine shop was not hurt and kept repeating to Nonno that nothing happened. I never understood then the subtlety of the vendor's statements to Nonno. How could this man lie, when there was blood all over the street and in the wine shop. The attitude in town was "Hear nothing"; "see nothing"; "say nothing", omerta. Nonno knew that and the vendor knew that, but I didn't know that. In a sense, the town was in collusion with the Camorra. Simply put, there was no law and order.

There were open gunfights between rival gangs not affiliated with the Camorra in Baiano and other towns in the vicinity. In a town, on the other side of Monte Avella, Cervinara, gunfights were an almost daily occurrence. Matters were made even worse in that ammunition in the police department was in short supply and pay for the officers was often delayed. The Questore, equivalent to a Major-general in the police department, was paid $40 a month, a Major $30 a month and a postman $14 a month. Typically, the salary of the chief of police was $30 per month. The salaries of the Carabinieri were artificially low for they were expected to complement their salaries by partaking of the "spoils" system. They tolerated the big racketeers of the Camorra and accepted protection money from the Camorra, but were relentless in their pursuit of petty thieves. Italians of the South lived on bread dipped in olive oil. Bread bought on the black market cost about 160 lire per kilogram (25 cents). Olive oil cost 450 lire per liter ($2-3 dollars), eggs 30 lire each and salt was not available at any price.

The Camorristi lived by their own secret laws, and recognized their own secret courts, which imposed only one sentence on the enemy or betrayer – death. Before the war there was some sort of moral authority, and justice, but soon after the war there was only criminality. If there was plunder to be had, the Camorristi were first in line and shared the spoils with friends and local police.

In Sicily bandits were looked upon by the Mafia as competitors; in the Naples area bandits and even scugnizzi were looked upon by the Camorra as slave laborers to generate plunder. The Camorristi tolerated the local police as long as the police kept the small-time criminals in their place, especially those who did not cooperate with the Camorra. Before the war Camorristi were thrown in jail by Mussolini, as the trials were rigged by Fascists Judges or sent away to islands or resettled in other places of Italy.

The "sister" city to Naples is Palermo, Sicily. Much like the Naples area, Sicily was settled by Greeks as far back as 800 BC. Also, Sicilians have seen invaders come and go for more than 2000 years; they have adapted to tyrannical invaders, and survived them all. So, the mind-set In Sicily was and is not much different from the Naples area. Like Naples, Sicilians have their own brand of underworld gang and it is often referred to as the Mafia. It has been alluded that the Camorra and Mafia organizations may be a by-product of overcoming all those invasions. For example, in the Calabria and Puglia areas, there is also another crime syndicate similar to Camorra and Mafia and it is called Ndrangheta. As in the other two regions of Southern Italy, Calabria and Puglia have been conquered by foreign armies for at least the past 2000 years. Nowhere else in Italy is organized crime as prevalent as in those regions.

In Sicily the AMG recruited locals to help them administer civil administration in towns. As in the Naples area, most of the local recruits for Mayor were Mafiosi and, in some cases Capo Mafiosi who returned from exile. Mussolini eliminated the Mafia in Sicily before the war by sending Capo Mafiosi to various small islands in the Mediterranean Sea near Sicily. Yes, things ran very efficiently in Sicily. I don't think anybody dared cross or mock a local Mafioso. Indeed, this must have been some sort of surreal situation whereby "the wolves were guarding the sheep". Where else in the world can a situation like this come up? I believe that the AMG governing Sicily at that time may not have been aware of the predicament local Sicilians were in!

As things were going very well in America for the Mafia in the 1920's and 1930's, Mussolini was about to clamp down on them in Sicily, as they were the main source of Capo Mafiosi in America. Besides the Italian Mafia, there were Irish and Jewish underworld gangs in America. Being a buffoon at heart Mussolini could not stand the thought of being upstaged by a Capo Mafioso in Sicily. Mussolini employed Cesare Mori to eradicate the Mafia in Sicily.

Mori was born In Pavia (north Italy) and had studied at the military academy in Turin. He had served two terms as police chief in Sicily before and after World War I. In 1924 he was appointed Prefect of Trapani (Sicily) by the Fascist government and in 1925 he was transferred to Palermo, the capital of Sicily. The title of Prefect is derived from the days of ancient Rome (Cicero) where a Prefect was assigned to major cities in the Empire. In modern times the Prefect is in charge of the Carabinieri (local police) over the province area, Publica Sicurezza (Public security police), Polizia di Finanzia (police of finances) and Interpol (international police). Trapani city is located in the western part of Sicily and Palermo is situated between Trapani and Messina. Most Mafia gangs were concentrated in the western part of Sicily and in the middle of the island. The influence of Mafia was less so in the eastern part of Sicily, but still significant. In the eastern part of the island there are still Greek settlements from ancient times. Sicily is to Italy as California is to America in that both are the fruit baskets of their respective countries. In addition, Sicily has maintained a steady export of olive oil and other produce to America for over hundred years. The Mafia has had strong control over these exports.

The mandate of the Fascist government to Mori was that the authority of the State must absolutely be re-established in Sicily and, accordingly, "If necessary new laws would be adopted to force subjugation of the Mafia". In his first two months Mori arrested five hundred Mafiosi, 450 in Palermo and more in the little hill town of Gangi, near the town of Corleone (made famous by the movie "The Godfather"). In addition, Mori butchered all the cattle, sheep and pigs in the town square of Gangi. This was the pattern for the next four years in the western and middle countryside of Sicily. Convicted Mafiosi were sent to islands near Sicily, like Lampadusa, and Stromboli. The Fascist government wanted to isolate Mafiosi from the people of Sicily entirely. As Mori stated: "These people have not yet understood that brigands and the Mafia are two different things. We have hit the first, who are the most visible.... but not the most dangerous one. The truly lethal blow to the Mafia will be given when we are able to make roundups not only among prefectures, police headquarters, employers' mansions and some ministries". By 1937 Mussolini believed that the Mafia was eradicated in Sicily and declared as much in public.

For Sicily, WW II was a total disaster compared with the rest of Italy. Ferryboats to the mainland and elsewhere were disrupted and, as such, the export market nearly vanished. Hence, the source of money vanished as well. The only thing that kept Sicilians from starvation was food produced naturally in their farms. This meant that there was a glut of olive oil, wine, wheat flower, almond products and fruits on the island. As such, it encouraged a barter system within the island, local bandits, and a black market on food products. This was an ideal setting for a Mafia comeback. Thus, by 1943 (after the Allied invasion) the Mafia came back stronger than ever to control the black market. Whatever Mussolini and Mori tried to achieve went all for nothing.

American intelligence, better informed than the Duce, realized that, in order for the invasion of Sicily to be successful, it needed the cooperation of the Mafia [73]. Navy and Army intelligence contacted Capo Mafiosi of gangland crime families in the United States. In particular, the Navy contacted Capo Mafioso in New York City, Salvatore "Lucky" Luciano, as he had already been in jail since 1936. He was jailed for running compulsory prostitution in the mid-west. Although he was in jail, he was still Capo, or in command, in New York City. He was chased out of New York and into a jail by former Governor Dewey of New York State.

In return for the commutation of his jail sentence Luciano ordered Albert Anastasia to protect the waterfront from dockworker strikes for the duration of the war. Also, Luciano contacted other Capo Mafiosi in Sicily with the instructions to help out on the incoming invasion by the Allies. Mafiosi were used to direct traffic, provide intelligence information about German strength, troop concentration and position, illumination of fields, tank positions and radio operators. Albert Anastasia was boss of the infamous Murder Inc. and controlled the American docks. He was killed long after the war by a gang-style murder in a barber shop. Luciano's sentence was commuted to ten years in jail and he was released in 1947. However, he was deported to Italy in 1947 as an undesirable. He was never allowed to return to the US and died in Naples in 1957. Interestingly, he was not welcomed to Sicily, although he was born there. The Mafia had benefited greatly from its collusion with American intelligence. Lucky Luciano's second in command, Vito Genovese, who was wanted by the FBI for murder in the US, was serving as an interpreter in Sicily and later in Naples. He was issued an American Army uniform with the rank of sergeant. He was caught running a major black market operation which involved stealing heavy trucks from American bases in Sicily. With the arrival of the Allies in Sicily most of the Mafiosi exiled to small islands, and returned to Sicily with increased authority and tried to make up for lost time. Mafia bosses were appointed by the AMG to responsible positions in city halls, as mayors, to police headquarters and security posts, since most Fascist administrators had been chased out of towns.

Military administrators were not interested in running cities in Sicily. They had their hands full running an Army. The German army was alive and kicking, although the Italian Army was no more after the invasion of Sicily. Basically, Mafia became the establishment or was asked to provide law and order over the farm, peasants and common people. Hence, in order to establish order over the people they could not afford to dilute their power with the Communist or Socialist parties which were active at that time.

Hence, the political alignment of the Mafia was with the Christian Democrat party, rather than with the Communists. In fact, the connection between Mafia and the Christian Democrat party extended to the time of Andreotti who was prime minister of Italy in the nineties [106, 107]. The Mafia needed protection from politicians to carry out their business and politicians needed the Mafia to build political power of their own. It was a mutual understanding between them [106, 107]. Over the years there have been many legal and illegal transactions between the Christian Democratic Party and Mafia, as reported in newspapers. Since the Mafia represented the "new" law and order in Sicily, they were obliged to concentrate their attention on eradicating banditry and/or brigandage. Bandits and brigands were sometimes Mafiosi and sometimes not. They operated in their own personal interests. The Mafia had no choice but to eliminate bandits in Sicily in order to give the appearance of maintaining law and order. This indeed was a strange situation for the Mafia to be in. The Mafia had a problem in carrying out this ruse for a particular popular bandit in those days, Salvatore Giuliano, a legend in his own time. In 1943 he was caught by the Carabinieri smuggling two sacks of black market grain. Giuliano shot one Carabinieri and escaped to the mountains. He then organized a gang of bandits by helping eight of them escape from jail. Newspapers in Italy and Europe were describing him as a modern day Robin Hood. He robbed from the rich and banks and gave little to the poor. This was not exactly a "Robin Hood" type of behavior, but newspapers needed a hero in those days.

The Mafia decided to put an end to "Robin Hood" for two reasons. First, since the Mafia became the establishment, they had to give the impression of providing some form of law and order in apprehending a "popular" bandit. Second, Giuliano was cutting into Mafia profits, as a competitor. The Mafia hired his best friend, Gaspare Pisciotta, to shoot Giuliano in his sleep. Pisciotta was later poisoned while serving a sentence in jail. In fact, all of the conspirators involved in the killing of Giuliano were shot as they emerged from jail.

After the war, Genovese consolidated his power in the Mafia by organizing the distribution of heroin and opium from Turkey to all parts of the world. These activities by him continued in New York City resulting in a new order and gang-land killings during the fifties. Many of the killings were portrayed in the movie "The Godfather", although the storyline had nothing to do with the facts behind those killings. In summary, the AMG created a totally corrupt civilian administrations both in the Naples area and in Sicily and declaring to the world that they restored these areas to normalcy, knowing full well that it was not the case at all. It was not until 1992 that magistrate detectives Giovanni Falcone and Paolo Borsellino of the special investigative office in Sicily that discovered to what extent the Mafia and the Camorra had infiltrated government, police departments and the justice departments in both regions of Southern Italy [106, 107]. The subtlety of this type of collateral damage due to WW II was never understood and reported. The hidden damage caused by these underworld syndicates has caused more misery globally than the war itself.

THE RECOVERY PERIOD, 1946-48

TWELVE
THE ARDUOUS ROAD TO RECOVERY

After the war, people in Avella were tired of "having a monkey on their back", like the local Fascist thugs. People just wanted to forget about the long nightmare and go on with their lives. For the first time in a long time they had the freedom to pursue their dreams and aspirations. They were in a hurry to catch up with the rest of the world and join the twentieth century experimenting with new ideas and business practices. I will recount the family businesses activities right after the War in Avella.

In the fall of 1945 and winter of 1946 a number of wine shops opened up for business in Avella. Nonno's shop and two other places within a block of each other set up wine shops. In addition, two wine producers or distributors next to the railroad station resumed business. One of them still produces wine for the label "Taurasi Wines" which is sold in the USA and Europe. A wine store in Avella, then, was not like a wine store that one finds in the USA. In the USA, a wine store stocks wine bottles from all over the world. Nonno's wine shop featured only one table red wine likely produced in Avella or nearby. The wine was contained in a 50-60 gallon glass flask to be sold in smaller quantities. In Avella grapes grow almost everywhere. White wine was not sold in his store. The large wine flask was placed on a table next to a cash register. However, the cash register was never used. Wine was sold by the quart or half-quart amount in a glass decanter container and could be drunk on the premises, outside on a bench, or taken home. If taken home, the buyer supplied the bottle.

The wine produced in Avella is different from that produced in the in the vicinity of Mount Vesuvius, Pompeii area. The wine produced in Avella is the ordinary red table wine found all over Italy, similar to the cabernet wine consumed all over the world. The wine produced in the Pompeii area is sweeter, more like a dessert wine. The difference in the wines may be due to the terrain or soil at the two regions. Over the years, ashes and lava from Vesuvius has covered the Pompeii area, but not in Avella and Avellino area. In the USA there are some wines under the label of "Avellano" and "Taurasi", and these wines are from Taurasi and Avella areas. The wine business is still booming in Avella exporting it all over the world. The town of Taurasi is located about 20 miles east of Avella. The grapes at the two towns must be of the same variety or are blended together. The wines produced from the Vesuvius area is marketed under the label of "Lacryma Christi Del Vesuvio". I would estimate that about twenty new small businesses were initiated in early 1946. Most of them have survived to this day, and today many more businesses are thriving in Avella.

Nonno bought his wine wholesale from the neighboring wine shop that produced wine in his courtyard. This was the same shop raided by the Goumiers two years earlier. Nonno helped the neighbor in the spring of 1944 in fixing the equipment to produce wine in his courtyard again. Large producers at the railroad station did not sell wines locally, but they made an exception for Nonno. He must have bought the wine on credit for I don't believe he had enough cash on hand to buy anything at that time. Their business relationship was based on friendship rather than business acumen. As business improved, Nonno purchased wines from the neighbor as well as from the ones near the railroad station. Thus, he would store wine from one vendor in one oak barrel and the other in another barrel. The two oak barrels were placed in a large room with no windows to maintain a constant temperature of the wines. Sometimes, he would mix the two wines to produce special blend of wines. Thus, the sales pitch to the customers was that he had a variety of wines in his shop, regular table wine and a little more expensive wines. Soon enough, all the wine shops were practicing the same "shtick". Some shop owners carried the blending too far in diluting wines with water.

Once all the wine in the shop was sold, usually by afternoon, Nonno would close shop and take a break by sitting on a chair, drinking a glass of wine, and watching a bocce game outside the store. His favorite thing was to dip peaches into the wine. I tried this combination myself and it makes an excellent dessert wine. Sometimes during break from the shop, he would take me along to visit friends and play cards in an orchard full of cherry, and grape trees, his favorite fruits. In the times that I was at Nonno's, I never saw the tax collector or any Finance Police checking on wine receipts. All business transactions were made in cash. Sometimes I helped out with sales.

Being prisoner of the Fascist economic system for so long motivated most everyone to try their luck in business and, most importantly, to return to normalcy. For example, Nonno expanded his business to making and selling pasta and bread. He already had a license to sell wine. He had an old recipe to make pasta and started to sell fresh tagliatelle and, later, spaghetti. He created a new recipe to combine fresh tomatoes, olive oil, garlic and toasted bread. He build an outside brick oven where the bread was baked. Left over dough bread (panini) were sliced in halves and put back in the oven. They were re-heated until they turned crisp and light brown in color. The trick was to moisturize the frisella (crisp panini) with oil and water and add tomatoes, basil leaves, salt and sometimes slices of cheese. Had he added mozzarella or grated cheese with tomatoes slices on the panini before re-heating them, it would have resulted into a pizza flavored panini. At least, this recipe could have been a prelude to modern day pizza or bruschetta.

At that time there was no pizza as prepared with molten cheese with tomato sauce in the Naples area. Today, the so-called Neapolitan pizza consists of a thin crust dough with fresh mozzarella, virgin oil, basil and slices of tomato toppings, not with a tomato base sauce. In some sense pizza is an American invention, not Italian. In fact, Pepe's pizza restaurant in New Haven, Conn., claims to have prepared the first brick-oven baked pizza in 1926. The owner of Pepe's pizza emigrated from Naples. Nonno's recipe sold like "hot cakes". Business was booming, and I was employed to work behind the wine counter.

Business was so good that the Sunday meals were getting better and better, since they featured more meat. Nonno loved to cook those meat dishes, and I loved to watch him cook sitting atop staircase steps leading to his bedroom. Suddenly, dried chicory plants started to be replaced by dried coffee beans and they were roasted in Nonno's house. I think now that they all looked forward to the day when they could smell those roasted coffee beans again. It seemed that everybody wanted to be in the room where the coffee beans were roasted. How ironic that only a year before chicory plants were used to make coffee and, now, we were surrounded by dandelions, daisies, and chicory flowers all over the farms, and it never crossed anyone's mind in those post-war years to cultivate, at least, the chicory.

The sweetest white grapes of moscato ever grown on this earth were cultivated on the roof by Nonno, but he kept a secret from me for a long time. He knew that once I got to know where the grapevine was located, I would have devoured it all. As I was able to get around to my aunts' studio, I would spend more time looking over what the aunts were doing with the patterning of dresses. I was fascinated by the geometric aspect of fashion as in the modification of templates of new fashions. In desperation to rid of me from the studio for I was getting to be a pain in the ass, my aunts told me about the location of the grapes and even showed me how to get to the roof.

It was divine, when I got to the roof. The grapes were big, almost the size of a golf ball, and had a golden color to them, and so sweet. From the roof one could see all the way to Mount Vesuvius. The farm adjacent to Nonno's house, belonging to Saint Peter church, seemed to extend forever. Now, I can see why the church was fearful of the Communists' idea of sharing farms in those days. The church was not about to share their land with anybody. Unfortunately, the rats on the roof also liked those grapes as well, and Nonno was concerned about them biting me. He and I made a peace deal and that was for me to bring the white grapes to him and save him the trip to get to the roof. In addition, above ground in the courtyard, he grew red grapes and that was easy picking for both of us and no rats to contend with. Nonno kept his wine business until he died.

The wine business was run solely by Nonno, whereas the two aunts were busy upstairs running the seamstress business. Their reputation as "miracle workers" in dressmaking spread throughout the area. The aunts were truly miracle workers for they made dreams come true in fitting the latest style intended for much slender women. Dreams rarely turned into nightmares as long as the aunts were allowed to work on what was possible. Most of the haggling between the aunts and the clients was about that. They were sufficiently talented to have survived in the competitive fashion world of today.

As business expanded, the aunts were spending too much time on the road to Nola in the purchase of various types of exotic fabrics, as these special garments and fabrics were coming available in shops after the war. Obviously, they were spending less time in the creative aspect of their business, and they were not happy. Francesca was hired part time for the expressed purpose of negotiating and purchasing fabric items, and she was good at it. Those expenditures represented the most expensive part of their budget. Francesca was "right at home" and the aunts knew that. That was the reason they hired her. As for Francesca, she was assuming the same role fulfilled by Imalda for the shepherds. Francesca must have learned some skills in dress making from the aunts. When she emigrated to America, she made all of her dresses until she died. However, she was not accustomed to fixed price policies in American stores. She always thought that it meant a starting point in negotiation. I explained to her as gently as I could that in America a fixed price means an end point in negotiations. That was the only thing that she was disappointed about being in America.

Down Main Street a new cafe and bar opened. The new feature of this bar was the billiard room and spumone gelato (ice cream). The bar was located across from Saint Anthony church, and it was centrally located on the "passeggiata" (social walk) route, Main Street to the central piazza. Espresso coffee aroma wafted all the way to Nonno's house, about two blocks away. In the morning, workers, on the way to the train station, would stop by to buy a pastry and an espresso. My favorite item in the bar was the spumone ice cream.

The bar attracted a lot of teenagers who gambled with cards and billiards for money after school hours; this included my brother. In the evening, teenagers were replaced by adults who played cards for serious money. However, there was a constant flow of people in and out of the bar, as people went for their passeggiata (social walk). In short, the bar did extremely well as people needed that outlet after being clammed up for years by the War in the evenings.

Down on main street, about a block from the bakery, a combination of pasta factory and bakery store opened for business for the first time. Pasta production occupied a large building and supplied dry pasta to all the grocery and pastry stores in Avella, Baiano, Sperone, Cicciano, and other towns in the vicinity. The owner was a former

Count who recently returned to Avella with his family. Besides these two businesses, he owned a factory that produced virgin olive oil which he shipped all over Italy and abroad. His huge farm was located immediately behind these three businesses and his residence. His residence was elegant, and I had a glimpse of it once during a recent demonstration in the piazza. The farm was cultivated for wheat, corn, and olives. I am sure that if there were fruit trees in the farm we kids would have raided it for fruits, although the farm was surrounded by a 12 feet wall. In addition to these thriving businesses, the count owned a cement and brick factory located near the creek in order to supply local construction builders in the area. These factories are still in place in Avella today. Prior to this factory bricklayers, like my uncle, made their own bricks, and cement blocks from heating rocks and pulverizing them.

For the first time the Farmer's Market Day was started in Avella in the winter of 1946. Before the war there was a similar market in Avella, but not during the War. This type of market was equivalent to nowadays to the a combination of Farmer and Flea markets in America. The market was scheduled for each Monday except for special holidays, such as Easter and Christmas. The market was located on Main Street, from the Cafe and Bar, near Saint Anthony church to City Hall, about five long blocks. Every imaginable fruit and vegetables in season were sold. Also, shoes, purses, bracelets, umbrellas, etc. were sold.

The ability to negotiate prices was paramount. Vendors expected customers to negotiate and for Francesca it was like being in heaven. She loved to go to the market for two reasons. She loved to haggle to the point of being embarrassing to me as a child, and she loved to visit a fellow shepherd family who sold all sorts of cheeses. Francesca knew everything there was to know about cheese making and both loved to talk about cheese adinfinitum to the point I would leave them. It didn't matter that I left; they were still talking when I returned. Vendors were mostly local farmers and from out-of-town shops peddling non-farm products. The market started at 6 am and lasted until 3 pm, and it seemed that the whole town turned out to shop. The market is in operation to this day.

The most popular outlet for the people of Avella was the Cinema Theater, built in the winter of 1946. It was located near Saint Anthony church. A German heavy cannon, of perhaps 88 mm caliber, stood in front of the Cinema entrance like a statue. The cannon was a souvenir of the German occupation of Avella. We kids climbed all over the cannon and often played cards on the metal plates resting on top of the cannon. Fortunately, it was not loaded to explode. Then again, we really didn't know for sure, if it was loaded. It was never moved out to scrap and it is still there.

The people of Avella were enthralled by the Cinema Theater. It played mainly cowboy and Indian movies. Randolph Scott and Buster Crabbe were the main actors in the films. The Marshall plan's money funded a lot of these movies. Soon enough the kids made wooden pistols to use in gun duels out in the streets. There was never a clear winner for every one claimed to be faster than the other, including me. Once in a while, sentimental Neapolitan movies, such as "Anema e Core" (Heart and Soul) were shown in order to make adults happy. Typically, kids sat in the front row of the theater and adults in the back and it was noisy, especially when the children were rooting for their hero. In those days there were no heroines.

My favorite movies were the comedy "slapstick" ones with Laurel and Hardy, Buster Keaton and Charlie Chaplin. In the late forties, comedies with the Neapolitan comedian Toto (Antonio De Curtis) appeared on the scene and they were popular with children as well as adults. His comedy was relevant to living conditions in the Naples area and, in some sense, may be characterized as being tragicomedy, that everybody in the audience could relate to. The Italian movie industry had a strong resurgence after the War. Their theme was to inject more realism into the movies and they began to replace the American movies at the Cinema. Italian audiences were receptive to the new vision of films and so was the rest of the world.

One of the by-product of cowboy and Indian movies was that the children started to make bows and arrows just like the Indians in the movies, and it was "hip" to walk around town with those wooden bows and arrows. Every kid in town had to have one. Gradually, the wooden bow and arrow graduated into a metallic one. The metal strips in an umbrella were used to make bows and arrows. One day we went to the creek to look for frogs or birds or lizards to spear with the bow and arrows. We found none of those animals, but we found a huge white snake. It was about 12-15 feet long and 6-7 inches wide. It moved slowly and we got almost on top of the snake and put two to three arrows through its head. The snake was deader than a door knob. The snake was so heavy that we had to carry it on a small wheel carriage through town as if we just saved the town from a calamity. We were waiting for applause from people in town just as in the movies. Well, we were not well received. People were swearing and shouting obscenities and invectives at us, especially the mothers. So, we took the snake back to the creek and buried him along the bank. That was the end of the bow and arrow period, and the beginning of scavenging for fruits in the farms.

In the spring of 1946 the picnic festival at the Fusaro fields resumed after a hiatus of seven or eight years, having being postponed for better times. Certainly, the spring of 1946 qualified as a better time than the war years. A contingent of Neapolitan families made the pilgrimage to the Fusaro picnic grounds in Avella. Nowadays, the Fusaro area is built up with restaurants, hotels and house settlements. A pizza restaurant is now located in the middle of the picnic grounds and a hotel across from the swimming pool.

Neapolitans have been fixated every spring to come to the Fusaro area for picnic, although there are many other similar places nearby. Neapolitans claim the following reasons for coming: They love the cool and clean mountain air at the foothills of Avella; this tradition goes back 600 years. Usually, Neapolitans come the first Saturday in May and the people of Avella schedule their picnic to the Fusaro the following Saturday.

Entrance to the San Michele cave. German troops set up a radio communication center above the cave. The cave is at the foothill of Monte Avella. The Clanio creek is below the cave.

The pilgrimage by Neapolitans to the ancient shrine of Cybele, near Avellino, has been going on for over six hundred years, since the miraculous picture of the Virgin Mary was presented to the shrine by Catherine of Valois, and it is seen by 60,000 or more devotees of this cult. Today, most if not all travel to Avellino by car. However, the devoted ones trudged the remaining few miles to the shrine barefoot. They then crawl on hands and knees to the altar of the shrine the last one hundred feet or so. After the religious festivities are over the pilgrims rush to the picnic grounds of the Fusaro and the cave of Saint Michael near the Fusaro.

Typical food prepared for the picnic was a pasta dish, meat, salad, pastries and lots of wine. The main feature and attraction of the picnic for the Neapolitans has been the presentation of new Neapolitan songs by aspiring vocalists who performed in the evening hours. In the morning people climbed up the mountain of Mount Avella. A third of the way up there is a huge cave with an entrance of approximately 10x100 square feet. The cave is about the size of a football field and at the center of the cave there is a religious altar and a statue of San Michele, the patron Saint of Avella. Mass is conducted at noon by a Catholic priest.

Before getting to the cave one must cross the creek. In addition, one had to be careful where and when to cross. At some places there were steep gorges and at the bottom torrential waters. At that time of the year, in May, the height of the water can vary anywhere from one foot to five feet, and the creek is at the bottom of a deep wooded canyon. It is treacherous at some places.

Nonno knew exactly where to cross the creek and where to scale the hill toward the cave. I became fatigued half way up to it and the cave went straight up. Even at that height it looked like "no man's land". When we got to the cave, in about one hour, I noticed wires dangling above the entrance. Only now, after 50 years, I realize the significance of those wires. They were the remnants of an antenna system, most likely installed as an observation post by German troops. This makes sense in that German troops were always in search of cave systems to defend against Allied superiority in the air during the War. However, this raises a point. If the Germans had an observation post about half way up Mount Avella, they certainly would have been aware of an American observation post during the Salerno landing. Therefore, the American observation post must have been as much as five miles east of the mountain top toward Avellino, but still on top of another mountain range. This hypothesis was confirmed upon further discussions with Dr. Richter who was in the landing. Dr. Richter was one lucky man, because the wooded terrain between the cave of Saint Michael and the Avellino mountain peaks are impenetrable by any means. The hills become steeper, the woods denser, water in the creek deeper, and in all the years that I lived in Avella I never heard of anyone going to Avellino that way. If so, it would have been news in town. Germans must have not been aware of the location of the Americans in September, 1943. Even, if they were aware, they didn't have the manpower to do anything about it. The terrain was too prohibitive.

The temperamental Clanio creek near the foothill of Monte Avella. The creek flows from the mountains of the Avellino area (east of Monte Avella). I usually never ventured beyond this point. In the summertime the creek is dry. The dams were built recently.

Inside the cave it was dark. At some places there were wells that were very deep and there was no protection from falling into it. At other places, there were corridors that never ended and it was too dark to go on any further. After the religious mass which started at noon, people started to head back to the picnic grounds, about one mile away. The only problem for me was going back when the water level suddenly rose another foot and the flow was very rapid. This time I needed help in crossing. Ever since then I never trusted that Clanio creek. It can be so beautiful in the summer, when the creek is dry, with the various species of birds around. That was the ideal time to set traps to catch birds. However, it can be so dangerous and tricky when the water flow was rapid and deep in the rainy seasons. At the bottom of the creek, the water comes at you from all angles.

Ever since that picnic day I have been upset with that creek. It was a love-hate relationship between myself and the Clanio creek. I hated the unpredictability of the water flow, rendering the passage of the creek problematical and sometimes extremely dangerous. I loved it when it was dry, where I set the traps for the birds. Little did I know then that in the dry limestone bed of the creek lay my future career in America, the magnetism of ferrite materials. The Chinese discovered magnetite during the Qin dynasty (800 BC) in dry limestone. The first compass was produced using magnetite particles. Greeks discovered the magnetism of limestone about 500 BC.

As we made our way back to the picnic area we saw seven or eight horses, a mule and a donkey, with riders, lining up for a race. Unbelievable! If Hannibal's descendants had been around, probably we would have seen an elephant and a zebra lining up with the horses. We ran back to the Fusaro area to place ourselves in the most advantageous spot to see the race. The jockeys were ordinary people representing different districts of town, much like the "Palio" horse race in Siena. The mule was ridden probably by someone representing the farmers. The donkey was ridden by a bride pulled by the groom. I am sure this type of diversification in representation may not be allowed at the "Palio" horse race in Siena.

We knew quickly who to cheer for and he won. The owner of the horse lived in a house next to Nonno's. Thereafter, I wa s allowed to pa t th e horse each time I passed the owner's house whenever I visited Nonno. The horse was tied up just outside the house so that anyone could feed or pat it. However, at night one could stumble into the horse for it was black in color. The horse took up most of the street and, sometimes, it was unavoidable to bump into the horse. It was a working horse used to pulling heavy rocks from the mountains. They used the rocks to produce cement powder for construction. I could not bear to see that sweaty horse pulling those heavy weights. It pained me to see that beautiful horse used that way.

The picnic site was located near the swimming pool built by the British Army Engineers. A lot of people went to the pool rather than to the cave of Saint Michael. The picnic grounds extended from the foothills of Mount Avella to the creek, a square mile and could easily accommodate 30,000-40,000 people at a time. The Roman aqueduct extended from the confines of the town to the Fusaro, where the water supply building was located. Water flowed via the Roman aqueduct to the fountains along the streets of Avella.

Most people settled down to eat by the creek where it was coolest spot. For me it was great, because that was where birds flocked. It gave me an opportunity to scout where a particular species of birds were nesting. Catching birds was part of a business that I initiated later. The creek about 70 feet below the picnic grounds, was full of 30 feet high boulders. One could hear the roar of the water rolling off those boulders. It looked and was treacherous to take a canoe down there. We ate ziti macaroni with meatballs the size of my finger nails and plenty of red wine. I drank wine diluted with water. The meal was prepared by Nonno in a carbonara style. There was roasted chicken with potatoes as a second dish. For dessert, we had a pie normally prepared for Easter Holidays – oatmeal, ricotta, rice, raisins, etc. A fire was started to brew freshly roasted coffee. How ironic with all those dandelions, daisies, asparagus, and chicory flowers surrounding the picnic grounds. Only a year ago roasted chicory plants were used to make coffee. It never crossed anybody's mind to cultivate the chicory flowers in those post-war days. After a meal like that there was only one thing to do – a small siesta.

The big event of the day was the soccer game sponsored by the Cafe and Bar located downtown Avella. It pitted most of the adults ranging in ages between 20 and 40 years against a team consisting of teen agers. The younger team was mostly made up of card players at the bar including my brother, Sebastiano, who was 12 years old. The older team was made up mostly of people from the O' Vicolo district, partisans and Communists. In a way it was a grudge match or a clash of classes. Interestingly, people representing the Monarchy and well-to-do (big land owners and large business) families did not show up at the picnic.

By far, Sebastiano was the best player. I was so proud of him. Before that game I actually never saw him play soccer. Amazing! That day it served as an impetus for me to become a soccer player and be as good as Sebastiano. He played center midfield and his game was pure finesse. Obviously, he had to be very delicate around older of getting hurt was very high. However, that style stayed with him throughout his career. If he didn't emigrate to America at the age of 18, he would have played for the major league club of Napoli. At the age of 16 he played for the Pompeii soccer club which was one tier below major league soccer. Yes, most likely I would have followed in his footsteps.

With the coming of summer of 1946, a new neighbor (Elena) arrived from Naples. Her house was located within the common courtyard adjacent to Nonno's. Five residents shared the courtyard, and it was connected to the outside street by a 60 feet wide tunnel. Usually, tunnels were closed off by a large portone (front door), but not this one. Elena owned a big villa in Naples and belonged to the aristocracy. Her husband died in Libya in the Italian African campaign of 1940.

The Italian army under the leadership of General Graziani was routed by the British Army in Libya. Many Italian soldiers preferred to be taken prisoners to prolonging the agony. Elena's husband's rank was that of a Brigadier General and his division was the "black shirt" Fascist armored division that fought in the battle of Tobruk (Libya). The Italian tanks in the armored division were very small, the size of a "match box", according to British Army staff. They lit up even from a rifle shot.

Elena was one of many former Fascist families who left their community to start a new life elsewhere and avoid Communists harassment in Naples. Her husband was an important person in the Fascist movement and was recognized as such in Naples. It was not safe for Elena to stay in her palazzo in the affluent Vomero district of Naples. That district drew too much attention from scugnizzi, communists and prostitution. In short, Naples was "no man's land" after the war. It had total chaos and 100% lawlessness. Elena's situation was not unique. There w ere m any local municipalities whereby important Fascist dignitaries had to leave town in order to escape from Communists or simply from muggers.

Elena had a daughter who was popular with other children. She spent a lot of time with my aunts modeling clothes that they made for customers. The daughter was a teen ager and was enrolled in Scuole Media (intermediate school). It didn't take long before Elena was inquiring about the dressmaking ability of my aunts and soon enough a nice friendship and business relationship developed among them. Elena was still in contact with people in aristocracy in the Naples area that had the means or money to buy dresses with the latest style or fashion at reduced prices. In short, Elena was able to produce a "rich" clientele for my aunts' special abilities in modifying the latest fashion style. Elena advised my aunts as to what the clientele wanted in terms of fashion and style. Elena knew a lot of the aristocratic families in the Avella, Baiano and Sperone as well.

Elena and the aunts would re-design a style to fit the "shape" of a customer. The aunts would cut the material based on the new modified template design. For me it was fascinating, almost like a mathematical problem in three dimensional geometry. Business was good for the aunts and Elena. As it turned out, a miracle was in the happening.

Elena needed someone to go to Naples once in a while to clean her palazzo and keep an eye on it. We needed money in the worst way at that time. The part time job of Francesca purchasing fabrics for the aunts was not enough to support us financially. Francesca was introduced to Elena by the aunts and a deal was struck. Halleluiah! Francesca and I took the first trip to Naples by train (21 km trip) and it was nice to get away from Avella. We were looking forward to the visit of the big city. As it turned out, it was not what we anticipated as a relaxing trip. There was one train station almost each kilometer (0.6 miles). Some stations were still totally devastated from the bombing during the War. Train wagons were parked on the side of the station damaged from Allied bombing. Railroad tracks were scrambled like spaghetti in a dish. At one station we saw an unexploded 1000 pounds bomb on the side of an abandoned train wagon. We froze and had chills up our spines. It was one thing to hear the explosion of a bomb from a distance, but it was a different matter to be so close to one and entertain the thought that it may explode at any time. Buildings next to the stations were, by and large, demolished from the bombings. Children and adults appeared to be crawling out of those buildings like rats. It was a shocking site. I thought that we in Avella went through hell and back, but these poor souls were still in hell. Destruction of buildings does not really explain collateral damage. It is the ramifications of the destruction of buildings that is worst.

It was like traveling in the twilight zone, even to the standards of a town like Avella. We in Avella had some damage from the bombing, but it did not compare with what we just witnessed on the way to

Naples. Most likely, those people occupying the destroyed buildings were scugnizzi and homeless people who had taken over the buildings. In general, housing complexes near railroad stations suffered the most damage by Allied bombings. However, surprisingly, the railroad station in Avella suffered very little. I surmise now that the damage due to Allied bombing was the greatest for towns near Naples' harbor, the main supply source for both armies. The train ride took about two hours, but it seemed to take forever in view of all the devastations. It was simply too much to take in as a child and difficult to comprehend how it was possible to have that much destruction in war.

As the train approached Naples, stations were getting bigger and bigger and people were cramming into the train more and more. Pick-pocket thieves were all over the train. At this time I could easily identify them for I was street-smart myself. I roamed the streets of Avella and I had pretty good idea who to stay away from, and we had no money to hide from thieves. At the Naples station there was organized thievery. Some thieves specialized in running away with suitcases under the pretense of helping out with them. Pick-pockets stationed themselves along waiting lines. Scugnizzi pimped prostitutes all over the station. It was simply a mad house where criminals were preying on visitors.

When we exited the station in Naples, all hell broke loose. For a split second Francesca disappeared into the crowd and I could not find her. There were wall to wall people all around us. Somehow, we reconnected and after a long walk we arrived at the villa. It was unbelievably beautiful. Vesuvius was right in front of us separated by the Bay of Naples and the sea. On the other side of the Bay, my friend Vito settled down with his family years later in Torre Annunziata and Torre del Greco. However, across the bay there appeared to be a lot of buildings totally leveled and the harbor was devoid of any activities. People were concerned that the harbor was still full of mines left there by the retreating German Army. Also, it was such a cultural shock to me. I didn't know that people could live in such luxury. The palazzo was located in the Vomero district overlooking the whole Bay of Naples. While I was exploring the villa and other places nearby Francesca started to clean the place. Yes, I did meet some scugnizzi in the streets. They asked me where I was from, for they detected that my dialect was not Neapolitan. They did not bother me for I had no money to give. One of the scugnizzi was no more than five years old. To this day I have wondered whatever happened to that child without a mother and father. By evening we headed home exhausted from the trip. Francesca was physically tired, but I was also mentally exhausted. Naples was no place to visit, but we needed the money. There were hustlers all over the place at the train station in Naples and in the streets. You name it, and it was negotiable. We were forever holding on to whatever luggage we had for our dear life. It was a constant battlefield among thieves. We managed to buy a ticket without being hustled and got on the train. It was a relief to leave that madhouse.

When we arrived home, Francesca received a cashiers check from grandfather Carmine in America for $150. At that time it was a lot of money, but it had to last for the whole year. There was a quota on how much money could be sent from America. The money order was cashed at the local post office for there was no bank in Avella then. Anyway, somebody was looking over our shoulders at that time, as we desperately needed that money. Nevertheless, mother kept the part time jobs with Elena and the aunts and I was spending more time with Nonno and in the streets. I became more like a scugnizzo roaming the streets of Avella on my own, foraging farms for fruits.

The timing of the money from America could have not been any better. We now had enough money to buy proper clothes to attend uncle Pierino's wedding in Avellino. His wife's name was Consalata Pagliuca, and she was from Montefalcione, near Avellino. Half the people of the town of Montefalcione are named Pagliuca. Many years later I met a gentleman in Boston, Mass., by the name of Angelo Pagliuca and he was born in Montefalcione. He and I were members of a bocce club in Boston. It turned out that he was Consalata's uncle. Small world! He relayed to me that he also lost his farm to the tax collector in Montefalcione for non-payment of taxes which was not true. I suppose our loss of the grazing field in Avella was not a single occurrence. I would venture to say that it must have been a common occurrence to landlords living in the USA after the war.

It was quite a journey to get to Avellino from Avella, a train from Avella to Baiano and a bus ride from Baiano to Avellino. From Baiano, the bus route was straight up the mountains. At one place the bus had to negotiate a hairpin turn on a narrow curve carved on the side of a mountain. At that point the mountain was pure granite rock and the width of the road was barely enough for the bus. At most, there must have been only 3-4 inches tolerance between the road and the bus. On one side of the road the bottom of the canyon was 500 feet straight down. At one instance around the curve the right rear tire was exposed outside so that only three tires were touching the road. Lucky for us, the bus driver was wise enough to empty the bus before making the turn. The creek below was the same Clanio creek that passed through Avella; by now it was my friendly nemesis. It was crazy. No wedding was worth risking one's life, but thank God we made it around that curve.

That was not the only surprise. On the way to Montefalcione, the bus had a difficult circuitous route to follow in order to avoid stranded, charred and destroyed German tanks, cannons, trucks, jeeps, motor scooters and benzene containers all over the road and this went on for a long distance. The destroyed vehicles appeared to be heading toward Salerno, probably as a supply convoy, and were bombed by Allied planes. If Dante were in that bus, he would have labeled the road as the one to "inferno". It was eerie. The smell of benzene was so powerful that it was difficult to breathe even two years later. The grass was charcoal black and did not grow back for a couple of years after.

Many years later, a throat specialist in thyroid conditions told me that many people who emigrated from the Avellino area have had an unusual number of thyroid cases, ten times more than the normal rate in Italy. Clearly, these thyroid cases must have correlated with the high concentration of benzene in Avellino area during and after the war. Benzene is now considered the most dangerous carcinogen. The other correlation to consider is that mountain people as in Avellino have little access to a fish diet, as is true in the Alps as well. However, thyroid cases in the Alps are much lower by a factor of ten less. Thus, lack of a fish diet alone does not explain the unusually high rate of thyroid conditions in Avellino. Most likely, benzene was the culprit. This is another example of collateral damage extending well beyond the war years.

The wedding was elaborate with all the rituals that go into an Italian wedding: Tarantella dancing, five course dinner, spumante wine, spumone, and cake. Francesca had a good time for the first time, since the outbreak of the war. Nonno and the entire family were there. This was a great wedding for Uncle Pierino who became a monk only six years earlier! He worked for five years in the Finanzia (finance police), and was promoted to Questore, chief of police of the Avellino area. He then moved on to Reggio Emilia to become Prefetto (chief of all police departments and Interpol).

When all was going so well, Nonno's store was robbed of pasta, bread, wine jugs, olive oil and money during the night. That was the death blow to Nonno's business. However, he did return to business in the fifties. In fact, at that time, there were a rash of robberies all over town. The other two wine stores just one block away were never robbed. Their entrance was protected by a heavy door similar to the entrance to a fortress. The door to Nonno's store was flimsy and easy to break into. Nonno reported the robbery, to no avail. The Carabinieri in town were ineffective. They took a lot of information from Nonno and that was the last time we ever saw them. Even my Uncle Pierino (Nonno's son and former monk) who was then Questore of Avellino (chief of Police) in charge of all police activities in the area of Avellino, could not find out who robbed Nonno's store.

In retrospect, it had the earmark of a Camorra's robbery where the robbers must have been out-of-towners. Camorra was in control of everything in southern Italy, police, politicians and legal and illegal business. They visited every business place that was doing very well, either in a formal visit or to rob it. There was no local government that could enforce law and order. Furthermore, no one paid taxes. The man who collected taxes left town in 1944, because he was a Fascist who would be chased by partisans or Communists. The new tax collector was a crook. In those days paying taxes was equivalent to paying bribery to the Camorra. Sooner or later the Camorra would have collected that tax money.
Unexpectedly, Francesca tried her hand at a business venture along with everyone in town who caught the capitalistic virus. Even vendors from out of town were increasing in numbers to sell their produces. Capitalism reached Avella with a vengeance due to so many years of suppression by the Fascist system. The money source for all these businesses was money sent from relatives in America. The drive to normalcy, like the rest of the Western world, was overwhelming.

There was more cash floating around town for people to spend, which served as impetus for business ventures in town. Francesca opened a store front to sell pasta, and baking flour. I was amazed that she dared open her store after Nonno's temporary demise of his wine business. I am not sure whether it was a gutsy move or the fear of missing out on the potential gravy train that some people were riding on.

Against the advice of Nonno and family, she opened for business. She bought pasta wholesale and combined it with flour shipped by grandfather Carmine. Francesca induced the shepherd community to sell their cheeses through her store. Her dream was to earn enough money to purchase a mechanical dough mixer and make bread, since she owned the brick oven in the portico. Eventually, with Nonno's help, she was going to make her own pasta, but she needed the machine. Hopefully, all financial worries would have been a thing of the past. Bread was the sustenance of life in towns like Avella after the war. Business was good and she was slightly ahead of breaking even. Sebastiano and I helped out from time to time. Francesca worked extremely hard to make the business thrive. In addition, she would go around town to advertise her store, especially to friends from the mountains, the shepherds, and Communist friends from the other side of the creek. Her hunch was right. Business was off the ground and moving along very nicely until the fateful night of March 15, 1947, the Ides of March. Everything was stolen from the store, even personal food supplies. None of us sleeping above the store heard a thing. The robbers broke into the front door easily and drove away in a truck. There were truck marks just outside the store. Naturally, Francesca could not contain her grief. As usual the Carabinieri showed up and took notes and walked away within a span of 10-15 minutes.

Francesca accused our neighbor's two sons of being involved with the crime. At that time I thought that it was an irrational accusation based on her intuition. I felt that it was improper and could only make our lives difficult with our neighbors, but she was adamant and insisted that the Carabinieri should track the brothers' whereabouts. I believe now that she was right.

The neighbors that Francesca accused were shepherds and knew my mother very well. The network of shepherd families was small, but tightly knitted. There was no secret among them. Indeed, if the two brothers were Camorra members, it was common knowledge among shepherds. After about a week, I saw Francesca serving espressos to both brothers in her house and laughing it up together. Even as a child, I thought that was strange behavior. Just a week before the brothers were accused of stealing from Francesca's store! She never explained or talked about either the robbery or the espresso meeting. My guess now is that she was compensated by the Camorra for the robbery in cash. The reason that I say this is because not once did she complain about the financial loss of the robbery. Yet, she complained bitterly for years for the theft of a chicken even when she emigrated to America. She did not re-open her store after the robbery.

For me as a child, the drive to make some money after the war was great. Perhaps, the home financial conditions dictated as much. I started two businesses. The first was selling kites. After many iterations in making kites, I learned to make good ones by admixing special ingredients for the glue. Otherwise, kites would break up while in flight. Stefano, my neighbor, who was also selling kites, taught me how to make the glue. He did not worry about my competition for I was not very good at making kites. Initially, the business was doing well until children started to demand bigger kites and fanciful designs which could be purchased from local convenient stores all over town. So, my business failed, but Stefano's stayed on. He was able to produce bigger kites at lower prices than the stores.

It was becoming a big sport to fly bigger kites for they could climb higher. The competition was to fly the kites higher and higher. However, the weight of the string, attached to big kites, got heavier and heavier, as the kite climbed higher. This invited some unscrupulous characters to stand on a roof and bring down the kite by twirling a rock attached to a string toward the sagging string. Usually, the roof in question was sufficiently far away for the miscreant to escape with the kite. As far as I was concerned, I got out of this business at the right time! It was getting too nasty and too technical for me.

My problem was that I needed to invest more money to make bigger kites at reasonable prices in order to compete with Stefano and the stores. It meant that I should have invested in special paper for making kites, longer cane sticks, and stronger glue in order to stay in business. I just did not have the money to buy these items. The second business that I started was the sale of birds. In Italy, especially around the Naples area, people are fascinated with caged birds, especially tropical ones.

The favorite local birds were canaries, cardinals and bluebirds. The demand for sparrows or ravens was low. The first item of business was for me to learn how to catch birds and the special locations where to find different types of birds, especially canaries. The latter type of information was top secret. No one who is in the business of selling birds will tell anyone else where to catch certain type of birds. At that time, the source of this type of information was none other than Stefano and his uncle. After badgering Stefano's uncle a number of times about locations of finding birds, he relented and was willing only to show me how to capture birds from trees and around the creek and foothills, using a trap made of net material.

The capture of birds from trees was rather trivial for me, but where to look for certain type of birds was an entirely different matter. Stefano's uncle was not about to divulge where to look. So, one spring day he, Stefano and I took a trip to the Fusaro area near the foothills. We got up at five in the morning and walked there, about a mile from Francesca's house. On a dry creek bed the Uncle set up the trap to catch the birds. First, he made a large bow strung together by a sturdy string. Second, he dug a hole about 2x2 square feet in area and one foot deep. The hole was partially filled with loose rocks and water. Seeds were spread all around the water hole. The bow was wrapped in a net and camouflaged with leafs. A string was attached to the bow and net and strung along to a hiding place. Every so often, the hole needed to be replenished with water.

The hiding place was a "piece of art". It had the appearance of a natural hedge among other natural hedges. The distance between the water hole and the hiding place was about 50 feet. All together it took two to three hours to set up the bird trap. This uncle was a true professional. Nothing was left to chance. He simulated bird sounds with a flute like whistle specially designed by him. I thought then that he was a little bit cuckoo for he was thinking like a bird in terms of what the bird "sees" and hears. He reminds me now of the character Papageno in Mozart's opera, Die Zauberflote (Magic Flute). Papageno was a bird catcher who wears a coat made of bird feathers whose calls on panpipes imitates birds' calling. Anyway, we waited about one hour and in one trap he pulled in three to four birds, but no canary. I knew enough then that if I wanted to start this business, I needed to feature canaries as part of the inventory. So, I asked the uncle, if he could sell to me a male and female canary. My plan was that if I failed to trap canaries on my own, at least, I could foster mating between the two canaries sold to me. He told me that he was short of canaries and would think about it. He never stopped thinking. I went out on my own to trap birds, following the instructions taught to me by Stefano's uncle. I went to the same area, near the Fusaro on the dry creek bed, but did not build the special hiding place of bushes, hedges, and tree branches. I hid behind a rock wall and tree branches. The most difficult part of the operation was the string mechanism to pull on the trap. If the string was pulled too hard, the trap would unhinge from the ground and birds would escape. Pulled too slowly, the birds' reaction time would be too fast. There was a learning curve in setting up the trap. Stefano' uncle had been setting traps for more than 20 years; he made it look easy. Nevertheless, the first time that I tried on my own, I caught a sparrow and a raven.

After a while I got the hang of it and could set up a trap system within two hours, including a hiding place. Every day I would venture more and more toward the top of the mountains along the creek route. I was getting deeper into the woods, and venturing toward the top of the mountains via the creek which slowly turned into deep wooded canyons and steep gorges full of wolves, and wild animals. This area was referred to as the Fontanella (little fountain) area. It was the old route from Avella to Avellino or to Monte Vergine before the highway was built that passed through Baiano. I knew enough that this was not the area to catch canaries. Canaries usually were found in dry, not moist, areas.

Nowadays, pilgrims to Monte Vergine from Naples and other areas take the highway. The old road, where I was setting up bird traps, was wild as it climbed up the mountain. In the wet season water flowed through the pathway or the creek, and the waterfalls spurted out from all sides. Wolfs, small black bears, and other wild animals were readily found there. It was truly "no man's land" in the wet season. Visibility was about 15 feet which was much less distance than needed to hide from the traps. I was desperate because, sooner or later, I needed to trap some canaries, if I was going to have a viable business. People were not interested in sparrows or ravens for these birds don't chirp like canaries. I was too proud to go back to Stefano's uncle and ask him where to trap the canaries. We were then competitors. What to do? I decided to head west from the mountains toward the old castle sitting on top of a small hill, and in dryer terrain. There were a lot of large rocks to hide behind, and also visibility was excellent. The only trees around were cactus. I discovered soon enough that the castle area was infested with rattle snakes. Almost every rock had a rattle snake underneath.

However, it was much easier to set up bird traps by the castle area. Once it was established that there were no rattle snake under a rock, the trap was laid out sufficiently far away to hide from the trap. The yield was much better and, within two weeks, I caught two canaries, one female and one male. The male was recognized from the fact that he has a longer central toe and the female has equal length toes. The intent was soon to put both birds in the same cage and let Mother Nature take over. Two eggs were produced but one baby bird did not survive. I nourished and fed the remaining baby bird special seed diets and liquids. For a while it appeared that the young bird was going to make it. In fact, the bird began to fly outside the cage, but all of sudden he died. I believe now that the canary needed another week of controlled diet before letting him fly outside the cage. For me, it was the beginning of the end for any more business ventures. I decided to sell the two canaries and all other birds and the cages. Yes, I learned a lot from those failures. One must have a product which is in demand and have the ability to deliver the product inexpensively. Also, one should have enough resources to counter-balance the ups and downs of business cycles. I was not willing to put more time or money into this business.

That was one learning experience, although I lost my "shirt". Francesca was in shock in the realization that here was a little "scugnizzo", me, in her household trying to hustle for money. She was reluctant for me to get started on this and made it clear to me that she was not going to put up any money. Once I got started and she saw my willingness to put in the hard work to make it happen, she was proud and encouraging when I needed that the most. Nonno was not aware of my enterprises for he lived on the other side of town. Sebastiano was too busy with school and soccer and friends to get involved in business with me. My aunts would have never supported me in business for they had their hands full with making dresses and worrying about another small business like mine. Besides, whatever "extra" money made from dresses went strictly to Sebastiano to keep up the "bella figura", good appearance. They did not have extra money to support my business.

In a way I was relieved that the businesses folded. This meant that I had more time for soccer and school.

In the fall of 1946, Religious festivals were returning to Avella for the first time since the War. The church was trying to get back to normalcy. Almost each church in town sponsored a festival. It a mystery as to the source of money to sponsor festivals after the war. The following churches in Avella sponsored the festivals: Saint Anthony, Saint John, Saint Peter, Saint Candida and Saint Joseph Churches. In that year there were only two festivals sponsored by Saint Anthony and Saint John. Usually, these festivals lasted three days, Saturday, Sunday and sometimes Monday, depending on crowd expectations.

Typically, on Saturday morning a tambourine player, a trumpeter and someone holding a miniature statuette or cross would march through the streets, playing their instruments as loud as possible announcing the festival. By the time they reached Francesca's house, it was early in the morning, but no matter I would get up and follow them all around town, rain or shine. I was so full of adrenalin that I didn't get tired following the tambourine man all over town. However, a lot of children followed the two-man band by the time it arrived at the church sponsoring the festival. Every time I hear the song now " Mister Tambourine Man" from Bob Dylan, it takes me back to Avella. In the afternoon, vendors would line up along the streets to sell toys, unusual handy things, whistles, cherry bombs and offer gambling. There really was no control over these vendors, and most of them were from out of town. One favorite food was slices of boiled pig with lemon. In the evening a temporary stage and orchestra pit were set up for opera music to be played in the piazza. The stage was usually on top of the closed water fountain near the palazzo of the Count. The orchestra was from the town of Montefalcione, where Nonno was once employed.

Since retirement, Nonno played in the orchestra only when a trombone player was needed. He was always ready, when called upon. He knew the scores by heart. The mass for the Saint was celebrated on Sunday. After the mass the procession of the statue of that Saint took place in the streets. People and store owners would attach paper money to the statue. There were sufficient people taking turns, to carry the statue around town. The priest of the parish followed the statue, blessing people along the way. Following the priest or priests were important dignitaries of the town, contributors and politicians, and town people. Only once did I see the Bishop of Nola come to one of our festivals. The procession never ventured into the O'Vicolo district, where Communists and shepherds resided. The procession followed a path on Main Street, where there were more opportunities to collect money from shops along the streets. Besides, there was friction between the church and the Communists with regard to the status of farms that the church owned. Eventually, the O'Vicolo district had their own festival sponsored by Saint Candida church, namesake of my Aunt. In the late 40s the festivals extended to Monday, but that was rare.

In late spring of 1947 there was a rumor in town that a large shipment of American baking flour was to be distributed to poor people in Avella. The American government paid for the shipment and needy families were to be the recipients at no cost. My friends from soccer informed me about it and, immediately, I told Francesca. Indeed, the rumor was correct and the shipment was due any day. Naturally, being financially strapped, a sack of flour could really help and we were convinced that we were on the list of recipients.

The flour arrived a week later on a Saturday, when I was not in school. It arrived by truck and the sacks of flour were dropped in front of the public school in the middle of the soccer field. There must have been 50-60 sacks, each weighing 70-80 Kg. Four or five bureaucrats from City Hall called names to come forward to pick up one sack of flour. I was standing there feeling confident that they would call our name. They never did. Our disappointment was beyond description.

Francesca demanded to see the list. Indeed, the list did not contain our name and she, of course, demanded an explanation. None of the recipients were poor and in need! Francesca asked bluntly, who made up the list? No answer was given and the administrators at the site handed the list to Francesca and simply walked away after parceling out all the flour sacks. We were devastated, to say the least.

We discovered later that none of the Communists from Avella received any flour, although they were the poorest of the poor. None of the shepherd families received any flour either. Some of the Communists and shepherds were good friends of mother. The flour went to people who were appointed by former Fascist administrators in City Hall, farm owners and relatives of camorristi who were in charge of City Hall at that time. These people were not well to-do, but they were not poor like some of us. There must have been somebody looking over our shoulders protecting us, perhaps God, or the belief that sooner or later a break would come our way. Two weeks later we received two shipments of baking flour at our front door! It was mind boggling. Where from? At first, we thought that it was part of the same shipment as before. It was post-marked from America and our grandfather came through. It was unbelievably relieving to the whole family. The flour was shared with Nonno's side of the family and Uncle Joe's family.

For the first time in a very long time the wood-burning brick oven in the portico area (above the pig sty) was put to use. Francesca made bread and rolls for the first time. It was a real treat to eat warm bread just out of oven. We had a steady source of bread for the next two to three weeks. That was a comfortable feeling for the first time in our lives. Thereafter, the grandfather from America shipped two sacks of baking flour and $150 cashiers check to Francesca every year until we left for America. That was enough to make do every year, enough to barely survive. The part-time jobs in Naples and with the aunts, it complemented our basic source of food and money.

Nonno's farm was beginning to be productive again so that in late summer of 1947, when the harvest was at its peak, everybody pitched in to help. A pile of corn cultivated in Nonno's farm was piled in the middle of the dining room in Nonno's house. The pile occupied the whole room and it was about six to seven feet high. I could actually touch the ceiling, when I was on top of the pile. Nonno put me on top of the pile and said for me to shuck them all. I did not mind, and I worked until I got tired. It seemed to take forever, and I took a lot of breaks. Finally, in the afternoon Nonno took over. I did come back and pitch in from time to time. From there, he and I went to the farm to pick watermelons, cantaloupes and exotic cantaloupes. That was fun for we got to eat few. Nonno would pick unripe special melons or special cantaloupes he would hang the melons on the wall above the balcony. By October or November the special melons would ripen sufficiently to be eaten.

The farm next door, where the colosseum was located, was totally enclosed by barbed wires. The farmers there were busy picking hazelnuts and olives. Hazelnuts were and are in great demand in Northern Europe. However, today Italy faces competition from Turkey in hazelnuts production. As is well known, the olive oil is produced all over the world and the business is corrupt. The only way to assure pure virgin oil is to produce it yourself. Nonno never cultivated hazelnuts and olives. I suppose, during the war, that business was not thriving, but fruit trees and vegetables were more useful to the family. Uncle Anthony from Boston reclaimed the farm, when he returned to Avella in 1957.

Christmas time was just around the corner and we kids were excited about the coming of Christmas as to how the Presepio was going to look in cousin Carmine's house. The year before, for the first time Uncle Joe put together the Presepio. Was he going to do it again? We wondered if it would be the same or if there would be any changes. If so, what will change? The anticipation was overwhelming. We soon had the answer from Uncle Joe. It was going to be bigger than ever and his good artist friend, Mastro Nicola, was going to get involved with the project. The children and Uncle Joe went to the foothills to look for the biggest tree trunks from which to build the Presepio. The problem was to cross the creek, when the water rapids were strong and cold. That year we had a lot of rain in November and December. I believe now that even if the water level was chest high, we would have found a way to cross that creek. We (cousins and friends in the neighborhood) were determined. The Clanio creek was not going to stop our mission. My Uncle must have felt like a Field Marshal with all those kids helping out looking for tree trunks at the foothills. In Nola Uncle Joe splurged and bought more figurines and a bigger star to pin on top of the Presepio.

The two artists put together a sketch of the Presepio. This time they added scenery of shepherds herding the sheep on the mountains and I liked that, being sentimental about shepherds. Mastro Nicola put the wood pieces in place, whereas Uncle Joe would shave off rough spots on the wood with his trusted chisel. All the while we kids were trying to figure out the next step in putting it together. Mastro Nicola put in his "magic" silver and gold paper over the wood and painted the sky as background. The grass scenes were actual grass and the trees were assembled from miniature branches. The mountain background, town scenery and sky background gave the Presepio a three dimensional realism. Uncle Joe and Mastro Nicola simulated Monte Avella in the background for the Nativity scene. They added restaurants, butcher shops, private homes, Nativity scene and a road system interconnecting all the scenes. It looked just like the town of Avella, except for the Nativity scene. Truly a piece of art. The whole neighborhood came to see it and marveled at the work of the two artists.

For the first time, cherry bombs could be bought over-the-counter for Christmas. Children enjoyed raising havoc all over town, especially near the monks' residence. I would toss them in the afternoon, when the monks took their naps in order to agitate them. Yes, I was in the spirit of Christmas according to tradition in Avella. Gifts were exchanged at "Befana" (the Feast of Epiphany). We received the usual candies and dry figs, but Uncle Joe rewarded the whole family with a radio and a bicycle. That was truly a memorable Christmas. Then, for the first time we could tune in to soccer games from all over Italy, including Juventus games, my favorite soccer team from Turin, North Italy. According to other kids in town, I was a traitor, because they were all fans of the Napoli soccer team, the local southern team in Italy.

The fundamental question to address here is to what extent did the Marshall Plan, 1947, help out in the economic recovery of Italy from WW II devastation and in particular a town like Avella which was so typical of towns in the Naples area. The quick answer is: not much, especially in the Naples area. Southern Italy received help from the USA as relatives in the USA were allowed, after the war, to send money and goods. This went a long way in the start-up of family businesses in many towns like Avella. Thus, the economic recovery would have occurred with or without the Marshall Plan. The Marshall Plan accelerated the recovery. The Marshall Plan [101] derived its name from US Secretary of State, George C. Marshall, after the war in President Truman's administration. During the War Marshall was a four-star General who was the main architect of the American war strategies in Europe and Asia. The plan was introduced by Marshal in a speech delivered at Harvard University after the War. The plan was also referred to as the European Recovery Program or ERP. In three years, under this plan, the US gave away $12.4 billion which was about 5% of GDP at that time. In today's dollar value, it would amount to about $900 billion dollars. The money was earmarked for industries, bank systems, infrastructures, food and minerals.

The recipients were: Britain ($3.4 billion), Germany ($1.4 billion), France ($2.7 billion), Italy ($1.5 billion), Netherlands ($1.1 billion), Greece ($0.8 billion), Austria ($0.68 billion) and smaller nations ($0.56 billion). Spain received no aid, since a Fascist government was in place then. The Soviet Union (Russia) and the Eastern bloc countries refused to participate in the Marshall plan. The counterpart to the Marshall plan was the "Molotov" plan which folded the economies of Eastern Europe with that of the Soviet Union. The Molotov plan was replaced by the "five year" plan whereby farm productivity was integrated in the Eastern European blocks and the Soviet Union. The problem in the communist countries of Europe was that there was no incentive to produce and increase wealth of the nation and the individuals at the same time. All production belonged to and was controlled by the State, Soviet Union. The economy from the Bloc countries never performed as well as that of Western European economy.

Seventy per cent of the American grants were given for the purpose of buying commodities from the US and Canadian suppliers. For example, $3.5 billion was spent on raw materials, $ 3.2 billion on food, feed and fertilizer, $ 1.9 billion on machinery and tools and $ 1.6 billion on fuel bought from the USA. The Organization for European Economic Cooperation (OEEC) decided where the products bought would be shipped and the Economic Cooperation Administration (ECA) organized the shipments of goods to various countries in Europe.

The US and Canadian suppliers were paid in dollars, whereas Europeans paid in their local currencies. Obviously, this situation lent itself to exchange rate speculations. If the value of the dollar, relative to European currencies, was low, suppliers were payed less for their export of goods. Thus, the size of shipments of goods regulated the exchange rate. In addition, the recipients of the grants were to match the grant money for future investments in their own countries. The aim of American policy was to raise the level of economic activities in Europe so that they could be trading partners with the US. Clearly, the Marshal plan planted the seeds for the European Union (EU) as it exists today. Although much credit is attributed to the Marshal plan for the economic upturn in Western Europe, the fact was that the infrastructure was mostly repaired by the time the Marshall plan came into existence. The effect of the plan was basically to create markets in Europe for the US to trade with.

In Italy, most of the grants went into re-building the industrial base in Northern Italy. For example, the Fiat Company was able to modernize their plants and compete with German and French auto manufacturers. Once the domestic market was controlled by Fiat, Fiat expanded to markets in Europe and the USA. As for Southern Italy, there was much infrastructure reconstruction, but no new investments in heavy industry or new markets. Part of the grant monies were spent on food supplies to Southern Italy.

There were no matching funds to invest in heavy industries in Southern Italy for there were no new heavy industries. Before the war the disparity in industrial capacities and markets between Northern and Southern Italy was uneven. After the war, the disparity was even greater and Southern Italy has never recovered since. In some sense, the Marshall Plan exacerbated a bad situation in Italy to make it even worse than before. It was not surprising that, after the War, there was a mass exodus of young people from Southern Italy to industrialized parts of Italy, Europe and USA. During the 1980s, Northern Italians wanted to separate from Southern Italy, because they felt that the financial burden to support the economy in Southern Italian was too great. These talks have abated today. Soon after the War, there was only one Cafe and Bar. Two years later, there were four more Cafes and Bars spread throughout Avella. Even, the poor section of town had a Cafe and Bar. I don't believe the aroma of an espresso coffee alone drove the desire for more bars. The Communist party started a combination of Cafe and meeting places for Communists and non-members.

Earlier, I mentioned that soon after the War, wine and pasta-making outlets were operating near the railroad station. Two years later farmers were getting active and rich. Shipments of onions, cherries, tomatoes, grapes, olives and hazelnuts were transported by truck toward the main highway to Nola and the railroad station. Wine and olive oil industries in Avella are booming. White/red cherries were transported from the farms to the train station in large baskets to be exported. A factory producing heavy farm machinery were being built in Avella in the fifties.

Tourism was picking up when hotels built in the Fusaro area with connecting roads over Monte Avella to Avellino after the War. The forbidden route through the thick woods to Avellino is now trespassed by a bus line from Avella for the first time. A paved road was forged through the woods in the fifties. Restaurants and pizza houses are springing up since the fifties in the Fusaro area as well as in town. Owners of the farm near Nonno's could no longer hide the colosseum. A boulevard was built over the dirt road and the earthquake fault-line leading tourists to the Museum. Another museum displaying ancient Greek art is located near the bridge blown up by the American soldiers. Finally, wind energy is being developed in Avella utilizing the constant wind blowing from the mountains. As such, a turbine factory is being built in town. The fundamental question to consider is whether such economic progress could be attained under Fascism? I don't think so. The problem was that a Fascist government interfered too much with people's spirit to be creative and, in addition, there was no reward to be creative. Only the state could reap rewards.

Farm production increased so much that women were beginning to be employed to transport farm products to the market. This type of work was usually reserved for male farm hands before the war. Women filled the gap of the missing men due to the War. Women who were carriers usually rested near the public elementary school building and lay the baskets full of fruits on an embankment. They carried fruit baskets on their heads, and they were extremely tired. We exchanged water or soda for some cherries and they liked that exchange. We knew that they were looking for that break in the afternoon, usually. The same exchange worked well with the watermelon vendors at the farmer's market. These vendors had no desire to take any watermelons back home to their farms. We were glad to take some watermelons out of their hands in exchange for water. The farmer's market on Monday grew exponentially with time. Initially, the market only occupied one long block of Main Street. Eventually, it extended for more than ten blocks, from the poor section of town to my house. The market was very crowded and it offered a variety of vegetables, fruits, and a variety of commodities.

Clearly, business was thriving in Avella, not because of the Marshall plan, but because people escaped the yoke of Fascism. They were fed fascist propaganda on a daily basis, and were tired of being told what was good for them. They wanted to have a feeling of experimenting life on their own terms, not on Mussolini's terms. Shipments of food from the Marshall Plan and money from relatives in the USA spurred small businesses all over Southern Italy.

On a personal basis the team of Uncle Joe and Mastro Nicola was doing exceptionally well. They were getting church commissions not only from local churches, but also from churches in neighboring towns. Their reputations as artists who could "repair" famous paintings from the Middle Ages grew rapidly. During the war there were many churches damaged by the bombings and many valuable paintings needed major repairs. Also, they were well equipped to repair building structures of the churches. In those days churches were the only customers who could afford to pay cash! Also, they collaborated on their own works of art.

Uncle Joe became part owner of the local cinema, which gave me free entry into the cinema. I must have seen every Cowboy and Indian movie ever made in Hollywood. There were not many original Italian movies for the movie industry in Italy was still in disrepair. It was not until the 1950s that the cinema industry in Italy began to produce their own movies. A number of times I was allowed in the projection room and the technician taught me how to splice the rolls of films. Sometimes, I was left alone to run the projector while the technician took a break.

After the War, ownership of a radio was very important for it connected us to the outside world instantly. In contrast to the past, news about the war and Mussolini arrived much later and, as a result, facts were always distorted or misinterpreted. Would that have made any difference in the outcome of events? Perhaps not. Finally, cousin Carmine and I could tune in live soccer games on Sunday. Without the radio we would have to wait for the newspaper on Monday to read about the games played on Sunday. It was also exciting to hear about the outcome of games instantly for all of us participated in waging bets on the so-called TOTOCALCIO. For 50 Lire (5 cents) one picked winners, losers and ties of Sunday soccer games. There were, in total, 13 games played on Sunday. Ties were also possible outcomes in soccer games. I considered myself knowledgeable about soccer teams, but the best that I ever managed was 10 correct picks out of 13. That was not good enough to win anything. Winner of TOTOCALCIO could win as much as 1 million Lire, $100,000. Besides the radio, Uncle Joe bought two bicycles, one for himself to get to work on projects and the other one for cousin Carmine.

Uncle Joe taught Carmine how to ride the bike and, in turn, Carmine taught me. The bike was a lot bigger than me. In order to ride I had to put the right foot through and below the supporting bar of the bike, a little bit awkward but manageable. However, as always, good things sometimes come to an end. I took the bike, with Carmine's permission, for a ride to Baiano. I never visited Baiano, although it was only one kilometer (less than a mile) away from Avella. Mentally, it felt like I was visiting the Soviet Union, because the mayor was Communist. It was a novelty to have a communist mayor in the area. I was curious to see how things looked like in Baiano under a Communist mayor.

The entry point to the town was the railroad station and the main piazza with its one coffee house. The town was on the main highway to Nola. The bicycle race "Giro D'Italia" and motor cycle races went through Baiano-Nola. The mayor was instrumental in building a modern structure for their cinema, and it looked avant-garde. Bravo for the mayor of Baiano. The town looked more built up with new housings and public buildings compared with Avella. They built a small hospital which was a rarity in a small town like Baiano.

Years later, I had an operation on my infected ear in that hospital. After all, in the 1946 election the Communist party polled at least one third of the electorate in Italy, implying that at least one third of the mayors were Communist. The moral of this story is that in those days it paid off to have a Communist Mayor in the post-recovery period of Italy. They got things done in their towns. The mayor of Avella, who was a Christian Democrat, built a road from the picnic area, called Fusaro, to the outskirts of town. After the first good rain storm the road washed away.

On the way back to Avella, I was moving at a fairly good speed with the bike circling around a curve beyond which the incoming traffic was hidden. As I turned around the curve, two donkeys pulling two wagons were galloping at full speed toward me. They were neck and neck in a race. To the left of one wagon was a barbed wire. To the right of the other was a ditch about five feet deep, where rain water flowed. In between the two wagons there was enough room to fit the bike. I aimed the bike for that gap. The wheel axle of one wagon caught the support bar of the bike, and I rolled over five to six times. I was bruised and scraped my knees and face, but nothing was broken. The continued their race. Naturally, Carmine was upset, because he had to explain to his dad about the broken bike. Francesca, Aunt Giovanna and Carmine invented a "cock and bull" story to tell Uncle Joe. Anyway, the made-up story worked. When Uncle Joe came home from work, he bought another bike for Carmine. However Carmine kept a closer tabs of my whereabouts with the bike.

Yes, the people of Southern Italy survived, once again, another wave of invaders in WWII. They shed the yoke of Fascism to lead a normal life to recovery. However, the real beneficiary of the hidden collateral damage was the criminal element in Southern Italy that took over the political vacuum created with the help of the AMG, Allied Military Government. To this day the whole world is paying dearly for that blunder.

THIRTEEN
SCHOOL YEARS

In the fall of 1945, Francesca enrolled me in the kindergarten school administered by the nuns. There were ten nuns administering kindergarten and elementary schools. Public Elementary school was free, but there was an entrance fee for the nuns' private school. Children from Avella and the town of Sperone were eligible to apply to go to the private school. Sperone was located on the other side of the railroad station, one kilometer away. The school consisted of a three floors building and a small church. Kindergarten students occupied mostly the courtyard, and rooms on the ground floor. The elementary school students occupied rooms on the top floors. The terrace was the place where we did physical exercises.

The view from the terrace was stupendous. It had the same view as the colosseum toward Mount Avella, but at a higher level. My favorite room was the kitchen on the first floor, where the nuns cooked. I loved to stand by the door and smell the cooking aroma drifting in the courtyard. Sometimes I would sneak into the kitchen just to see what was cooking. The one time that I got caught in the kitchen I was punished severely. The nun picked me up by the ear lobes and literally lifted me off the ground.

Francesca negotiated the entrance fee with Madre Superiore, the mother Superior and director of nuns' order. The argument was about whether or not I was entitled to a half or full scholarship due to the death of my father. I learned one thing from that exchange, although I turned different shades of red from being so embarrassed. I learned that nuns were tough negotiators, but Francesca won out. There was nothing soft about nuns, when it came to money. They were in the same predicament, financially, as the rest of the town's people.

Francesca negotiated a full scholarship on the basis of our being poor and my father's death in Libya. The nuns negotiated a bad deal for I was unruly. There was not a single rule that I did not break voluntarily or by accident. Each time I violated a rule I was punished severely. A short and stiff wooden paddle was used to slap the back of my hand and it left an imprint on my mind and hands. I was made an example of what not to do in front of all my classmates.

Being raised by a shepherd family with their free spirit did not prepare me well for the nuns' disciplinary methods. By that time, I enjoyed my freedom to roam the streets and raid farms for fruits. And the foul language that I was accustomed to must have either entertained or made them blush red in their necks. Thena g ain, I will never know for their necks were always covered. The regiment as a kindergarten student was pretty much the same every day except on Wednesday afternoon w hen we either walked in a single file to the church in the nun's building or to Saint John church which was about eight blocks away. We were to exercise tranquility in church and sometimes mass was served by a priest.

Private school administered by nuns. The terrace was facing the small hill where Germans were camped. Photo courtesy of Anmarie Vittoria, 1981.

As a child, I was bored stiff on these excursions to church. When I lined up in a column with others on the way to church, I would position myself to be last in line by jockeying with other children in line. With the flick of an eye I would scamper away to a field and play soccer with other children who were not in kindergarten. The trick was to get back in line, when the nuns and the rest of the children came out of the church and look like an angel with the rest of the children. Only once did I get caught, and the penalty was, as usual, stiff. Nothing was going to stop me for trying again and again. It really became an exercise in timing, getting out and being in line at the right time and at the right place. Francesca protested about me being punished with a wooden stick, but to no avail. It didn't help her cause or lessen my physical pain, when she used foul language to the nuns. I was embarrassed in front of other children.

The morning routine consisted of projects with other children: painting, clay work and singing. Exercise on the terrace followed the morning sessions. Lunch consisted of soup, pasta e fagioli (beans), spaghetti, fruit and powdered milk. For me, it was the main meal of the day and, most times, the only meal. Nuns were really saints. At lunch there was so much noise, commotion and confusion among the children. To this day I don't know how the nuns were able to organize something like 200 children to eat at the same time quietly and not to throw any food at each other. There was a constant motion of children from one end of the dining room to the other.

In the afternoon sessions, the nuns engaged students in being able to communicate, introduction of the alphabet, and religious stories. I was truly interested in the religious stories to the point that I asked too many questions, mainly about the credibility of what I was told. That infuriated the nuns. The worst part of kindergarten was the sanitation in the bathrooms. It was terrible and I will spare the reader the details. I am certain now that it was the cause of much sickness in children then. In one of the excursions where I skipped attending Saint John church with the nuns I got hurt playing soccer. A kid kicked me in the right shin. It was a deep gash wound and I still have a scar from it. I washed it and mother bandaged it, but it got infected. Yellow pus was coming out of the wound and Francesca was really worried. Only three years earlier my sister died from a scratch on the knee. So, she took me to the local doctor. After examining the wound he thought that I might have cancer. Anyway, he gave Francesca a bottle of alcohol and a bottle of peroxide in order to clean the wound. Obviously, these two simple medicines were not available, when my sister was hurt. My leg healed and I went back to playing soccer with a vengeance. The following year Francesca worked in the political campaign for the doctor's bid to become Mayor of Avella. In June 1946, kindergarten school was coming to an end and I was at an age to be admitted to first elementary school. There were two impediments for my attending first grade. First, I developed a small stutter. I don't know to this day how and when the stuttering started. No one in our family ever had such an affliction. Perhaps, the strain of adapting to the school system of education and the discipline meted out by the nuns was too much for me to overcome. I was raised as a "wild goat" where every other word was a swear word and I used to roam the streets of Avella alone, as a child. Francesca was holding three part-time jobs, helping the seamstress aunts, making cheese for a shepherd family near our house and cleaning houses. It was barely enough to support the family. As far as Francesca knew, Nonno was to keep an eye on me while working. The nuns were strict in carrying out their discipline and did not tolerate my language or behavior. They advised that a delay of one year may be helpful to me. Francesca was offended by their attitude and decision for she worried about how I would react. They suggested that I be transferred to the public school system, as the nuns were overly concerned about my condition. In the public school system stuttering was not an issue for one of my friends was not held back in grade level because of it.

There were two reasons for this decision. First, the nuns were fed up with the free spirit of a "goat" (me); second, the nuns were under pressure from the parents of other children in the school to get rid of me. All of the parents of the other children were of well-to-do families. In those days not many families could afford to send their children to a private school. Not even Uncle Joe could afford to send his children to private school, although he worked full time after the War on lucrative contracts from the church, and the construction business. The only reason we could afford it was that we received a free scholarship. So, there was resentment by the parents of my presence, especially of my background. It was not just the bad language, my clothes did not exactly meet the standards of other children in school. Although other parents had some misgivings about me, the children in school couldn't care less about what the parents were saying or thinking about the situation. Being fiercely independent and free spirited, I stuck out like a black sheep among the affluent kids in school. Francesca, standing right in the middle of the courtyard declared to Madre Superior that Michele (that was my name then) will "stay put". These discussions were being held in front of me and it was not a pleasant exchange, but very terse. I had a feeling that Francesca had little respect for nuns. She thought that it was an unnatural behavior for women to labor in a convent in order to serve a male society of priests. Her attitude did not help me in improving my relationship with the nuns. Knowing full well her attitude, I dreaded each time she made an appearances in school for whatever reason.

In the fall, I returned to the kindergarten school, determined to do well in school, especially after that exchange between Francesca and the nuns. I was very conscious of the stuttering. On the first day of school Nonno took me to school instead of Francesca. Nonno wanted to relax the atmosphere with the nuns. Francesca went to Naples for her part-time job, cleaning and dusting an apartment belonging to Elena. Elena collaborated with the aunts in dress-making. She left Naples to avoid harassment from Communists. The nuns greeted me like "the return of the prodigal son". They cuddled me and were genuinely happy to see me. Even, "mustacciola", the nun with a slight moustache, who was the cook, was very nice to me. Whenever she would stare at you with hands on hips, her pose could strike fear in anyone's heart. However, when she smiled, the whole courtyard would "light up" like a ray of sunshine. At one time she took me to the kitchen and allowed me to stir her favorite dish of sausages and red peppers. She did not offer any, but that was ok with me. I was very respectful of the art of cooking as Nonno was a great chef and I adored his food. However, helping mustacciola was like being in heaven. I used to watch Nonno for hours. As soon as he turned his back I would try to stir the frying food. Nonno did not mind.

Slowly but surely the stuttering problem was becoming less of a problem and less conscious of it. I was invited by my friends from school to visit their houses. The friends lived in palazzos with plenty of food all around. The kindergarten consisted of about 30 students. One third of the kindergarten students came from the town of Sperone and there was little socializing or interaction between students from Sperone and Avella. The students from Avella were sons and daughters of industrialists, business, lawyers, and former Royalists except for one student, Andrea, who came from the O' Vicolo district. I am certain now other children do in other school systems.

that he was supported by a special scholarship due to his father being killed in the War, although his father was an active Communist partisan. His father belonged to the partisan insurrection group which was operating in the hills of Rome and preceded Don Camillo as leader of the partisans in Avella. His uncle was Don Camillo who followed in the footsteps of Andrea's father, and was a shepherd. He was also a distant cousin of Francesca.

Although friends came from higher social class, I was genuinely happy for them and they knew that. I just wanted them to accept me with my stuttering and all. For example, my friend Paolo, whom I mentioned earlier, would often invite me to his house. His play room was as big as mother's apartment and we would play soccer in the courtyard. One large room contained a bowling alley where Paolo and I spent a lot of time bowling. His older brother, Agostino, would join us and teach us some basic skills of soccer. Thus, the relationship was on equal terms. Agostino went on to become a major league soccer coach at Bari. I don't remember exactly when, but the stuttering went away just as it appeared. To this day I don't understand why I had the stutter in the first place and why it disappeared all of sudden.

Most of the time the parents of my kindergarten friends were gracious and welcoming, but some were outright nasty once they heard "Cicchella" (a chirping owl) was my mother's nickname. That was the nickname grandmother Imalda gave to Francesca. However, one friend who remained a friend for life was Vito. I was the only one who could call him Vituccio (little Vito) for he was small for his age. He was a little guy, but no one dared to intimidate him. We had respect for each other and basically we protected the kids from Avella from the bullies of Sperone. Everyday there was always some sort of spat between children from their respective towns. I never understood the hassle between the two groups.

His family lived in an apartment diagonally across from our house. His grandfather rented grazing land for his sheep from my grandfather Carmine. Often, they herded sheep together. His father did not pursue a life of shepherding, but became a businessman dealing with real estate in the Naples area. Vito was apprehensive about being small in size. There were more midgets in the shepherd community than the rest of town. Eventually, he grew to normal size and played major league soccer in Italy.

The other good friend was Paolo. I knew him from the times I played soccer against his older brother, Agostino. His father was a count and a judge, and were well to-do. The family owned a farm of ten acres in the middle of Avella. His family was always happy to see me and that was not pretense. They did not look down on me because my family was poor. In fact, Francesca warned me not to be a "pain in the ass" to this family and not to socialize too much with them. Remember who you are, I was told by mother many times. Class consciousness had been alive in Italy then and now. I believe that class divisions only exists among adults. Children don't think in those terms. I certainly didn't think that way and neither did Paolo. Besides Paolo and Vito, I knew the rest of the classmates very well, but did not socialize much with them. Initially, the three of us would run around the farms pillaging fruits from trees in the summer time. Years later, we were joined by Bruno, who introduced us to foraging farms growing cactus fruits in his area. We avoided picking hazelnuts for there was a real danger of being shot by farmers.

The winter of 1947 started out with a bang. Vesuvius erupted and continued for about a week. From Avella, we could see that it was a horrific sight. The smoke, clouds and ashes rose to about forty thousand feet into the sky and measured many miles across. Tremors could be heard all the way to Avella. It looked like the end of the world. In addition to the eruption, the wind coming off the hills was so strong that I had to hang on to the walls of Saint Anthony church in order not to be lifted off my feet. It was like a wind tunnel effect as the wind from the hills came straight down on Main Street. By the second day, ashes were falling all the way to Sorrento, Capri, and Ischia. On the third day lava was flowing on the outskirts of the towns of San Sebastiano and San Giorgio. An image of San Gennaro was smuggled into the town of San Sebastiano for the purpose of stopping lava flow into the town of San Sebastiano. San Gennaro was implored to perform a miracle. However, on the fourth day the lava stream into the town of San Sebastiano slowed down considerably. Half the town was under thirty feet of lava, but the town was saved from destruction. Was that a miracle? Nah, just luck.

We tried to sleep at the edge of the entrance to the bedroom for fear that the ceiling may fall on us while sleeping. There were tremors the next two nights, but nothing catastrophic happened. We survived that winter, and spring brought a lot of rain, so much so that the streets were flooded. Apparently, the water level in the creek increased to about 20 feet and flooded the town of Avella. Soon after, I got sick with scarlet fever. That was strange, because most kids in those days got sick with typhoid fever. Fortunately, this time there was anti-biotic medication and the local doctor was able to prescribe it at the local pharmacy. A new pharmacy opened in town in January of that year and actually had the medicine in store. It was a miracle that medicine was available for I desperately needed it. The whole family was concerned for we never heard about this strange sickness. Cousins, Aunts, Nonno, friends and even Don Camillo visited me. The sickness was a mystery to them as well.

The recovery was very slow and I was in bed most of the time. When I got back to school, I promised myself to behave for I didn't have much energy. I remember, in one of those excursion to the church, where I remained in line with the group, that I noticed a black child in a shoe repair shop. At first I thought that children must come in different shades, but, certainly, I didn't know how. After I established that this kid was a fixture at that shop, I asked Francesca whether she was aware of that black kid in the repair shop and if the boy was their son. Her answer was that it was a fluke of nature and it was their child. It made sense to me and I did not question her further. What did I know to doubt anything she related to me about nature?

Many years later, when I was living in USA, I learned about the unhappy circumstances. The wife was raped by the Goumiers while the husband was a prisoner of war in a British camp in North Africa. I can now just imagine how it must have been, when the husband returned to Avella. However, I am happy to report to you that that child was well loved upon the husband's return from North Africa. His name was Bruno and with Vito, Paolo and I spent a lot of times together foraging farms all over the foothills. Bruno's house was located at the bottom of the hill where the castle was located. I would hide in his house, when the nuns took us to Saint John church. Most times, we would go toward the medieval castle and look for cactus pears to eat. Those fruits really stung, if one was not careful. The trick was to bring along a napkin and grab the cactus fruit with the napkin and cut it with a knife. The cactus fruits could be found along the road to the castle.

The castle had a commanding view of all the area surrounding it. One could see as far away as Naples (21 km) to the west and Avellino (10 km) to the East. Also, it was easily defensible at any angle of attack.

Every time Bruno or I would lift a large rock, a rattle snake would be popping up. It was not a friendly place where one could have a picnic. He attended the nun's school and we overlapped for one year. He eventually took over his father's shop.

As summer approached, the school year was coming to an end. The recommendation from Madre Superiore was that I had progressed sufficiently and, for whatever reason, the stuttering went away. As such, she allowed me to advance to first grade. For me it was a tremendous relief. The whole kindergarten class made it to first grade. However, some kids transferred to public school for the parents could not afford the school fees. Soon after school was over my mother sent me to work on a farm that was owned by her uncle who lived at the foothills near our house. The arrangement was that the farmer would pick me up at six in the morning and transport me to the farm by riding a mule. The farm was located near the picnic grounds of the Fusaro. At seven in the evening the farmer transported me back home. The dirt road to the farm took me past the creek, a shepherd neighborhood where Vito lived, the slaughter house (formerly the German headquarters), the pool, the former Goumiers' camp, the Roman aqueducts and finally to the farm near the Fusaro grounds.

Farming was hard work and the food was atrocious, beans and pork at all meals. Also, it took time away from soccer and friends. I was upset, to say the least. The only good thing about getting up so early was that the shepherds were on their way to the market to sell their ricotta and other cheeses. Their ricotta was still warm and it tasted so good in the morning. I loved eating fresh ricotta early in the morning on a fig leaf. The work at the farm was menial. I weeded the vegetable garden, tended the grape vines, rotated the watermelons, etc. and the worst part was being bitten by snakes.

A revolution was brewing in my mind then. After one week of farm work I told Francesca that she had two choices: 1) send Sebastiano to do the farm work, or 2) she can work there herself and can stay there the whole summer. Francesca realized that she was dealing with a talking and stubborn "goat" and also knew that whatever gig or agreement she worked out with her uncle, it was over. The rest of the summer I played soccer from morning until night.

I didn't even go home at lunch or dinner. I am not sure whether I was still upset about the farm work or I missed my friends in the summer time.

In late summer of 1947, I needed a new wardrobe for school, since I was to attend first grade at the nuns' school. The school uniform was black with a white collar item around the neck. It looked like a kitchen apron. We had to buy the materials for the uniform, pants, shirt, etc. and shoes. Francesca was going to sew the clothes with the aunts, the professional seamstresses, helping out. The only place to buy these items was at Nola. Off we went to Nola.

It was impossible to go by the Cafe and bar without having an espresso. The aroma alone pulled a person up in the air floating to the Cafe and Bar. Yes, the smell was that intoxicating. The Cafe was located less than a block from the train station in Nola and I am sure the owner, being an astute person, realized the benefits of being close to the station. For me it was quite an ordeal to go through all that bullshit haggling with the merchants that my mother loved to do. I always wondered as a child whether or not the merchants were equally engaging about negotiations. To this day I cannot answer that. Finally, we returned home and the aunts and mother got busy making the school uniform for my first grade appearance in September.

It was embarrassing to be the oldest student in first grade and worrying about the stuttering coming back. Francesca managed by various means to secure a full scholarship for me to attend private school administered by the nuns. She paid a price by campaigning with the local medical doctor to help him get elected to be Mayor. In those days there was no central government and all decisions were delayed until a new government was elected. It is amazing to me that Francesca was able to secure a full scholarship.

The nuns were sticklers about discipline as much as their religious beliefs. I was raised by a widow who, half the time, did not know where I was in town. I was no different from a scugnizzo roaming the streets and farms. I was undisciplined to be in school. Almost on a daily basis I was reprimanded for one thing or another. The first couple of months we spent time learning the alphabet and how to count. It seemed like every nun was keeping an eye on me, watching every move that I made.

However, the first grade teacher was easy going and patient with me. I needed that and tried very hard to do well in school. The other good thing about first grade was the free lunch. This was secured from the Marshall Plan via City Hall.

It was a strange paradox in that a private school should be subsidized, but not a public school. Certainly, it was not a national policy, since money from the Marshall Plan was intended for everyone. It had a lot to do with local politics of the times. Some influential person who had a child in our private school must have had an input on the distribution of the Marshall Plan food on local institutions. In those days, no policy, nationally or otherwise, could be carried out without the "blessing" of the Camorra in Southern Italy. This implied that someone who lived in Avella and was associated with the Camorra had a child in the nuns' private school.

The Communist party in Avella objected during the elections the support that the nuns' school received from America, since it benefitted well-to-do children. Don Camillo later rescinded the protests once he learned that his nephews, Andrea and I, attended the school. In retrospect, Don Camillo was more of a Socialist than a Communist for he understood the plight of poor people and shepherds in Avella. I don't believe he understood the international Communist movement as outlined in the Communist Manifesto.

The routine in first grade was that we went over the verbal part in the morning, alphabet, writing skills, talking skills and numbers. The lunch break was about one hour and all the children from second through fifth grades and kindergarten were combined into one dining hall. It was noisy, but the nuns were able to control the crowd and the noise very quickly. Noisy kids had less time to finish their lunch. They were detained in a separate room until they calmed down. After lunch, we were taken to the roof terrace to exercise. Sometimes the routine was changed so that the exercise came in the morning and we had a small siesta in the afternoon. After lunch, geography was taught. The teacher would cover a country on the map and one student was called upon to demonstrate that he or she knew the location of the country in question and location of rivers and mountain chains, among other details. Sometimes, in the afternoon, the nuns would recount a religious story and explain religious implications of the story. Other times the nun would cover a historical person in ancient Rome and

Greece. I excelled in geography and recounting historical facts and stories, but mediocre in verbal skills. In second grade the verbal portion of the instructions picked up pace. Grammar was introduced and writing a full sentence was required. Soon after, composition of essays was introduced. We were required to write nice things about Madre Superiore or mother or some relative. If I really wrote what was in my mind about Madre Superiore, for example, the nuns would have put me in stockade and throwing away the key. I wanted to write serious things about historical heroes from ancient Roman times that I heard about. At that age, the verbal skills lag well behind the thought process of a child.

In late spring, students were required to write an essay about a theme to be chosen by an academic inspector of the Catholic school system. Before the arrival of the inspector, the teacher assigned as homework a theme to write on and to hand it back to her for corrections. Indeed, when the inspector came around, the theme that he chose happened to be exactly the same topic that we were assigned earlier as homework. Was that a miracle? Nah. I was tense and anxious about writing anything on paper, and I hid the essay in the desk drawer prior to the inspector's coming. I had the feeling that it was going to be the same theme as assigned. I did not want to skip any words of the original essay that I practiced as homework. The essays were turned in to the inspector and all of us passed with flying colors.

Madre Superiore was livid, when she found out that I was using the essay from the homework assignment hidden in the desk. Her point was that it was cheating, and if it happened again she would expel me out of school. I was also penalized and the teacher placed donkey ears made of paper on my head in class. That was very embarrassing and demeaning. It encouraged not to put anything on paper. Besides, who was really cheating?

After this incident I was despondent in class and refused to read books out loud in class. Again, I was penalized and smacked with a wooden ruler on the back of my hand. Ouch, that hurt. The nuns kept me after school so that I could be practice to reading from books assigned in class. As such, my soccer teammates expected me on the soccer field after school and they were upset. Francesca was informed and let me know in no uncertain terms, what lay ahead for me, tending sheep the rest of my life, if I didn't buckle down and do right there and then that I was going to be numero uno in school. I was too terrified to be roaming around on those mountains. During these tough times Paolo and Vito were in my corner and shielded me from insults from classmates. Words like ciuccio, jackass, were hurled at me quite often.

Unquestionably shepherding on the mountains was hard work as well as dangerous. On a camping expedition to search for mushrooms, Sebastiano's friends and I roamed around a small hill next to the creek. Avella is well known for its white onions (similar in taste to Vidalia onions in USA) and big porcini mushrooms and exotic mushrooms. Each of us was handed a basket with the hope of filling it up by noon with mushrooms. We got up at five in the morning and headed for the hills. When I reached the top of the hill, I came across a German shepherd dog. It was one huge dog, only 30 yards away, and it was staring at me. I didn't think much of the situation for I thought that it was a guard dog for some local shepherd. There was no one nearby to yell for help. I thank God now that the dog moved on, as someone was approaching me.

When I asked the others whether or not they saw a large dog, no one saw it. I was told that there was no reason for a dog to be there. Besides, I was told, shepherd dogs usually were not in this vicinity, but across the creek on the high mountains. Then, like a thunder bolt, it occurred to me that what I saw was not a dog, but one big wolf, my size. He would have torn me up in a matter of a millisecond. I froze and panicked just thinking about what happened. From where I was, I could actually see Francesca's house from a distance, and ran down the hill as fast as I could.

Of the 15-20 big mushrooms (six to seven inches in height) that I brought home, Francesca selected only two porcini mushrooms to be eaten. The rest were poisonous, although they looked exotic and ready to be eaten. Obviously, sheep and goats are very selective about mushrooms, as Francesca learned early in life. The two mushrooms were unbelievably tasty, but I was never going back there again.

The first opportunity to redeem myself in school came soon enough. The teacher assigned the multiplication table to study and be ready to be tested the next day. In addition to memorizing the multiplication table, I realized that there was a simple rule to square any number that ended in five. For example, the square of 65 is equal to (6x6 +6)25 or simply 4225.

I extended the rule to other numbers in general. The field of numerology studies has a lot to do with numeric patterns. This is often practiced by non-academicians in the middle-east and far-east.

So, the next day the teacher tested all of us and I did extremely well. I did so well that the teacher went beyond the multiplication table assigned to us the day before and asked me the square of 15. I promptly gave her the answer. I will never forget her amazement. I explained to her the simple number pattern or rule as well as the numerology, or pattern, for other sequence of numbers.

It impressed her and it changed the nuns' perception of me. Paolo and Vito were ecstatic about my sudden ascent in academics and respectability with my fellow students in class. I was no longer the ciuccio of the class. My reading prowess picked up, for I was spending less time on soccer fields. I loved to read ancient Roman stories and Greek philosophies. Usually, the mornings were dedicated to recitation of historical events in front of the class and I looked forward to reciting stories of Roman heroes of ancient times. I discovered that when I wrote things about historical stories, my fear of writing disappeared. I have always admired writers who have to write for a living. The report card for that year was near perfection. A score of ten was considered perfect. I averaged a score of 9.5. According to the nuns, it was the highest grade score ever registered in second grade. For behavior I received a score of 10. Was that a joke by the nuns or what? I will never know. I was just determined to erase any lingering effects from the past.

In third grade there was a new teacher and her name was sister Felice (happy). She was stern but very fair. I immediately liked her no-nonsense direct approach to mathematics. She showed us how to add, subtract, multiply, divide and square root of numbers. Also, she introduced basic geometry. It took me about one month to get the hang of it mathematically. Also, her dialect was Florentine and there was a period of adjustment in terms of communicating with the class. It took her many years before she made peace with the Neapolitan dialect. At the time that I was there she insisted in her dialect and the students eventually adjusted to it. The morning routine was to have students recite history lessons individually as well as math lessons. Sometimes the morning recitals extended beyond lunch hour.

In the picture above, Vito is in the first row (fourth from the left); Santina in the second row (first left); in the fourth row, I am sixth from left. Paolo is to my left and Raffaele (from Sperone) is on my right. Suora Felice was our teacher.

One day, before lunch, Suora Felice came to me with a stern look. I said to myself: "What now". With the most pleasant smile ever from any of the nuns at school, she said: Capitaniello (little captain), in very affectionate terms, I need to talk to you about the arithmetic lessons. When spoken in a Florentine dialect, it comes out in a sing-song manner, almost like singing. It was pleasant to hear her in that tone of voice. I was flabbergasted for nobody addressed me that way in town unless they were family or dear friends of the family. Not even Vito or Paolo addressed me that way. Otherwise, it was Michele. I recovered soon to think that, perhaps, Suora Felice was talking about me to Madre Superiore, my arch nemesis, in that tone of voice. Ever since she admonished me I tried to avoid her with a passion. I thought that Suora Felice was going to reprimand me about the fact that I was skipping on the church visits scheduled every two weeks at local churches. My thought process was going at 100 miles an hour and my attention turned to how best to cover my tracks better the next time I skip the trip to the church.

It was nothing like what I was thinking. Suora Felice said that there is not much that she can teach me in arithmetic or geometry and it was a waste of time for me to come to the board and show off my skills in arithmetic and geometry. At this point I was totally clueless as to where she was going with this. Is she sending me home to face Francesca again? She suggested that I take over the duties of overseeing classmates do the arithmetic exercises on the blackboard while she supervised the recitations of the history lessons. What? I couldn't believe what she was saying. There was a practical side to her reasoning. Our class was consistently late for lunch, because of her desire to cover too much material in the morning sessions. With me helping out we had a chance to be on time with the rest of students in other classes at lunch time. For some of us, the lunch meal was important for it could have been the only meal.

That evening I told Francesca about it. Her reaction was, "So, you are no longer the ciuccio, eh?" Her main preoccupation was the rate at which I used up shoes playing soccer. I was consuming one pair of shoes every six to twelve months. In those days, soccer shoes for children were not available anyplace in the Naples area. Francesca was tired of cajoling local shoe repairmen to fix my shoes. The next day I was at the blackboard calling each classmate's name to come to the board and do various arithmetic or geometry exercises. Initially, there was some reluctance on the part of students to come to the blackboard. They were dragging their asses. However, Suora Felice was keeping an eye on me as I was explaining to my classmates how to do certain arithmetic operations. Effectively, I was the mathematic student assistant at a very young age. Suora Felice did not ease up on me. If anything, she demanded more of me in other courses. She knew about me more than I realized at that time.

She demanded that I write an essay about everything and anything every week and required me to turn it in to her. It helped me to overcome the fear of writing. In fact, when the inspector of schools came around and picked a theme to write on I had no fear at all in putting some writing together. The practice of rehearsing theme writing before the visit from the school inspector was still in place, but it was the option of the student to rehearse or not. I didn't rehearse for I felt confident. Historical recitations were demanding as it was not enough to give details from the book, but style of presentation mattered to Suora Felice. At that level? In retrospect, Suora Felice tried very hard not to show favoritism toward anyone.

The classmates were surprised and flabbergasted as much as I was at the role assigned by Suora Felice. After a while they understood, like me, that I had no choice in the matter and I didn't derive any special benefits from this situation. We worked hard to improve our math skills and they realized that I didn't feel superior. Sometimes, I felt deprived and got upset when schoolwork kept me from playing soccer. I must admit that my friends, Paolo and Vito, were treated special, but I couldn't help myself. They informed me a priori, when it was convenient for them to be called upon. I was proud of them as much as they were proud of me. I treated the children from Sperone and Avella the same way, although in general there was much bickering between the two groups.

There was not much fraternization on a daily basis between the kids of Avella and Sperone. The problem was that they lived about a mile away from the railroad station, too far to socialize with them on a daily basis. Besides Sperone was a very small town compared with Avella and there were no soccer fields. The only attraction was a small Cafe on the highway to Nola. It may be compared to a rest stop on a turnpike in the USA. As in Avella, they too got away from coffee made from chicory after the War. Being in that special position did not change me as a child for I had been already through hell and back. This special situation was nothing for me to brag about. I was too grounded by the nuns and Francesca to behave any differently from before. "Once a goat, always a goat". However, as a result of this episode, schoolwork became priority number one and soccer number two. I liked the responsibility of being relied upon.

The routine of assisting classmates continued into fourth and fi fth grades. Advanced geometry was added to the arithmetic lessons. I believe now that showing classmates how to do things in mathematics was more beneficial to me than to them. I gained insight and confidence in myself doing mathematics. However, this confidence did not carry over or translate to the time I was introduced to algebra in America. I remember telling the teacher in the US that I could add, subtract, multiply, divide and determine square roots of numbers very well, but I had no clue as to what he wanted me to do with the variables x and y. I was totally perplexed. My friend Rigo (short for Enrico) tried to console me by saying that algebra was for scientists and not for people like us. The nuns instilled confidence in me, and I was not about to let them down. The Neapolitan survival skills kicked in, and I began to look for riddles or tricks to solve algebraic problems, instead of reading up on algebraic rules in the book and apply them. The problem was that I could not read English yet. The teacher said to me:

whatever you are doing, keep doing it. Whereas I looked at problems in algebra as exercises in survival, the teacher looked at it as mathematical techniques. We reached a satisfactory détente.

Some parents of classmates in Avella went out of their way to be nice to me, since they heard the special role I was playing in school. They even invited me, for the first time, to visit their homes to do homework with their child. It was annoying to me to be bottled up inside a house, when I could be playing soccer outside with friends or roaming the streets or raiding farms, which I enjoyed more. In one instance one classmate invited me to his house to do homework. However, when his father who was a reputable lawyer showed up in the study room, he started to ask me how I learned arithmetic and what my parents' background in academics were. I felt like I was in the zoo being looked on like other animals. I was under the microscope being investigated for my background. I did not care for that at all and that was the last time I spent time with my friend or any other friend. I had better things to do and that was playing soccer in the afternoon or stealing some fruits in the farms.

Usually, homework preceded anything else. Francesca's concern was where the next meal was coming from, when I was attending fourth and fifth grade. As long as she didn't hear of any disciplinary problems from the nuns, she was happy about school. There were no more discipline problems in those years, 1949-1950, and, as a result, I did very well in school grade-wise. I even got along with Madre Superiore, my former nemesis. I could not get away from her fast enough for she wanted to hug me every time she saw me. What a f....g nuisance.

At this point in schooling I had a choice to either pursue an academic classical route in school, Scuole Media (five years) or more technical schooling, referred to as Scuole Ginnasia (five years). The classical schooling consisted of the traditional Greek and Latin languages literature, complemented with math, science, history and Italian literature. The practical training leaned toward learning technical skills including engineering. Sebastiano and I enrolled in the classical training. In Avella there were no schools beyond elementary school, private or public. Higher education schooling was located in Nola. In addition to Scuole Media, Scuole di Liceo was also located in Nola. The next step in education was the University in Naples. Realistically, the best that I could hope for in those days was the completion of the Lyceum (Liceo) School.

We simply did not have the means of ever attending the University; that was mainly a place for the rich and affluent, but not for "goats".

In a way it was sad for me to leave the nuns' school. They prepared me well for the Scuole Media and I felt confident of the next step in education. The nuns were proud of me and told me that by far I was the best student in a long, long time. Still, I had apprehension about the next step in education. Sebastiano was already in the Lyceum School and I knew how hard he studied for school. He was fluent in Italian, Latin, French and Greek, and I was fluent in Neapolitan dialect which nobody could understand outside of the Naples area. Believe it or not, I had to learn proper grammatical Italian as spoken in Florence, for example. That transition in dialect was going to be painful. For example, I loved to swear in every imaginable way using the Neapolitan dialect but, then, I had to give it up in order to be fluent like the rest of the student body. Cousin Carmine was attending the Ginnasia School system and trained to be an electrical engineer. He graduated from the public school system in Avella. At the time that he was ready to attend elementary school, his father (Uncle Joe) was in the Italian Army and the family could not afford the entrance fee to the nuns' private school. The other cousin Giannina (Jenny), however, attended Scuole Media in Nola and was two years ahead of me.

Nola was 10 km away from Avella by train, which left Avella railroad station at 8:11 am precisely. That was the only good thing that Mussolini instilled in Italy; trains ran on time even after the war. I would walk to the station with my cousins, Carmine and Jenny. The route to the station depended on the season of the year and whether or not we had money for an espresso. In the winter time we could never walk on Main Street by Saint Anthony Church, because the wind was so strong that at times it would lift one of us off the ground. We had to hold on to the wall for our dear lives. It was more like being in a wind tunnel.

The wind came straight from the high mountains in the East. The town of Benevento, which translates as "the good wind", is above the mountain peaks of Avella. So, we were forced to walk on side streets and farm roads all the way to the station on windy days. I enjoyed walking on the farm roads especially when fig trees were full of fruits. That was the "goat" in me. When it was not windy, Main Street offered an advantage in accessing to a coffee house. There was no bus connection from Avella to Nola. School was free to attend and a train pass (abbonamento) for a year was purchased at minimal cost. The train that went to Nola was on the same rail line also directed to Naples. The train station in Nola was about 10 blocks from the school.

Next to the station in Nola, there was a coffeehouse that roasted and brewed their own coffee beans. The coffee smell was so intoxicating that sometimes I would stop by and have an espresso. If I had an extra lira or two I would buy a pastry with it. That was heaven after smelling that chicory aroma for so many years during the War. Across from the coffee house there was a huge field, sometimes used as a soccer field. Surprisingly, Nola did not have a minor league soccer team, although it was ten times bigger than our neighboring towns of Avella and Baiano. The other small town that had a minor league soccer team was Pompeii. Sebastiano was a member of that team. Pompeii could be reached by train via an exchange of trains in Naples (called Vesuviana exchange). Sebastiano spent a lot of time on these trains in order to play soccer as it took him two hours to reach Pompeii by train from Avella. A Gypsy camp was located across from the coffee h ouse. O bviously, the Gypsies traveled mostly by train at night all over Italy, right after the war. It was the only means of transportation, although most train stations were bombarded during the war. Some train stations on the way to Naples were totally destroyed, for example. Although I loved soccer, I dared not play on that field for Gypsies were too close for comfort.

Francesca implanted in me a story about a child from Avella being kidnaped by the gypsies in Nola who was never returned. I don't believe now that it ever occurred. As a matter of fact, one day I ventured into the gypsy's camp and observed for myself. It was like entering a whole new world. People were living in tents, kids out of school running all over the field, men and women were half dressed, musicians played a strange metallic instrument with their tongues, casino type gambling was here and there and there was the sale of anything on the black market. It was fascinating, but also a little bit out of the ordinary. This was no place for me to hang around. The gypsies appeared and disappeared in Nola almost randomly. It was never the same gypsies in camp from one day to another. I have wondered often why gypsies came to Nola and no place else. Nola was at the crossroad to the south (Calabria, Sicily), east to Bari, north to Rome and west to Naples. Most of those gypsies seem to have emigrated from Romania or east-bloc countries before and after WW II. A lot of them have settled in Italy, in big cities, and gypsy camps can be found readily.

Coming from a farm town like Avella, it was exiting seeing people shopping. Two years earlier, when I visited Nola, it was like a ghost town. Obviously, things were pickingup there as well as elsewhere. Nola was and is on the main artery from Rome to Sicily. All of the communication electrical wires during the war passed through Nola. In June the whole town comes to a standstill for the celebration of the Feast of the Lily. For the Festa (feast), eight enormous high wooden towers, these towers are referred to as the lillies, are built and decorated with flowers and are carried through every street in honor of Saint Paulinus who, in the fifth century, invented church bells in this town. The spectacle lasted for three days. The religious procession is usually led by the Bishop of Nola.

On the first day of school (Scuole media) books were handed out. When I learned those Latin prayers as an altar boy, I had no idea of the language structure of Latin. I was just parroting what I read in a prayer book. Compared to the Italian language, Latin is more grammatically structured. I was never a literature buffo, but I was ready for the challenge. My classmates came from towns surrounding Nola, and most of the towns were in the province of Naples. Avella was then a province of Avellino and by all rights I should have attended the Scuola media in Avellino. However, there was no bus or train transportation from Avella to Avellino.

Yes, we came a long way from the devastation of war, but still not back to normal. I loved Nola. It allowed me to wonder and dream how the outside world could be in a normal situation after seeing so much human misery in Avella and surroundings. The family visited Avellino before and we knew how extensively it was bombed by Allied airplanes. I certainly did not want to go to school in Avellino. My studies in Nola only lasted four months until we emigrated to America.

Sebastiano had a much longer career in the school system at Nola. Like me, he went to the nuns' school for five years of elementary school, where he had a full scholarship to attend the nuns' school. Now, I understand the reluctance on the part of the nuns to give me a full scholarship. According to the nuns, Sebastiano was the opposite of me. He was well versed in verbal skills, but not so well in mathematics.

However, his math skills were still above average and he was well behaved in school. When he entered the Scuole media he truly excelled in literature: Italian prose, Latin and French. After three years, he graduated with honors from the Lyceum School. I loved to see Sebastiano at home studying on a desk that my mother inherited from Imalda in Avella.

Sebastiano would take the time to explain to me what he was learning and he loved to recount Greek mythologies. I think now that he wanted to scare me a little bit about those Greek mythical stories that were not of this world. That was why I later became interested in Greek philosophies by Plato and Aristotle, and Roman authors like Cicero. However, Sebastiano had another life besides schooling. Twice a week he would go to Pompeii and practice with the Pompeii minor league soccer team. Pompeii's team was affiliated with the major league soccer team of Naples (Serie A). I knew then he was a good soccer player, but I did not know he was playing at that high a level and being so young (sixteen years old). In the town of Avella he rarely played soccer. On Sunday he would disappear from sight in Avella. He was playing soccer for Pompeii and was paid minimal money. He did extremely well at the Scuole Media in Nola, and was promoted with honors to the Lyceum.

Lyceum school of three years is a requirement for University entrance. Roughly 10% of students finishing elementary school attended the Lyceum. On average, it took five years to finish the three years of Lyceum. Again, as in Scuole Media, the emphasis was the classical training- Greek, Latin, Italian and French languages. Science and mathematics instructions were, at best, minimal. Sebastiano did well in the first and second year of the Lyceum. Sebastiano did finally finish the third year in the Lyceum school at a financial drain for the family. It cost money to be accepted to the Lyceum and there was no scholarship to support him. The aunt-seamstresses were very helpful in supporting Sebastiano's schooling. He was ready to attend the University of Naples, when the family emigrated to America.

FOURTEEN
CHURCH RECITALS AND SAN GENNARO

The urge to earn money and help the family was strong in me at a very young age. Pierino told me during one of those many soccer games that he was an altar boy and was earning money at weddings and funerals from tips. The priest at Saint Peter was too cheap to pay for normal Mass duties. I was interested, and immediately went to make an appointment with the priest's secretary. I was told to obtain letters of referral from my mother and Madre Superiore. I told the secretary that Francesca could not write and asked if it would be ok for my mother to talk to her or the priest. I was trying to do a favor for Francesca; she only went to third grade in public school. I am sure she could have written something, but it would have proven to be embarrassing for her.

Francesca thought that I wanted to become a priest. Also, she was apprehensive about priests even in those days, and was often outright derogatory toward the clerics. She would say: did you see that SOB priest visit the nuns today, implying something sinister. I didn't want to hear any of that and I explained to her my real motive, to make some money. She was overjoyed and went to see Madre Superiore for the referral letter. It seemed forever for Madre Superiore to write that referral letter.

Hesitation on her part was understandable. I skipped more than half of the excursions to churches sponsored by the nuns. I am sure that she thought: This kid is no angel. The referral letter finally arrived and I was called in to see the priest. The priest sat himself behind a desk in a way that he would be looking down at me. When you looked up at him the crucifix was behind his head. It was eerie. I did not know whether to genuflect or make a cross, as I looked up at the priest. I sat there for a while, as he appeared to be busy about fiddling with some paperwork or something on the desk. Finally, he spoke to me. I swore then that these priests went to acting school. He knew everything about me and the family. Any acting on my part to pretend that I saw a special vision was a waste of time. He was surprised to see that I wanted to be an altar boy and dismissed me. He simply did not want to hear any cock and bull story from me. My reputation preceded me. In retrospect, Madre Superiore must have informed him as much.

I was assigned by the priest to work with Pierino and help out with Sunday Mass. Pierino was the logical choice, since I mentioned his name in our conversation. Then he asked me, if I knew Latin. I said that I was introduced to Latin grammar in school. So, I lied a little bit. He never mentioned about helping Pierino out at weddings and at funerals.

The church of Saint Peter in Avella. The soccer field is behind the bell tower. Photo courtesy of Anmarie Vittoria, 1981.

After the priest informed Pierino that I was assigned to him to work on Sunday Masses, I could tell that he was not pleased to train me. He did not care to share with one more altar boy tips money from weddings and funerals. As a trainee, I questioned him as to why it was so important to know Latin, when I barely know the alphabet. He said that there were two reasons: The Mass was conducted in Latin. So, in order to know what to do during the mass you need to know some Latin. Secondly, every year the priest sponsored a visit to a convention iof altar boys that competed in the recital of prayers from the Mass. In those days, the Mass was conducted in Latin. Usually, the convention was held at a resort beach near Naples: Sorrento, Amalfi, Castellamare, Capri, Ischia, etc. Wow! The beauty of it was that it was all paid for by the church. However, for that year the convention or congregation of altar boys had already been held in June at Castellamare, near Naples. The city of Castellamare was and remains headquarters for the Camorra. Being born at the foothills of the mountains, it is the dream of every local, someday, to dive into the waters at those beach towns. I was under the impression that the tips would be split between Pierino and me. However, I was corrected by Pierino. The tips must be declared to the priest and the priest assigned the money to the altar boys! I was disappointed to say the least. That night I could not sleep for I was thinking of clever ways and schemes to short-change the priest. For me it was strictly business, nothing religious or personal.

At the Sunday Mass I was with Pierino and another older altar boy. In this particular training session on Sunday Mass, Pierino instructed me to sit on the side and watch the two of them work around the altar. The nod of his head was the signal for me to bring the little bottles of water and wine from the side of the altar to him, and no one else, and return to my chair. However, sit, genuflect and stand up, when the congregation did the same. So, here I was looking intently for Pierino to nod his head. He didn't nod his head, but flashed his middle finger in my direction. I looked around to see who he was flicking his finger at. Only the statue of Saint Rocco was behind me. I concluded it could not have been the Saint that Pierino was flicking the finger at. The next thing I saw he was giving me the Italian "famous" fist salute. I concluded that he wanted the little bottles quickly and I brought them over. There was a sigh of relief from the priest and a smirk on Pierino's face. I told Pierino later to make sure the priest doesn't see those signs in the future. Otherwise, the priest will fire both of us. Future Masses went smoothly, as I was beginning to get the hang of it. I knew, without signaling, when to bring the water and wine, but I was still in training. The next phase of training was to actually be next to the priest on the altar and ring the small bell at the right time, and genuflect, and standup in unison with church goers.

The timing for ringing is very critical. The bell is rung, when the priest raised the altar bread or the chalice above his head. Furthermore, the ringing should be in bursts rather than a continuous ringing and only two bursts, before and after the raising of either the altar bread or the chalice. Yes, I learned those procedures the hard way. Initially, I watched Pierino do it and it appeared to me so trivial that I did not pay attention. This time Pierino and I were at the altar working around the altar. Apparently, I graduated from apprenticeship to the main show. The third altar boy was a trainee, sitting on the side of the altar waiting to bring the water and wine to me at the altar. I would signal to him, when to bring the two small bottles. Pierino was to signal me, when to begin and stop the ringing of the bell. I thought at that time it was going to be a "piece of cake". Well, he did signal impolitely as usual, and I began ringing the bell and looked at him when to stop. He never gave me the signal to stop. Usually, the ringing should only last about five seconds, at most. Here I was at it for at least 10-15 seconds and the priest discreetly motioned for me to stop. It was rather awkward for the priest to raise the altar bread with one hand while motioning with the other hand for me to stop ringing. The next ringing was to be timed with the raising of the chalice.

I lost all confidence in myself and Pierino and was ready to choke him right there in church. I stopped only because the tip money was on my mind. It became obvious that I was in the hands of a "nut" case. After a minute Pierino gave me the usual signal for the second ringing, when the priest raised the chalice above his head. There was hesitation on my part as I did not trust Pierino anymore. The priest was raising the chalice with one hand and waving to me with the other hand to ring the bell. Again, he turned toward me and motioned with his hand to ring the bell and I finally did it. It was comical entertainment and shocking to the people attending Mass, but the priest neglected to laugh. He was livid. After Mass, the priest took Pierino aside and wanted explanations. Pierino was despondent and was reluctant to give any explanations. He was too upset about sharing tip money with me and told the priest as much. The upshot of the exchange was that Pierino was fired. The priest never inquired about all the screw ups and the dirty gestures from Pierino. He turned to me and said: Next time you are going to be by yourself at the altar. The priest then dismissed me. The conversation between Pierino and the priest was all about the tip money. Nevertheless, Pierino and I remained friends on the soccer field and laughed about it then and now. Pierino just got tired of being an altar boy and training new ones given that the priest was cheating him out of tip monies at wedding parties. I had no intent to share any tips with the priest either and I had a plan. A revolution was brewing.

Few months later, by default, I was in charge of the funeral and wedding duties, since Pierino and the older altar boy left the group. The priest came over to me and explained that whatever tips collected were to be declared to him only. He would then distribute the money to the altar boys who were present at those functions. Everything was left as murky as dirty water. No definition as to who gets what and how much, depending on duties performed. I thought long and hard about the new situation. Besides the normal duties, I would be training new ones in the program. I casually mentioned to Vito and Paolo about the two openings for altar boys. Vito was enthusiastic about joining me in the revolution, but Paolo was not allowed by his parents. Also, Vito's interest was to visit resort towns like Amalfi at conventions. I clued him into my plan and explained to him, that at funerals and weddings, we would declare to the priest half as much as collected from the tips. Among ourselves, we would split the collection evenly. He suggested that he collect the tips to put the priest at ease. We were of the same mind.

By the following year or two I was able to perform all the chores required of an altar boy without any instructions from anyone. I was even learning some Latin prayers so that I could compete at the summer convention of altar boys the following year at Sorrento. Sorrento, as it was and is a well-known resort town located on the other side of the mountains from Amalfi. It is also known from the famous Neapolitan song "Torna a Sorrento". In order to arrive at Sorrento from Avella, we had to board two trains, one from Avella to Naples and another one from Naples to Sorrento. It is the same today.

We were housed in a dormitory where we slept four in one room. On the first day, at 8 am, the examination of altar boys began and we were tested on the proficiency in reciting prayers in Latin. Our priest lined about 12 altar boys from Avella in front of a desk where an examiner (another priest) was sitting. He appeared to be bored. Our priest would line up the experienced altar boys at the front of the desk and the less so in the rear. I was in the rear. The hope of our priest was that the examiner would call upon the altar boys up front. I believe now that the whole thing was rigged. The examiner only asked questions from the boys lined up at the front desk in front of the examiner. It was a way for priests to recruit potential altar boys for priesthood. As far as I was concerned the only thing that mattered to me was the whereabouts of the beach for I never visited a beach before.

We went to the beach as a group but soon dispersed all over the beach as any child, under those circumstances, would have done. It was a repeat the next day except soccer games were scheduled between altar boys from different cities. On the third day, we returned to A vella and my mother wanted to know everything, especially about the beach, which she had never seen before. I told her that there was no white beach, but it was a beautiful town with a lot of lemons on trees. There was a British pub right on Main Street. The owners were the remnants of the British invaders of the Salerno Beachhead in 1943.

Altar boy duties lasted for about 4 years. It is important to relate the following story for it illustrates the living conditions in Avella after the war. Besides altar boy duties I was assigned by the priest to collect money during Mass. A small twine basket was used for this purpose. During mass, well before communion, I would take the basket beside the altar and walk toward the first row of parishioners. The basket was handed to the people in the first row in order to collect money, and the basket would move along the row of parishioners and return on the second row.

Then, I handed the basket to the third row and repeat the process to the very last row. Usually, the basket was full of money before the last row. This particular day, just before the last row, the basket was full again and I handed the basket to the last row. On the return of the basket, it was empty. Yes, it was empty! It is difficult to describe my feelings then and now. It was hard for me to fathom thieves committing a crime in church? Stealing from the church! How was it possible? I stared very hard at all the men in the last row, as I walked past them. I checked their hats and/or loose items on the chairs. I remember asking some people where did the money go. Certainly, money did not have legs on it! They all gave me this angelic look and stared at me as if I were a mental case. They put their heads down and resumed their prayers. What a f..g joke, I said to myself. The feeling of been had by a bunch of goats was truly terrible. Those faces are still imprinted on my mind to this day. In retrospect, I believe now that it was not a man that took the money. It was a woman with a shopping handbag and most likely the handbag was hidden under the skirt between her legs. It was not physically possible to stuff all that money in a man's pants pocket or jacket in less than two to three seconds, especially when I was looking for bulging pockets and kept an eye on the basket as it moved down the aisle. The money did not disappear in thin air. I surmise now that it disappeared within one to two seconds and that could only be achieved with the help of a handbag. If the transfer of money from the basket lasted more than 2 seconds, I would have noticed. I did notice three women bunched together at the end of the aisle, and I knew one of the husbands was the Communist party leader in Avella, Don Camillo. In those days Communist leaders did not attend mass, but their wives did. I have a good idea now who that person was, one of the three women sitting in the end of the row of chairs. So, I took the empty basket to a place near the altar. After the Mass the priest inquired about the collection, as he was about to take off the robe and I showed him the empty basket. I explained to him what happened in every detail. I will never forget his demean and comment. He calmly stated that whoever took the money must have needed it more than the church and that was it! How can he be so cavalier about it, when he was so cheap about tips earmarked to altar boys at weddings!

When I told Francesca about this incident, she asked me if I recognized anyone in that last row. I said that our lady friend from "O' Vicolo" and her friends were at the end of the aisle, Don Camillo's wife. The shepherd community was a very close knit community whereby every shepherd knew everybody else's business. It was somewhat puzzling that most of Communist men never attended any church, yet most of their wives did. It was their way of maintaining the party line or discipline which was a position of anti-church. Their dream was to parcel out church's farmlands to Communist members.

Francesca just smiled and walked away as if to say: Good for them who took the money. I was shocked and perplexed to say the least. Now after many years, I understand. She knew damn well who did it, but what good would it have done for me to know at that time! Giving the money back to the priest was no solution to poverty at that time. Obviously, as a child, I was clueless as to what was happening in town and even in church, and the priest wasn't clueless either. He knew very well who was sitting at the end of the aisles. In ordering me to collect monies during Mass, it was like sending a sacrificial lamb to the wolves in asking for church donations from the Communists.

However, that was not the end of it. After the theft episode in church, we altar boys were no longer allowed to be tipped directly at church weddings and at funerals. Pierino warned me about it and that was the reason why he left the altar boy service. Usually, a wedding ceremony was a long religious affair and it was customary for the family of the groom to tip the altar boys directly. Furthermore, altar boys were invited to wedding receptions whereby upon recognition more tips were collected together with the priest. At funerals and, after the religious Mass, altar boys walked to the cemetery carrying a wooden cross for about a mile. Invariably, the altar boys were tipped by the family of the deceased. The honor system required the altar boys to give the priest the tip money or defer collection to the priest on our behalf. The priest then disbursed the "net" tip money to us which was significantly less than what was donated. It was almost enough motivation for me to convert to Communism. In my house every lira counted as we didn't have much money. For me, it was strictly a business venture to get whatever little money I could to help out. I had no intention of becoming a priest or any religious person, although I was a very serious student in the catechism classes taught by nuns. As a student, I would question the teachings of the church to the point of arguing with some of the nuns, as I was interested in historical connections. Soon after the theft incident in the church, the priest kept most of the tip money by forbidding us altar boys to collect any tips directly. The decision made no sense to us. In retrospect, the priest must have connected us to the people responsible for the theft or trying to make up for the loss. The priest knew that we came from the shepherd clan and most likely some shepherd took the money. I guess we were guilty by association. Thus, the only reward for being an altar boy was the late spring trip to the beaches in order to attend the convention.

However, one wedding was memorable to me. Mastro Nicola invited Uncle Joe's family and my family to the wedding and were allowed to share prime seating arrangements next to his own family. What made this event so memorable was that, for once in a long time, we were enjoying ourselves and forgot all about the War stuff and everyday struggles to survive. It was a beautiful feeling for a change, thanks to Mastro Nicola. At the wedding I was the altar boy in charge of the proceedings around the altar. It was a Catholic wedding, since the bride was Catholic. She was from Baiano and was the daughter of the Communist Mayor of Baiano, and her name was Violetta. If I were to put two and two together today, my guess is that they met when Mastro Nicola was inquiring about road construction plans from Baiano City Hall. Violetta was the receptionist to the Mayor's office. The Mayor of Baiano was a good friend of the Maestro, as they both worked at San Carlo. According to Uncle Joe, the Mayor behaved more like a Figaro figure in trying to "match the couple" rather than a regular Mayor. I informed Mastro Nicola that if he was going to tip me not to do it in front of the priest. "Quillu fetente se piglie I soldi", "that ass hole will keep the money". I could speak honestly to Mastro Nicola, because of being Uncle Joe's nephew and I knew him well enough to talk that way. I said, also, that the tip money should be collected discreetly by the other altar boy, Vito.

The maestro (Nicola's father) liked what I said about the priest, being a communist for a long time. He had been studying the Karl Marx brand of Communism for many years and had little use for priests. He was responsible for bringing opera singer Beniamino Gigli at one local festival in Avella to sing a number of arias. For the wedding he brought some musicians from San Carlo Opera House to play music in the courtyard for Tarantella dances. The affair was very private and truly memorable. Beniamino Gigli was one of the leading tenors in the world during the 30s and 40s. In the opera world, he was referred to as Caruso number two. He bristled over that characterization. He preferred to be known as Gigli number one. During the war Gigli mainly performed in Rome opera houses for Fascist audiences. This was like keeping a canary caged, since permission for travel abroad was denied. He was labeled a Fascist, because of those appearances. In retrospect, Gigli was no Fascist, because a Communist like the Maestro could never get along with a Fascist politically or otherwise.

The Maestro came over to Vito and stuffed money in his cassock pocket and said, "Tell the priest to go to hell, if he asks for the tip money". Vito was surprised, to say the least, someone of the stature of the Maestro would seek him out to stuff his pocket with money. We did not pass the message, but kept the money. When the priest asked for the tip money, I told him that I did not get tipped. The priest knew that was the truth for he kept an eye on me. He was not aware of Vito's whereabouts. He stared long and hard at me and I stared right back, classic stalemate. Priest or no priest, I was not going to hand over the money. He owned 100 acres of farmland in the middle of town, adjacent to Nonno's courtyard, and he didn't share one iota of farm goods during the war years with Nonno or anyone else in town! I, the poorest of the poor, was going to share with him? Hell may have frozen over, but, in no way, I was going to hand over the money. That's how I felt as a child toward the priest. The money shared with Vito was spent by me on starting new businesses that failed. Altar boys looked forward to these conventions whereby a competition among them was set up to recite Mass prayers in Latin. Initially, I was not very good at reciting anything, even in Italian. So, the priest placed me in the last row, when it was our turn to be interrogated. It was well understood that the examiner was not to call on any altar boys lined up in the last row. I "graduated" from the last row to the first row after three years when I was called upon to recite Mass prayers in Latin. I remember doing very well and was well regarded by other altar boys and by our priest, but there was no financial reward. The only reward was the time I spent playing soccer after the competition and the times on the beaches at Sorrento, Castellamare, Ischia, etc. Basically, at that point in time I was training the next generation of altar boys while the tip money was drying up.

I started playing soccer, when I was about six years old. I would play the game after school every day. On weekend and holidays I would play from morning to night. Sometimes I didn't go home to eat. The biggest problem was that I would ruin my shoes within six months and we simply could not afford new ones.

On one summer day, Sebastiano broke his arm in a soccer game in Pompeii. He revealed that he broke the arm as he tried to do a dangerous kick called the "scissor" kick. The scissor kick involves a somersault motion whereby the ball is kicked when the ball is up in the air and above the head. One flips the body around in a scissor or somersault motion to kick the ball. It was a dangerous maneuver, if the rotation of the body is only partial. One either breaks an arm or back. It is used in games as a last desperate effort to shoot on goal. After I heard what happened to Sebastiano I went to the soccer field to practice the scissor kick and, yes, I got hurt but not enough to stop practicing it. However, I did master the kick and thought then that I was ready for the big times. There was no future in going to a University. There were too many young men, who graduated from the University of Naples, walking the streets of Avella without a job. I would see a lot of them in the train to Nola, neatly dressed and carrying smart briefcases, as there were something important in them. It was really sad. I guess the pressure from the families and the desire to work was so great that it drove them to pretend. For sure, I did not want to go that route.

As I got older, I began to realize that making a career in soccer was my ticket out of Avella. Sebastiano at the age of 16 was already playing soccer for the city of Pompeii which was a minor league team owned by the major league soccer team of Naples. I had no desire to be a farmer or a shepherd or a barber or any other semi-skilled position. I tried but I was not very good at most apprenticeship jobs. Since we were so poor, attending a University was out of the question. One thing about the war was that one learns fast what the options are in life. There weren't many for my family. After my kite and bird businesses folded, I had more time for soccer and school.

Normally, I played on a bigger soccer field near Saint John which was located further away from home, and the competition was better. At Saint John field I usually teamed up with Pierino and Pipino and the three of us and some "scamorse", inferior players, could beat any team in town, teen agers or older. I flip-flopped between the two soccer fields at Saint John and Saint Peter and sometimes played soccer from morning to night. My mother was furious every time I came home with brand new shoes totally scuffed up in one day.

Fortunately, Francesca knew a shoe repairman, Mastro Antonio, who was a dear friend of the family. He was Godfather to my father and his son and both died in Libya. Before the war my father's barbershop was located next to Mastro Antonio's shop. The two would engage in pranks on each other. For example, my father trained a canary to chirp a special song just as Mastro Antonio left his shop on an errand. The chirping was triggered by my father's whistle. After the War, I would sometimes walk past his shop and hum that special tune and he would shoot out of his shop and throw shoes after me. He would threaten to hang me from the highest tree, if he ever caught me humming that tune again.

The truth of the matter was that it hurt him too much to hear that tune. It reminded him of the past with my father and his son. I never realized then the deep emotions he had for my father. I did it because I liked to hear him refer to me as capitaniello, little captain, even though it was in a threatening manner. After all that bravura Mastro Antonio charged minimal money only to cover the cost of materials used to repair our shoes. That was very important to us for the price of shoes after the war was extremely high. Mastro Antonio was the best in town and the title of Mastro was well deserved. He could simulate the latest style of shoes and improvised on the style and made it better. He was very proud of his art or craft and we loved him as a man with a good heart, but we loved to tease him like Papa.

Even among kids playing pick-up games, there was a tier system. Either one played with scrubs, not talented, or talented players. By the age of 8-9 I began to play with players who were very serious about the game. In particular, it was during a pick-up game that I met Pierino and Pipino on a soccer field. They both attended public school and were one year older than me. Pierino had an older brother whose name was Salvatore. Pierino's father was a tailor and the mother worked in the same shop. The shop and one room housing was located on the main street, one block from Saint Peter Church. Their bedrooms were located away from the shop, inside a courtyard shared by five other families.

Most times, there were just enough children to field a team of seven players (one goalie, three defenders and three forwards). The standard number of players on a soccer team is eleven. In those days the popular formation adopted by professional teams was the so-called 2-3-5 system which designated the first number as the number of defenders, the second number as mid-fielders who can be utilized as defenders and forwards, and the last number as forwards. The goalie is not designated in this numbering scheme. This system is no longer adopted by any professional team, and major evolution of systems have occurred every ten years since. I have adopted some of the newer systems, when I was coaching children from the age of four to forty years for more than twenty five years in the USA.

The most rewarding part of coaching soccer is to see skills, practiced during the week, displayed on game day. After many years of coaching I may summarize my experience as follows. On the average, one half instruction can be imparted to a four years old, one for a five, and two for a six. For most teen agers in the USA no instructions are helpful. My favorite group is the five to six years old, although they tend to bunch up in games. They give it all on the field. Most times soccer becomes monotonous, as the skills practiced are repeated over and over again in game conditions. However, sometimes, suddenly and out of nowhere, a child on the field exhibits moves that were not taught. Where did that come from? I call it creative learning and it also occurs in classrooms. A coach or teacher can see creative learning or thinking, but is not able to predict it in a child. Basically, the child has transitioned from a state of acquiring the skills to a state of applying the skills, much like a transition in Quantum Mechanics between two physical states. That is almost impossible to predict when that occurs in a child. As one would say, something clicked in his or her brain. It does not occur to every child on a field or class. That moment in soccer is truly magic for a coach.

Pipino, Pierino and I made up the forward line. Pierino was the equivalent of a "striker" in today's terminology, and, as such, it required for him to be a finesse player making the right pass to me or Pipino. In contrast to Sebastiano or Pierino, there was nothing cute or finesse about my game. My attitude was: Pass me the ball and get out of my way. However, if I drew too much attention, I had no problem passing the ball to others. Pipino, on the other hand, had a problem passing the ball to anyone even if he was guarded by ten players. He loved to hog the ball. For that, he was reprimanded by everyone, including his mother. We had different temperaments and personalities, but we worked together like a clock.

Salvatore was part coach, mentor, advisor and bull-shit artist. At games he would draw up plans for attack and defense. Also, he would give individual advises as to what to practice when not playing games. However, most times, he would admonish us three not to be selfish on a soccer field, especially Pipino. Sometimes, the whole team would chase Pipino all over the field and hold him accountable. We needed him on the team, because he was the only left-foot kicker on the team and a good one at that. Yes, it was that serious. The team began to outperform other teams consistently, adults and teen-agers, but only when we picked up a fourth member on the team to complement the three of us.

Vito was small, like me. Unbelievably, he preferred to play the mid-field. Most kids liked to play forward, but not him. He and I had something in common. We both came from shepherd families and attended the nuns' school. We had a beautiful plan in dealing with the priest, when he became an altar boy. It was I who pushed him to be in our team. It didn't take long for him to dominate the mid-field which was solid as the rock of Gibraltar with him there. He was small, but no one dared to push him out of position. Every offense moves were generated through him. Most importantly for me, he fed the ball to me more often than Pipino did. We beat every team including the ones that Sebastiano played with in Avella. No team in Avella from various districts wanted to play us anymore. It was not so much the losing aspect, but the manner of style on the field. We were the youngest, but were intimidated by no one and it showed in our playing style. Vito, indeed, eventually became a major league soccer player for the Naples team for 12 years.

After each soccer game we rested at Pierino's house and usually played cards. Sometimes, we listened to radio transmission of soccer games. Salvatore was too big to be agile in soccer, but he was intelligent in a soccer sense. Also, he was wise enough in a soccer sense to put us on the same team when competing against others. He put me at right wing, Pierino at center forward and Pipino at left wing. Pipino and his older brother lived with their grandfather, Mastro Antonio, and mother in a two room apartment right next to Pierino's house father's shop. Pipino's father died in Libya about the same time as my father.

Mastro Antonio and Pipino's father were shoe repairmen. Mastro Antonio trained Pipino's older brother to be a shoe repairman as well. The intent was to keep the craft in-house from generation to generation. However, Pipino's older brother wanted no part of being a shoe repairman. Often, I would hear squabbles among family members about the business of the shop, when I visited Pipino at home. Pipino's brother was determined to learn another trade, and he joined Mastro Nicola and Uncle Joe as an apprentice. Mastro Antonio was disappointed, to say the least. Pipino eventually attended the University of Naples and became a lawyer. The family tradition in shoe repairs ended with Pipino and his brother looking elsewhere for employment.

We took on players of any age and beat them soundly. In one game we played players who were in the in twenties, representing the best soccer club in Avella. We totally controlled the game from beginning to end. After the game we had to run for our lives for they were so upset with us. They chased us off the field. As a result, we could no longer schedule a game in Avella. We started to hit the road: Nola, Cimitile, Baiano, Sperone, and all the towns along the rail line.

The problem was to get all team members to come and play away from home. When all showed up, we were unbeatable. We were that good at such young age.

The highlight of our travel to the soccer games was our visit to Pompeii, where we saw Sebastiano play for the minor soccer league team in Pompeii. It was a long journey to get to Pompeii by rail. Pierino, Pipino and I took the train to Naples first for about one hour. From there, we switched to the Vesuviana Railroad company line to get to Pompeii for another forty minutes. It was worth it, because Pompeii was the main minor league team for the Naples team, which was in Serie A (Italian major league soccer).

Sebastiano played the center half position which may be the most important position on a soccer team. That position controls the midfield, and, therefore, the flow of the game. Sebastiano was truly a gifted center half as his passes were exquisite and on the mark. I was very proud of him. Sebastiano introduced us to the coach after the game. I am sure that Sebastiano must have given a scout report about us to the coach. The coach set up a little pickup game between the three of us from Avella against some scrubs (reserves) from the Pompeii team. It was no contest. We totally dominated them. After the scrimmage the coach talked to the three of us and said that when we turned sixteen years of age, we should return to his team in Pompeii. I was sky high. That was my dream and my ticket out of Avella.

It was our dream to eventually play soccer together at the major league level. By the age of twelve we knew each other's moves so well that it was nearly impossible to defend against us. For example, Pierino was very good at recognizing the right situation to make the type of a pass I wanted from him even before I made my move. Basically, he created open space on the go. A mid-fielder or a center-forward has a split second decision to "see" the open space. He reminded me today a lot of center forwards Rumenige (German National) and Boniperti (Italian National) with similar moves. They were great players for many years in their own country. They invented the art of finesse in soccer. There was no question that the coach was impressed, but to what extent or commitment, I didn't know. Certainly, when we reached the age of sixteen, he would have looked us up. Today, I still think about those days. It was a magic moment that I am very proud of.

Salvatore was Pierino's brother and he was five years older than Pierino. Also, he was responsible for scheduling soccer games with other towns. We shared our love of soccer as well as that of watermelons. On market day he organized a scheme in negotiating the price of watermelons with vendors. Salvatore would approach a vendor and start the negotiations. One person would draw the attention of the vendor away from Salvatore by walking behind the wagon full of watermelons. At the same time a third person would walk past Salvatore and stuff t he w atermelon i n a shopping bag. When the vendor returned to negotiate with Salvatore, the outcome of the negotiation was either the watermelon was put back or it was bought at a ridiculously low price. Most times we walked away with two watermelons bought at very low price. Yes, it was not fair haggling, but that was the lunch meal for the day. We had nothing else to eat in those days. However, when times were better, we bought as many watermelons as we could afford, fair and square. A feast on watermelons was enjoyed by all of us at a meeting place, usually on the German cannon by the Cinema. Ironically, Salvatore became Maresciallo (chief of police) in later years in Avella and he inspected the market place for security!

When I came to America, soccer was a very foreign game, and I certainly did not want to appear foreign. I was told by American friends, in no uncertain terms, to never bounce a basketball on my head, period. So, I adopted the games of basketball, baseball and football with the same fervor I did with soccer. Usually, I practiced basketball, for example, from morning to night, in cold or hot weather. It was not until ten years later that I touched a soccer ball as a graduate student in USA.

Pierino became a popular singer and Pipino became a Judge. It is interesting to note that Salvatore also stuttered. I used to ask him how it started, and he really did not know when it started. Also, I asked him whether or not he was held back in public school because of his stuttering. Again, he said that stuttering was not an issue at all in public school. What a relief for me. I thought at worst I could always enroll in public schools, if things did not work out in private school. However, I sympathized with him for I knew the pain that he was suffering.

It was advantageous to be associated with a soccer team as we were always the first ones to hear the latest rumors, especially about the return of military prisoners from far-away lands. That was because someone on the team always had a relative shipped away to war by Mussolini. Whenever I asked the adults about the rumors, most of them were not aware of them. However, Francesca always seemed to know all the details. She knew who they were and what district they lived in town, etc. To this day I don't know why she made it her business to be aware of these sad things. In a way I was annoyed that she kept up with the past, when I really wanted to forget about it. Perhaps, that was one more reason that I was totally committed to soccer after the war.

The goal post on the soccer field at Saint Peter was located right in front of the entrance door to the residence of the priest. Often, the secretary would come out to the field and asked us to keep the noise down so that the priest could take a siesta. It was obvious to us kids playing soccer that the priest was not a soccer fan. Perhaps, he got hurt playing soccer for he had a noticeable limp. We tried to be quiet, but it was impossible to do that on a soccer field with kids playing. The net result was that there was some bad karma between the priest and the neighborhood kids about the shouting on the soccer field.

One memorable day I shot the soccer ball so hard that it went through the window on the second floor, where the priest's bedroom was located, and shattered the glass pane. Remarkably, the secretary did not come out at the entrance door inquiring as to what happened or who did it? This went on for at least two weeks and not a single pip out of the priest. However, one day as I was drinking water from a water fountain near Saint Peter church, the secretary sneaked behind me and informed me that the priest wanted to see me about the window at nine in the morning the next day.

When Francesca heard about the incident of the broken window, she was furious. The whole neighborhood knew about the broken window and who was culpable. She said not to promise to pay for anything. I did not sleep at all that night. The next morning, I went up the steps to the priest's office. Again, my chair was facing the priest behind a large desk, and he was looking down at me. The crucifix of Jesus was placed right behind him in a way that as you looked up at the priest, the crucifix was behind his head. It gave the appearance, as if he were on the cross. He stared right into my eyes and started to explain the various types of sins. After he finished explaining, he asked me, if it was I who broke the window. I said in the name of and respect for San Gennaro I did not break his window. Saint Gennaro was the patron Saint of Naples and he was never canonized by the Vatican. Again, I adopted San Gennaro as patron Saint of Avella, showing false humility to the priest. San Michele, the Archangel, is the patron Saint of Avella. Promptly, the priest said that San Gennaro was no Saint. He bit his tongue for he meant to add: Neither are you.

San Gennaro had confined his miracle-working to Naples for fourteen centuries since his martyrdom at Pozzuoli and it was believed of him that only Naples would be saved from destruction by the volcano Vesuvius. In 305 AD San Gennaro was thrown to the lions inside the colosseum in Pozzouli. This colosseum is one of eight colosseums built by the Romans. The lions did not devour San Gennaro, but he was beheaded by a gladiator. The blood of San Gennaro was saved in a container (ampulla) ever since. If it solidifies in the first week of May, it will bring good omens for the year. Otherwise, bad luck. San Gennaro had been "hired" to keep the fires of Vesuvius at bay in Naples.

Naples had tried to change loyalty from Saint Gennaro. During the French occupation of Naples in 1799, a French staff officer went to the priest and gave him ten minutes to produce the miracle or be shot. The miracle consisted of the liquefaction of San Gennaro's congealed blood taking place on the first Saturday in May. A slow liquefaction is considered an ill omen for the ensuing year and complete failure of liquefaction is taken as a sign of the Saint's extreme displeasure. The blood promptly liquefied and San Gennaro was charged by the Neapolitans as a traitor, since he was wishing good luck to the French. It also implied a long occupation of Naples by the French. The statue of San Gennaro was thrown into the sea and replaced by San Antonio Abate. With the first eruption of Vesuvius, San Antonio was not able to prevent the flow of lava toward Naples. Fishermen were sent back into the sea to search for San Gennaro's statue. A statue of San Gennaro was found on the Maddaloni Bridge in time to stop the flow of the lava. With this "miracle" San Antonio was no longer the savior Saint of Naples and San Gennaro was back for good. Near the end of WW II San Gennaro's blood liquefied slowly signifying ill omens for the Neapolitans implying more suffering which, indeed, occurred in Naples after the War. Liquefaction of the blood has nothing to do with miracles, but a lot to do with the temperature of the blood in the ampulla. Obviously, Neapolitans are very superstitious.

The priest then said: How do you explain the soccer ball has your name on it. Apparently, the priest figured out that the word "capitaniello" written on the soccer ball implied my ownership. I replied: It is true the soccer ball belonged to me, but it was not me who kicked the ball into the window. Furthermore, I said: Teen agers took over the field and the soccer ball, and I was waiting to get my ball back. I did not volunteer to say who kicked the ball, although he never asked me to name the person. He was incredulous and I knew right there and then that he had no proof that I did it. No one turned my name in to the priest. As the secretary handed the ball to me, she casually said that the priest wanted to talk to Francesca about the incident. She wanted to give the impression that the matter was over and the priest just wanted to inform Francesca. I knew better. It was like the calm before the storm. Then the conversation shifted toward a conciliatory tone.

He said that it would be nice, if I came back as an altar boy once in a while to train the new kids. When I informed Francesca about the priest wanting to see her about the incident, she expressed some sentiments that I cannot put in print. She never went to visit the priest. In fact, we changed allegiance from the church of Saint Peter to Saint Anthony which was closer to Nonno's house. Nonno liked that, because he had been a member of that church for a long time. Besides, he liked to remind me to go to church anytime I was at his house. He knew that Francesca did not care one way or the other for she rarely went to church. The first Communion ceremony was celebrated in Saint Anthony church with Nonno being the sponsor.

On my last visit to Saint Peter church for Mass, the priest put me to work at no salary. I was assigned to assist a paid worker to attach ropes to the bells placed at the top floor of the tower. This meant going up and down six flights of stairs tunneling ropes through a hole in each fl oor. What a pain. That was the last time I visited Saint Peter church for Mass. Thereafter, I attended Saint Anthony church exclusively for Sunday Mass. The nice thing about Saint Anthony church was that it had a big soccer field right outside and the monks' bedroom quarters were far away from the soccer field. During the Mass on Sunday, soccer was prohibited for us kids who were supposed to be in church! In the courtyard there was a palm tree full of ripe dates. How sweet they were and the monks did not mind sharing their dates with people after Mass. In addition, their garden was like the garden of Eden (as relayed to me by the nuns), full of fruit trees, fig, pomegranate, pear, grapes, apple, cherry, etc. The monks really worked hard to maintain their garden. I could see them working in the garden from Nonno's house, which was next to the garden.

The monks were very protective of their garden. Not even rats were allowed in the garden. An eight foot stone wall surrounded the garden and the wall was attached to the church structure itself on two sides. In effect, there was no entry into the garden all around the property. They had horses and donkeys in their stable in order to pull heavy equipment in the garden. During the Easter holidays the monks went around town with a wagon pulled by horses or donkeys to ask for donations from the people. By and large people were generous after the war. Usually, special Easter cakes were donated to the monks and sometimes money. I never saw the monks going around town during the War. No one had anything to give. For me the temptation of the pomegranate tree extending over the wall was too great. In the summer, those pomegranate fruits were smiling at me and very inviting. They were red and big and they "winked" at me.

Using a small ladder, the wall was climbed. I grabbed two to three pomegranates from the tree that were hanging over the wall. As I put the ladder back in Nonno's courtyard, he saw me with the fruits and inquired as to where I got them. I said to Nonno: You know very well where I got them. He said: First of all it was not nice to do that to the monks who worked so hard on their garden. Also, you can get hurt climbing the wall. I explained that the climbing part was easy for I used the ladder. "Well, don't do that again". Nonno and I shared in eating the fruits.

Soon after, Nonno got permission from the monks for us to visit the garden. That was not easy. I am sure it would have been easier to visit Fort Knox in USA than such a visit. Once inside the garden, there was a palm tree full of dates in the courtyard as well as in the garden itself. Naturally, I stuffed my pockets with dates and each time I picked dates on the ground Nonno would reprimand me. There was too much scugnizzo in me for I could not help myself. In the garden every imaginable fruit tree was there and all the fruits Nonno and I adored and worshipped. At the time of our visit the monks were making wine from the grapes cultivated in the garden. It was clear to me then that these monks worked very hard and, indeed, that was the message Nonno wanted to convey to me without saying a word. In all honesty, I knew what Nonno was trying to do, but I was too incorrigible. Obviously, Nonno was very religious. As for me, being around nuns and priests cured me of that special halo on their heads.

Nevertheless, the administration office of Saint Anthony church was too accessible for anyone to come and go. The administration office and the courtyard was open to the public except at night. If the church was located on an isolated hill, the monks could afford such a liberal attitude. It was located downtown Avella, where people were starving and no means to make a living. In addition, most, if not all, of the young people congregated at the bar next to the church. It did not take long for one young man to ransack the administration office for money. The timing of the robbery was coincidental with the afternoon siesta of the monks.

Obviously, whoever stole the money must have scouted the comings and goings of the monks in the afternoons and had knowledge of the interior layout of the convent. In short, it was an inside job. The amount of money involved was about $50. In those days it was a lot of money for a young man to possess. Monks were and are very devoted religious people, but are also astute. It did not take long for the monks to figure out who did the robbery. Instead of going to the Carabinieri (local police), they invited the young man to the office. It was useless to go to the local police, since they were more corrupt than the young man. Besides, why ruin a young man's life over $50, when his only intent was to help out his family. The young man confessed and all was forgiven. As penance, he was assigned to Mastro Nicola, assisting him in the painting of the Madonna of Monte Vergine. I was privy to those negotiations via my brother Sebastiano who was a close friend of this young man. They often spent times together at the bar across the street from the monastery playing cards. The young man would often bring espresso coffee to the monks who had ordered from the bar.

FIFTEEN
POLITICS AVELLA STYLE

The winter of 1946 was rather mild, without even a trace of snow on Mount Avella. Communists were brandishing their red flags marching down Main Street from City Hall singing their revolutionary songs. None of them were clients of my seamstress aunts, implying that most of them could not afford much. Most of them lived in the part of town where shepherds lived near the bridge blown-up by the American soldiers in 1943, the O' Vicolo district. There were about 100 of them and they were outright nasty and outspoken. Shouts and insults followed everywhere they went. In the end, they would congregate in the center of the main piazza and interfere with anyone doing business in City Hall or any place else near there. Their objective was to draw attention to their cause, which was the overthrow of the Monarchy. They were noticed, but I felt that there was a better way to draw attention from the people, instead of being a pain in the ass and obnoxious. In retrospect, elimination of opposition in piecemeal fashion is often expounded in the "Communist Manifesto". Thus, they were just following orders from Communist leadership to eliminate one more opposition, the Monarchy, on their way to power. Their demonstrations were in regard to the coming referendum on June 2, 1946 concerning the abolition of the Monarchy, and the title of King in Italy. Also, local and general elections were held.

In 1946, spring came early. The favorite pastime for me was to catch birds from the nests on trees, when water flow in the Clanio creek was quite strong. Sometimes in the spring it looked like the treacherous rapids of the Colorado River. Amazingly, most times it was dry, especially in the summer. At this time, shepherds hurtled their sheep into a big pool of water (50x100 square feet) to wash the wool and drive ticks and fleas away. At one end of the pool the water was 15 feet deep and at the other end it was at ground level. The water was drawn from the creek, as the water rolled down an artificial dam. The sheep were herded up a ramp into the pool, from deep water to shallow. The pool was located next to a large building where they butchered horses and cows. The building served as German headquarters, when they camped in Avella. After the bath the sheep were sheared of their wool coats. It was fascinating to watch, but the work involved was tedious and laborious.

On the same afternoon, tending the bird trap near the creek, a squadron of planes flew over. I was terrified, thinking, oh no, not again and dove into a thick bush to hide. I imagined all sorts of possibilities. However, the planes were dropping leaflets written in English and candies were also dropped from the planes. I took the candies home and ate some of them and saved others. The next day I was walking toward Nonno's house, past the nun's school, where there was some commotion down the street. Some Communist fanatics were on loud speakers telling people not to pick anything dropped from the planes.

Apparently, the communists graduated from riding donkeys to riding cars. They claimed that the candies may be poisoned. This was their way of undermining the Allies. All of sudden, the Allies were our enemies, according to Communists propaganda. This was a prelude to another war, the "Cold War" between the Soviet Union and the USA. As in the "Manifesto", each Western country was to be isolated and taken over by the Soviet Bloc. I knew better for I had eaten candies the day before. That day, again, I saw the planes dropping leaflets and candies. I calmly went about picking up candies and ate them in front of other children. Suddenly, school children at the nun's school rushed for the candies. The next day all of us children waited for the airplanes and waited and waited. The planes never showed up again. The message on the leaflets was related to the election on the referendum. For us children, it meant only missing out on more candies.

In the final phases of World War II, King Victor Emmanuel had tried to save the Monarchy by nominating his son, Umberto, "Lieutenant General of the Kingdom". This move was equivalent to an abdication of his throne to his son. The King promised that, after the end of the War, the Italian people could choose its form of government through a referendum. The head of state in early 1944 was General Pietro Badoglio who had explicit support of the British and Americans.

In the months of April and June, 1946, the people of Italy were preoccupied with the coming election of the General Assembly in April 19, 1946 and the referendum on June 2, 1946, about the disposition of the Monarchy. The main purpose of the Assembly was to draft a new Constitution of a new government and they had two years to do it. A "Yes" vote in the referendum implied the Monarchy or King Victor Emmanuel III could form a post-war government similar to the British form of government. A "No" vote implied that the Monarchy or the King would be exiled from Italy. The Communist and Republican parties were active against the King. The Communist Party in Avella headquartered next to City Hall. They held a rally almost every day up and down the main street and would carry a red flag, singing Communist revolutionary songs, and a trumpeter to get people's attention. Typically, the group consisted of 30-40 Communists.

It was not what it appeared like, a political rally. They would send out communist politicos to seek out children and talked to the kids about how beautiful Soviet Russia was and became friendly with them. I know about these recruiting excursions for they talked to me about the beautiful living, dolce vita, in Mother Russia. Once the attention was drawn to themselves, a Communist party member would break away from his "comrades" in the flag waving group and engage a child into a conversation about anything of current interest. The approach was very smooth and informal. Soon enough, the conversation drifted toward diatribes against the church, government, USA and anyone opposing Communism. In my case, we talked for a long time sitting on a comfortable bench across the water fountain in the piazza. These conversations were exhaustive, but in the end, the arguments presented to me were flawed even to a child. In retrospect, the Communist view in Italy at that time was long range; they were preparing for a long political and class struggle by indoctrinating youngsters with the Communist movement. The election in 1946 would be one of many.

The scourge of Communism in Italy has lasted more than fifty years, but nowadays the threat of Communists taking over the Italian government has subsided. They have gone through a re-definition of ideology from what Karl Marx intended. I am sure Karl Marx is not happy in his grave about what is happening in Italy with Communist ideology. For example, farm communes could never be possible in Italy for ownership of farms has always been very dear to family traditions and identities. The Russian concept of farming is very strange to Italian thinking. Italian farmers do not like to share their farms or produce with government overseers. The Communist party was the only one in Avella demonstrating against the King. I remember one man who was in charge of the Republican Party headquarters in Avella, next to the Cafe and bar, putting up many posters on the wall advocating abolition of the King. The Republican Party in Italy advocated a return to a government and Constitution, similar to when Italy gained independence from France and Austria. Clearly, the Republican Party in the USA represents totally different beliefs: Belief in the US Constitution and State's Rights. The king had mild support in Southern Italy only because he resided in the South during the Referendum. North Italy was solid against the King. The outcome was inevitable and the referendum did not carry.

The Monarchy was supported by a local person in Avella operating out of his house. He represented the Monarchy Party and it was supported by the Count in Avella, and plastered posters near the Café and along the passeggiata route, Main Street. It did not help. In the referendum election, the "No" vote barely won in Southern Italy, but Northern Italy voted overwhelming No. That was a strange result in view of the fact that the house of Savoy (King) came from near Turin (North Italy), since 1870. The King and wife were exiled to Egypt and he died in 1947, with little notice in Italy. The son, Umberto, was exiled to Portugal. The Monarchy Party is no longer viable today. The following year, 1947, the new constitution was drafted and passed by the General Assembly with a vote of 452 to 63 against.

The General Assembly, voted upon in April 1946, was in place between June 1946 and January 1948 [102]. Each party had run separate candidates in the 1946 general election and the DC (Christian Democracy) received 35.2% of the votes, but PCI (Communist Party) and PSIUP (Socialist Party) together received 39.6%. Effectively, the Communist, "left" leaning, representation in the Assembly outnumbered the DC party representation. In a compromise move by De Gasperi (DC) the PSIUP and PCI received some ministerial posts in a DC led coalition cabinet. PCI's Palmiro Togliatti was appointed minister of Justice. However, USA President Truman took exception to these appointments by De Gasperi and put pressure on the Italian government. The final outcome was that the PCI and PSIUP were excluded from the cabinet formed by De Gasperi. The PCI and PSIUP decided to unite in 1948 to form the

Popular Democratic Front (FDP). Basically, the Communist Party had marginalized the Socialist Party into a meaningless entity and reduced its political influence. This was another example of "divide and conquer" as taught by Communist doctrines (Manifesto). The Constitutional Assembly was in place from June 1946 to January 1948 and it wrote the new Constitution of Italy which took effect on January 1, 1948.

General elections were held in Italy on Sunday April 18, 1948 to elect members of parliament, Chamber of Deputies and Senators of the Republic. Italy was no longer reigned by a King, since the referendum of 1946. There were something like 60 parties nationally. The major parties included the following: Christian Democracy, Communist, Socialist, Social Democracy, Social Communist, Monarchy, Liberal, MSI, Liberty, Leaf, Republican and few other minor parties. The Christian Democratic Party was supported by the Catholic Church and the Church wanted people to believe that it was a sin to vote for anyone else, especially Communist. The party leader of the Christian Democrats was Alcide DeCasperi. The Communist was supported by the Soviet Union, although they denied their acceptance of financial aid from the Soviet Union. The Communist leader was Palmiro Togiatti. Pietro Nenni was leader of the Social Communist Party and Pertini the leader of the Socialist Party. He was one of the partisans chasing Mussolini on his way to Como. The other parties were of minor importance. The MSI (Fascist) Party had the same platform as the Fascist Party prior to the war. The Monarchy party dreamed of bringing back the King. However, King Victor Emmanuel III was dead in 1947 and his son Umberto was exiled to Portugal. There was no hope of bringing those people back to govern Italy.

The elections were heavily influenced by the "Cold War" between the United States and the Soviet Union. The USA feared if the Communist Party won, Italy would be drawn into the Soviet Union's sphere of interest. It was a dirty and vicious political campaign. The Christian Democrat campaign claimed that, in Communist countries, children send parents to jail. The CIA gave two million dollars to centrist parties. The PCI was also funded by the Soviet Union and the Cominform. Ten million letters were sent by Italian-Americans urging Italians not to vote Communist. The Christian Democrats won with 48.5% of the vote and 305 seats in the Chamber of Deputies and 131 seats in the Senate. The total number of Deputies in the Chamber was 574 and 237 in the Senate. The Popular Democratic Front (FDP-Communist Party) under the leadership of Palmiro Togliatti and Pietro Nenni gathered 31 % of the vote, 183 deputies and 72 Senators. Most of the support for the Communist party came from the so-called "Red Triangle" region of Emilia, Liguria and Savona-Bologna-Reggio Emilia area, which is still predominantly "red" or Communist.

The year in politics, 1948, started out with the major parties inviting national politicians to come to Avella and give speeches at their rallies. Usually, the speeches were delivered on a temporary podium built on top of the water fountain in the piazza, in front of the buildings owned by the local Count. Water was turned off to accommodate the podium. The podium faced the entire piazza near City Hall. The Communists brought their "big gun", Palmiro Togliatti, to give a speech. The piazza was full to the limit. This meant that people from other towns also attended the speech. For example, there were Communist groups from Baiano and Sperone as well as Avella. The towns of Baiano and Sperone have voted Communist since 1946. However, the people of Avella have never voted in favor of the Communist Party since. Other politicians who came to Avella were DeGasperi (Christian Democrat) and Nenni (Socialist). For each of those speakers, the piazza was full. Based on the capacity of the crowds it was clear that the two parties in contention for the next prime minister of Italy were the Communist and Christian Democratic Parties. The side walls on the main street of Avella were plastered with posters from every party. There was not a clear spot on any wall due to the plastering of the posters. The most offensive poster, to me as a child, was the one where the Communist Party depicted Giuseppe Garibaldi as one of their own with a red bandana around his neck with the slogan "Viva Bandiera Rossa", long live the red flag.

Giuseppe Garibaldi has always been every child's hero in Italy. He was the hero of the Italian revolution in 1870. He started his campaign of uniting Italy in Sicily and ended up in Rome where he drove the Papal Army into surrender. Prior to the revolution the Pope occupied vast amounts of property, banks, farms and buildings in Italy [12, 18, and 46]. The church ceded about 20,000 square miles to the new Republic of Italy except for a square mile of land in Rome, the Vatican. The Communists tried to make the point that Garibaldi was anti-church, just like the Communist Party. Those insinuations had nothing to do with historical facts. Garibaldi was a very religious man and a revolutionary, but not a Communist. When Garibaldi started his first revolution (~1840), there was no Communist Party, well before Karl Marx's ideas on Communism were published. The earliest publication dated in 1844 did not deal with the doctrines of Communism. Garibaldi was a true revolutionary. There was not a revolution that he did not believe in. He even went to Uruguay in 1839 to partake in a revolution. He started the Italian revolution in Sicily and combined the "kingdoms" of Sicily and Naples into one state to be combined with the northern regions of Piedmont and Lombardy regions.

His main motive was to fold his hometown of Nice under the umbrella of the new republic of Italy. The Italian revolutionaries had a lucky break when the German King, Otto Von Bismarck [104], attacked France and Austria to form a new state of Germany. As a result French troops withdrew from the Papal state of Rome and the Austrians from Veneto (Venice). The Italian revolutionary troops simply walked into Rome and Veneto to declare the new nation of Italy under King Victor Emmanuel I. As soon as Italy was united, King Victor Emmanuel I, informed Garibaldi that his services were no longer needed. This was typical of a king, dispersing unwanted attention to others or not willing to share the limelight or glory with the popular Garibaldi. The point was that Garibaldi may have been a revolutionary, but he was a republican at heart, never a communist! Garibaldi finally d id realize his dream of having Nice annexed by Italy. Clearly, the Communists tried to re-write history in that campaign of 1948. Spin-doctors existed long before modern day politics.

If the Communist Party won the election in 1948, Italy would have become another satellite country of the Soviet Union. The election result was not close, and the Democratic Christian Party won by 48% to 38%. The other parties split the rest of the votes. It is interesting to note that if one added all the votes of the Communist Party and other Socialist parties it would have surpassed 50%. Yes, it was a close election and, fortunately, the other Socialist parties were not allied with the Communist party. These election results changed slightly for the next 35-40 years until the downfall of the Berlin wall. These election results implied that Italy was very much polarized politically for years for years to come and as a result the central government was not stable. There was, on the average, a change in the prime minister's office every 15-18 months. In most western countries the change in leadership in the central government occurred every four years. The problem was that, with a small change or perturbation of the above electoral results, it affected dramatically alliances needed to obtain a majority in parliament. A Prime Minister needed a majority in parliament to govern in Italy as well as in other western countries. Since 1948, Italy had the largest membership in the Communist Party of the Western Democratic countries. The Communist Party was not able to gain sufficient vo tes th ereafter foItaly to become a member of the Soviet Bloc.

There were only two candidates for Mayor of Avella, the local doctor who ran under the banner of the Christian Democratic Party and a person from the poor district of Avella under the Communist Party banner. The local Communist Party of Avella accused Francesca of taking bribes from the leaders of the Democratic Party, including from our beloved doctor. They would make statements in public saying that they saw Francesca walking in the streets with loaves of bread under her arms. Those comments hurt. What hurt even more was that those comments were made by Francesca's cousin Don Camillo, who was still herding his sheep on my grandfather's grass fields on the mountains.

Although Francesca's background was from the shepherd community, she wanted nothing to do with the Communist Party in the coming local election for Mayor. Most of the shepherds were diehard Communists. She was of the opinion that if they won, the Communists would take away the special scholarship perks that the nuns granted to poor people like her. That was the rumor in town. She decided to enter the political campaign to get the "good" doctor elected mayor of Avella. He was the same doctor who treated Caterina and many other family members. She was very good at convincing some of the Communist diehards and shepherd friends to vote for the Christian Democratic Party for she knew a lot of them, when she worked helping grandfather Carmine shepherding on the mountains. Her role was to contact directly the main competition, Communists, and convert them over to vote for the Christian Democratic Party (CDP). The campaign for Mayor was tough. The Communist Party put up a strong campaign, since, in those days, there was a lot to complain about in town. The number one issue was corruption at all levels. The Communists were promising to share farmlands of the landowners and the church. That was appealing even to me.

Those comments invigorated Francesca even more to visit every single shepherd family in Avella. In one instance, a Communist agitator grabbed me by the shirt and started shouting and shaking me to tell Francesca to stay out of politics and stop talking to people in the "poor district". I never delivered that message, because she was hell-bent in delivering the shepherd's votes to the Christian Democratic Party. Nothing could have stopped her. I knew that. The only problem was that some of these shepherds were illiterate and mother spent a lot of time instructing them how to vote and how to sign their name on the ballot. Also, some of them never voted before.

Interestingly, the election returns for the local election were much better than the national election returns. The Democratic candidate was elected with a majority of 56% versus 31% for the Communist candidate and 13% for other candidates. This was a surprising result in view of the fact that towns all around Avella, Baiano, Sperone, Cervinara and Cicciano, voted for Communist Mayors. This result was due mostly to Francesca's efforts in the poor community of shepherds. The Communist Party put up a candidate who was not even a resident of Avella. He lived near the cemetery which straddled the border between Baiano and Avella. The town of Baiano was almost totally Communist.

In Avella the Communist and Christian Democratic parties were the two major ones vying for the mayor's position. Francesca was deeply involved in politics. I did not understand her allegiance to the Democratic Party given her background in shepherding and being financially poor. Also, most people who tended sheep were diehard Communist. A lot of her relatives and friends were Communists. A lot of her Communists friends tried to convert me by exulting the beauty of "Russian farm living". Even as a child I thought that these people were either delusional or brainwashed. Francesca would plaster posters of the Democratic candidate on walls near where we lived. The local doctor, Mario Biancamano, was still attending medical school at the University of Naples. The counterpart to Francesca, in the Communist campaign, was Don Camillo who cleverly plastered Communist posters over the ones Francesca posted up for the Democratic candidate. It was too dangerous to venture from home any longer without some escort. She was accused by the Communists, throughout the campaign, of taking bribes from the Democratic Party and the church.

They should have known that she hadn't gone to church in years. Politically, it was a nasty time. We were looking over our shoulders for possible trouble or attacks. The "good" doctor won the election and was very appreciative of the efforts by Francesca. She "moved a mountain" politically for the "good" doctor. After this brutal election, she reminded me that the Communist leader in Avella, Don Camillo, was still our long distant Zio and deserved our respect. He may be misguided, but he was still our "goat".

One of the first acts of the mayor was to fund a road project near our house. Francesca has pleaded innocence about this project for years. The engineer in charge was a student who was a freshman student at the University of Naples. This was nothing less than a political payoff to supporters. A freshman student in civil engineering at any western University school barely has initiated specialized courses in civil engineering. Most likely he may have taken an introduction course in physics. If so, he was not qualified to build a road and pave it. In a small farm town like Avella, a person who attends a University, automatically is referred to as Dottore. It doesn't matter, if the person is attending the first or last year of his studies. In some sense, it biases townspeople's opinion about the qualification of that person. This may explain why the Mayor was able to push through this ruse. There is a foundation, dirt filling, etc. and paving in the construction of a road. It must have been some form of payola involved between the Mayor and the engineer's family. This family included the new tax collector, who purchased grandfather Carmine's land on Mount Avella, and financially supported the Mayor's campaign for election.

Again, it was difficult to rationalize the decision by the Mayor. Fortunately, Francesca suggested to the young "engineer" that he hire Uncle Joe and Mastro Nicola, the artist, to help him out. This is hard to believe, but it really happened. So, the three of them got together and planned the construction of the road. According to Uncle Joe, the poor student had no clue as to what to do. It was almost like "the three stooges" constructing the road. Somehow, they got hold of some plans at City Hall in the construction of roads in Avella and Baiano. The Communist mayor in Baiano refused, at first, to release the plans, but eventually yielded.

Uncle Joe and Mastro Nicola searched for road construction plans in Avella's and Baiano's City Halls. The road plans found in Avella were outdated, since the last construction was more than fifty years old. Fifty years before, roads were built for horses and wagons. Newer roads were built during German and British occupations, but they didn't leave any road plans behind. Hence, Mastro Nicola focused the search for the plans at Baiano's City Hall. A paved road leading to the soccer stadium was recently built there. They secured a letter of introduction from the Mayor of Avella, who was a Democrat, requesting permission to access road construction records in Baiano. The receptionist to the Mayor of Baiano dismissed the letter outright by throwing the letter in a waste basket, stating that they would need a letter of introduction from the Communist leader of Avella. She was somewhat abrasive. Nevertheless, she said that she would show the letter to the Mayor, as she retrieved the letter. Mastro Nicola thought that the receptionist looked familiar, but could not place where he met her before.

Francesca arranged for the two artisans to talk to Don Camillo about a letter of introduction. Apparently, Francesca and Don Camillo patched things up after the election. They were stuck together, as they were relatives. Don Camillo did more than writing a letter. He promised them that he would come along with them to see the Communist Mayor of Baiano. After all, he was also a Communist. When the three of them visited the Mayor, they were all surprised. The Mayor greeted Mastro Nicola as his lost son, and introduced formally his daughter, the receptionist, to Mastro Nicola, not to Joe and not to Don Camillo. Mastro Nicola had a smile from ear to ear, and she appeared meek and not abrasive as before. Apparently, the Mayor knew Mastro Nicola's family well. Before the war, he was stage manager of the San Carlo Opera house. Often, he and the Maestro would ride the train together from Naples home. The Maestro would get off at the Avella station and he, one stop later, at Baiano. They had much in common. Both were Communists and anti-Fascists. To what extent they socialized, it is not clear. With the appearance of German troops in the area, the future Mayor joined a partisan group covering the Avellino-Nola area and the Maestro and family went into hiding for about a year.

After the small talk was over, the gathering broke up into serious negotiations about the road plans, but Mastro Nicola spent time re-acquainting himself with the receptionist. They (Joe, Don Camillo and the Mayor) struck a deal. Don Camillo and the Mayor would supply the laborers for the construction of the road and a list would be made available to the Dottore, the "engineer", via Mastro Nicola and Joe. In return, recent road plans would be made available to the Dottore. At the end of the meeting, the Mayor instructed Mastro Nicola to return to the receptionist's office or to his daughter to help him find the plans. Obviously, the Mayor had another agenda, besides a political one. I believe that the Mayor and Papa would have gotten along just fine, if Papa were alive. They were of the same mind set, true Figaros.

The Mayor of Baiano was bribed in many ways. Most of the laborers put on the road construction were members of the Communist Party who had never worked on road construction and were unskilled and were residents of Baiano and Avella. Due to the war there was very little skilled labor in Italy and more so in Avella. The day-to-day operation was handled by Uncle Joe and Mastro Nicola and they were in charge of delegating work. The titular head of the project was the young engineer. He basically kept tabs on who should be paid on the project and accounted for the flow of money to workers. The project was finished in a year to pave about two miles of road that ran from my house to the Fusaro picnic area. Mayor Biancamano retired soon after the road was built for he finally got his medical degree and moved to Naples to practice in a hospital near there.

An out-of-town person was installed as the new Mayor. The people of Avella never knew where he came from and what his party affiliation was. There was a lot of speculation as to who he really represented: Camorra, Government in Rome, a Communist or a Democrat. The Mayor pretty much kept to himself and didn't do much of anything for the rest of the term, which remains the case of the Mayor of Avella today. In the following election for Mayor, Francesca stayed out of the election campaign – thank God. We did not need any more headaches. The local pharmacist ran for Mayor against the Communist Party candidate, Don Camillo. Francesca voted for Don Camillo for he was a good shepherd and a good man, and, besides, he was family. Basically, Don Camillo was more of a socialist looking out for the poor people of Avella. The pharmacist ran under the Republican Party. There was no candidate from the Democratic Party. The pharmacist easily won and was able to stay in the office as Mayor for four years. After all, people needed medicine more than ricotta from Don Camillo.

The Communist Mayor of Baiano funded a project to build a soccer stadium near the cemetery of Avella less than 1 km from Avella. It took about three months to build and, more importantly, a professional soccer team was organized from local talent in Baiano. No players were chosen from Avella, although some played at higher level soccer teams in the area. The team at Baiano was the lowest tier soccer level, class D; Serie A is the highest level. In addition, to a soccer field the Mayor of Baiano funded the construction of a modern Cinema which eventually was drawing viewers from Avella and vicinity. Obviously, the Mayor of Baiano was more successful in securing funds from the central government of Rome, although the Prime Minister and President of the Republic were Democrats. The implication here is that parliament controlled the disbursing of moneys to small towns, not the President. Competition between these two towns dates back to Roman times, when the Appian Way cut through Baiano rather than Avella. In those days Avella was a much bigger city than Baiano.

SIXTEEN
AMERICA THE BEAUTIFUL

The U.S. immigration laws [105] of the 1920s resulted in long waiting lists for the small number of visas available to those born in Italy. Exactly 249,583 people were waiting for admission into the USA after the war. The annual quota allowed for immigrants from Italy was 5,666. When WW II came to an end in 1945, an estimated 7 to 11 million people were displaced from their homes in Germany, Italy, Austria and the rest of Europe. However, US attitude towards Italian immigration to America was dramatically affected by the new wave of refugees from Southern Italy, especially.

The Truman administration supported admitting a number of European refugees over and above the existing immigration quotas for that region of the world. The law passed in 1948 authorized the entry of 200,000 displaced persons over the next two years. In 1950 the entry to USA increased to 415,000 displaced people. The law stipulated that preferential treatment be given to people who were in resettlement camps, or refugees. It also gave preference to relatives of American citizens who had housing available for displaced people or refugees.

In the late 1940s a number of my friends were leaving Italy for the USA and South America. As I have mentioned earlier, my friend Bruno's older brothers left for South America as early as 1945. The two brothers were excellent trumpeters and played beautiful music from South America, tango, samba, etc. I was truly sad to see them go. I am not sure what compelled them to leave, when they could have made a living any place as musicians. I don't think the fact that their family adored Mussolini had anything to do with their departure. The adoration part was due to the fact that the perks from the Fascist government were great before the war for a large family. Honestly, no one in town cared about past political allegiance of anyone after the war.

Raffaele from Sperone was one of the earliest people I knew who emigrated to America. We were classmates at the nun's school and was extremely pleased to inform me that the family was able to qualify as refugees whereby they did not have to wait long to immigrate. However, they never interned in a refugee camp. They left town in less than a year after he informed me, and settled in New Jersey.

Besides Raffaele, an avalanche of people from the local area were leaving town for the USA. Few of the refugees had relatives in USA to sponsor them, and most of them were refugees taking advantage of the new immigration laws for displaced people. As for us, we were not aware of any special laws in immigration that we could take advantage of. None of us was holding a job for there were no jobs. The only financial support was the $150 a year and two sacks of baking flour from our grandfather in Ambridge, Pa. Although everything around us was bubbling with business success, we were not part of that. We barely survived.

My main concern was the desire for a pair of shoes to play soccer. I would venture to say that most people who were affiliated or sympathized with Fascism during the war left town for South America, North Italy and other places in North Africa and the Middle East. It did not take a genius to realize that trouble was brewing on the horizon for former Fascists. In fact a lot of them did not survive that period of time, 1944-1947. Some of the Fascists did not even have a trial before they were killed by partisans or some seeking personal revenge. Sebastiano was basically supported financially by our seamstress aunts. Whatever clothes or money in his possession was provided by the aunts - even gambling money. He was entering the Lyceum school system which meant that in three years he would be eligible for University. School was tuition free, but there were expenses, such as train transportation, books, food and clothing. Also, he needed tutors from time to time to help him pass examinations at the end of the year. The Lyceum school system was very academic. Fortunately, Sebastiano was academically inclined and had no problems with the classical work in the Lyceum.

Usually, people who attended the Lyceum would enter the University and I am certain that he would have done so, if we stayed in Italy. There was no guarantee that he would have made it to the majors in soccer. As for myself, I was attending the nuns' school and was planning to enroll in the "Scuole Media" which was five years of preparatory schooling for the Lyceum. I was of the mind set "Lyceum or bust". The point was that, for both of us, our future in Italy was pretty much settled. The only question was whether we boys wanted to pay the price of attending the Lyceum and on to the University.

The problem has always been that there were not many jobs awaiting for University graduates in Southern Italy. Usually, those students that got a real job were recommended by some influential person in government, police and church and there were not many jobs like that. So, the handwriting was on the wall. The future was bleak in academics unless you knew someone influential. Nothing has changed to this day. Our only hope was to make it big in soccer and the probability of that occurring was between slim and none. In a way it was like a class system. If one was born in one class system, it was nearly impossible to climb out of it.

Out of desperation Francesca wrote to grandfather in Ambridge, PA, requesting sponsorship to come to USA, as required by immigration laws. In truth it was I who wrote the letter, as Francesca dictated as to what she wanted to say. I was ecstatic about the possibility of going to USA. After all, "money grew on trees there". I had a naïve view of America. I thought that I would meet Indians for the first time and wondered what language they spoke. I wanted to ask them, if they knew Buster Crabbe, my hero. More importantly, I thought all these financial worries would, once and for all times, go away for the first time in our lives. This way I could concentrate on my studies.

However, when I informed Nonno about it, he appeared very sad, almost in a daze. I promised him that I would visit every year on my birthday. He cried and went inside in the house. I was told by my aunts that he never recovered his composure from that day until he died. But then again, the aunts were always so dramatic, being artistically inclined. So, I gave little credence to what they said.

Sebastiano's reaction to coming to USA was totally negative. He preferred to remain behind in Avella. He had established a long list of friends throughout Avella and vicinity, and was popular in the Café and bar scene playing cards and billiards. In addition, he was a professional soccer player with reasonable potential to become a major league soccer player. From his perspective, the future looked bright. From my perspective, it was just the opposite. After all these years, I now understand where he was coming from and I respect that. At that time it made no sense to me, even though I was much younger than he. In fact, Francesca and I were planning to leave him behind. The response from my grandfather in Ambridge took "forever", two to three months, and we were ready to go. The reason that it took so long was that he needed someone to write the letter for him, as he never had any formal schooling in Italy. Probably, his father kept him in the mountains shepherding from the day he was born.

With the sponsorship in hand Francesca went to look for a lawyer to prepare the paper works for the immigration office in Naples. It was a nightmarish experience in dealing with lawyers in Avella. We made an appointment with one who resided in one palazzo on Main Street. Outside the palazzo it was bustling with cars and people shopping on Main Street. It was modern times like the twentieth century. Inside the palazzo it was like entering into the middle ages. It was dark and full of statues at the center of a small courtyard, with a carefully manicured garden. We climbed up the steps for about five floors and knocked on the door and waited.

For a minute I thought Count Dracula was going to show up for it was so spooky. Finally, an old man showed up immaculately dressed and invited us in. Coffee espresso and cake were offered along with small talk. Frankly, I was bored stiff and apprehensive as to the drift of the conversation going nowhere. It was like watching one of those scary Count Dracula movies at the Cinema in Avella that I often saw. Finally, we got to the business on hand and he promised that he would contact a lawyer in Naples who worked in the American Consulate, who would "recommend" us. I was very happy to leave that spooky place. In fact, I ran down the stairs. I really thought that this man was an incurable nut case.

When we were outside the palazzo, I berated Francesca for securing the service of this lawyer. Since then, I have forgiven her, because she was venturing into a professional world that she was not accustomed to. Anyway, we never heard from this lawyer. It was difficult to fathom how this man made a living as a lawyer. I believe now that this man probably was not a practicing lawyer at that time. What he had to offer was special contacts, via the Camorra, with influential people in Naples. Apparently, he must have determined that it was not financially worth his while to do anything more for us. Hence, we never heard from him.

After the first lawyer, Francesca selected another lawyer in another palazzo on the same Main Street. Again the same spooky scenery as the other place. Again, the same ritual with the espresso and small talk before getting to business. This time however, the lawyer had a set of application forms that we had to fill out and return them back to him. We filed the paper application and returned the forms back to the lawyer. The application forms were for a special refugee consideration rather than a traditionally sponsored program of the 1920s. That lawyer was of the opinion that we could emigrate to America quicker that way. Again, that was the last time we saw him or heard from him. He was paid in advance after he promised a quick resolution. It was really an exasperating experience, even as a child. Obviously, our great desire to emigrate was not matched by the efforts of these two lawyers. The results infuriated us. We felt despair for it was like a situation of the blind leading the blind. How is it that others were able to pick up and go to the USA so quickly? We didn't know what to do.

In the meantime, my grandfather from Ambridge was wondering what was going on, and we really did not have good answers for him. Time was of the essence then. Grandfather was diagnosed with some incurable disease, often identified with steel or coal workers. Now, we know it to be the dreaded "black lung" disease common in the coal mines and steel factories areas of West Virginia and Western PA. Grandfather was treated medically at his home. Thus, there was an urgent need to get to America as soon as possible, but we were spinning our wheels with no progress to show for our efforts.

Life for Sebastiano was changing fast. A lot of his friends were emigrating to USA, leaving town in order to secure employment in other cities, mostly in the north of Italy. He got himself into a fracas with some shepherd boys over their sister. In shepherd's traditions there were protocols in relationships with shepherd girls that he did not follow, according to Francesca.

Of course, she knew all about those protocols. It was amazing how history repeated itself. My father fell in love with a shepherd girl and so did my brother. Papa solved the problem by serenading Francesca. After the war serenading was taboo. The twentieth century came upon us fast. People did not want to live in the past, and, for sure, not the shepherds. Eventually, Francesca patched things up with the other shepherd family. They spoke the same "goat dialect". Perhaps, Sebastiano should have honed on that language instead of Latin, Greek, Italian, French and English. In the meantime every single bone of Sebastiano's body was hurting. The girl's two brothers performed chiropractic surgeries on Sebastiano's joints.

To add to his woes, his closest friend who was a shepherd died in a freakish bike accident to add to his misery. On the way to the annual pilgrimage to Monte Vergine in Avellino his friend was run over by an on-coming bus. Sebastiano was also on a bike right next to him. Somehow, he barely survived. With all this happening to him he came to the conclusion that it was time for a change in scenery, the USA. Finally, we had an active participant in applying for emigration, Sebastiano.

Astonishingly, some of Sebastiano's friends were young and influential lawyers. One, in particular, was the son of a high court judge in the Naples district. Even more astonishing was the fact that they were related to Nonna Caterina (grandmother). For the life of me I don't understand today why Francesca turned to some unknown lawyers who did not know much about the new immigration laws. For example, my uncle Pierino in Reggio Emilia (near Florence) who was a former judge and Questore (superintendent of police and Interpol) would have those immigration papers finished and expedited within days. Here we were after two years and we made no progress whatsoever toward emigrating to USA.

Sebastiano was able to secure the service of his friend to handle the immigration papers. His friend's name was Giulio and he was nephew to Nonna and he was a registered lawyer. Giulio, Sebastiano and Sassano (another friend) were inseparable. They were like the three musketeers. They often played in Sassano's bowling alley inside Sassano's house. Besides these three friends, there was another group of teenagers that hung around together in coffee houses, billiard rooms and card rooms. This group preceded "La Dolce Vita" long before it was made fashionable by director Fellini.

Giulio was a serious student and the family expected nothing less than a University degree. Giulio was assured of a career in the future. His father was a big-time judge in Naples and nepotism was alive and well in Naples. The timing for the change in lawyers helped us with the immigration papers, since, right about this time, the quota for immigration to America from Italy doubled.

The exodus to America was just beginning. Within a short time Giulio arranged for an interview with the American General Consul stationed in the American naval base in Naples. This base was huge and it was located in the harbor of Naples. The base had its own military airport separate from the Civilian one. Sooner or later, every American ship that navigated in the Mediterranean Sea, the Red Sea, or near the Middle East would be stationed in the Navy base in Naples. It employed 5000-10000 civilians from the Naples area. However, it was and is the source of much of the merchandise peddled in the black-market.

The interview with the American Consul was very friendly. I am sure it must have been a cultural shock for him to be stationed in Naples. The contrast between Mid-Americans and Neapolitans is like between living on the moon and earth. Whereas mid-Americans dwell in the simplicity of life, Neapolitans are intrigued by everything that they see or imagine.

The Consul was a tall person and rather young, 35-40 years old, and came from the mountain state of Wyoming. He just wanted to talk to me, not Francesca or Sebastiano. He asked me what my plans were going to be once in America or what I wanted to do in America. There was a translator in the room who spoke perfect Italian. Of course, I replied that I wanted to be a soccer player. He just smiled and talked about something else. I don't remember exactly what was said but somehow the Consul did most of the talking, as he liked to talk. Francesca fell in love with the crew-cut look of the Americans that she saw in newspapers, and she was determined to give us kids the same look once in America.

She was tired of the Neapolitan-Camorra hair style. According to Francesca we Neapolitans needed to be modern like the Americans or get with it. She loved America even before she arrived or landed a foot in America. It was her ticket out of that misery in Avella during and after the war. When in America she loved to make cakes from recipes in a box. She thought that it was the greatest discovery ever made, since the discovery of America. In Italy it was a major undertaking for anyone to bake a cake from scratch, especially when it required a lot of eggs. Eggs were expensive during and after the War.

After the interview it was a matter of waiting it out before a precise time for our departure was set. For the first time in our lives we could relax about our future and about life in general. I think that ever since I was born, my family was under pressure to survive almost on a daily basis. Our anticipation of what to expect in USA was very naïve. Perhaps, being exhausted from the daily drudgery of life in Avella gave us a false sense of what to expect in USA. We expected to morph into money and have no more worries the rest our lives and money grew on trees. We all know that was and is not true, but we wanted so badly to believe in that dream.

With the visit to the Consul over it allowed us to relax and enjoy whatever days we had left in Avella. Francesca began to plan to visit places that she always wanted to visit as a child that she had heard so much about: Capri, Sorrento, Amalfi, etc. Also, we looked forward to hearing for the last time the Neapolitan concerts to be held at the annual picnic ground at the Fusaro area of Avella. Every spring 50,000-60,000 Neapolitans came to the pilgrimage at the ancient shrine of Cybele, near Saint Michael caves at the foothills of Monte Avella.

As with so many Black Madonna sanctuaries, this one also started out as a Pagan holy site dedicated to the goddess Cybele. Tradition says that in the early 11th century, when Paganism was still practiced in remote parts of Europe, St. William of Vercelli, the patron saint of Irpinia, decided to turn this mountain shrine to Cybele, the Great Mother of the Gods, into a sanctuary of Mary the Most Holy Mother of God. He gathered a little band of monks and occupied the place for Christianity. The first real church was consecrated in 1124. It was destroyed and rebuilt several times. The current monastery, guest house, and sanctuary date from between the 18th and 20th centuries. Architecturally, they are not very interesting, but the basilica is richly decorated and the whole place lies in breathtaking mountain scenery.

People gathered for picnics at the Fusaro grounds after religious Mass in the morning. In the evening hours a concert of Neapolitan songs were held at the Fusaro. For us from Avella, it was an early peek into up and coming Neapolitan songs and singers from Naples who would perform at the San Remo Festival near Genoa, Italy. Perhaps, it was the pre-cursor to other festivals as well where future songs and singers were displayed from throughout Italy. At the Fusaro, only Neapolitan songs were featured. For example, songs like "Anema e Core" and "Scalinatella" and singer Giacomo Rondinella were heard for the first time at the Fusaro picnic grounds.

When we returned from the concert that evening in May our neighbor, Serafina, was all excited and eager to talk to us. She said that a distinguished and good looking Neapolitan and his wife came about an hour earlier wanting to see us. He inquired about our whereabouts and said he would be back in the morning at about 9:00-10:00 am. We had no idea who could that be. I don't think we slept that night. The next morning was Sunday and, therefore, no school. We ate breakfast early as we were anxious as to who that person could be.

Our neighbor Serafina and her sisters were hanging out their windows to get a glimpse at what was going on. In a way it was exciting. As we were waiting for the mystery guests we were systematically reviewing people whom we had met in the past five years and dismissing all the ones who were not possibly be "distinguished". We narrowed down the list of potential persons to three or four "candidates". As it turned out, we were completely wrong in our guesses and unbelievably surprised.

Around 9:00 am a sporting Alfa Romeo car pulled up next to our house. The car itself was ascending onto us like a spaceship. In all the time that I lived in Avella I never saw an Alfa Romeo, but I did hear things about it from other kids. Of course, we heard about the Ferrari racing car and other cars as well, but nothing like this. A man and woman came out of the car and walked toward our house. As Serafina said, he looked distinguished in a linen suit and wearing a tie. Nobody wanted to know who the wife was. He was the split image of Amadeo Nazzari of the movies. For those of you who don't know who Nazzari was he looked like Omar Sharif of today's movies. He politely introduced himself and his wife as Carmine and Carmela Iaccarino and they were from the Vomero area of Naples.

He went on to say that during the War he was Captain of the Italian Army stationed in Cirenaica, Libya. The Army also operated an Air Force base there near the hospital at Agedabia. He was the commanding officer in charge of maintaining and operating a military hospital for the Italian Army, where he and Caporale Michele Vittoria, Papa, were stationed. Francesca almost fainted. She lost her composure and started crying uncontrollably. Serafina and her sisters were no longer hanging from their windows for they started to come over to our house and gave my mother support. It seemed that the whole neighborhood was at the doorstep of our house. Sebastiano and I were not in tune with what he was saying. Francesca was in no condition to do anything. So, Serafina started to make espresso for the guests and provided some morning cookies from her house.

Signore Iaccarino went on to say that he wanted to personally give his condolences on the death of Caporale Michele Vittoria and it was the saddest day of his life when he died. They were planning to leave Libya together on a plane, but Papa died the day before the scheduled departure. Transport by boat was not possible for it was patrolled by the British Navy. Thereafter, there was small talk about this and that, but I can't remember exactly what was said. Finally, my mother introduced both Sebastiano and me as Capitano and Capitaniello as how the town knew us by name, but our real names were Sebastiano and Michele. He stared at us and it seemed forever. I could tell that he was deeply moved for his eyes were watery. He wiped his eyes and stood there motionless, almost in a trance and speechless. then, he embraced us. By this time my mother recovered her composure from her shock and introduced some of our neighbors to the captain and wife. Finally, there was a name associated with that title. It was an amazing turnout of people in the neighborhood wanting to see this man and wife.

Neighbors were standing by the front door peering through the door and window. Obviously, it was a reflection of how much the people loved Papa and wanted to hear everything. Somehow, word spread throughout the neighborhood. He must have been a true "Figaro" as in "Barbiere di Siviglia". He invited us to come and visit his family in Naples and left a business card behind. We were impressed, for we were never handed a business card before and invitation to his house in Naples. He was so modern and very strange encounter for us kids. That sad encounter was over and our thoughts turned to America once again.

Francesca was hell-bent on taking excursions to Sorrento and Capri before leaving for America, although we could not afford the excursions. We left at about six in the morning, in a rented car that Mastro Nicola drove. He was the only one who could drive a car. The logistics for the planning of the trip was a nightmare that it is not worth recounting now.

Suffice to say that Uncle Joe and family, we three and Mastro Nicola and wife took the trip to the resort towns. We got to Sorrento mid-morning and viewed many vistas.

A small colony of British tourists at a local pub were enjoying espressos in the main piazza of Sorrento. A former British soldier who was veteran of the Salerno invasion owned one of the pubs. Remarkably, they featured a dish called "shepherd's" pie. Out of loyalty to the shepherds of the world, we almost stopped by and ordered the pie, but changed our minds and stuck to pasta dishes.

Years later, when I visited Sussex University, my colleague there prepared the pie for me at a dinner invitation. It was an interesting recipe, but once was enough. For me, it was equivalent to what we call in USA, "sloppy Joe" hamburger meat covered with a thick layer of mashed potatoes. At noon we had a big lunch at a restaurant on the hill overlooking the whole Sorrento Bay. I did not know it then, but my elementary school teacher, Felice, retired at Santo Agnello Convent one to two miles from Sorrento. In the afternoon, we took a boat ride to the island of Capri. The view from Capri toward Naples and Sorrento was stupendous. I can imagine even now how it must have appeared to someone in Capri, when Mount Vesuvius exploded violently in 78 AD, destroying Pompeii. The philosopher in ancient Rome, Pliny the elder, described the eruption of Vesuvius from the island of Capri as the beginning of the end of the world.

It was and is remarkable to me that no wall was built next to the Hadrian "fall". Emperor Hadrian would invite "special" guests that he did not care for to take the view near the edge of a high scenery point. He then pushed them over the edge as the visitor took on the view, 500 meters below. After the visit to Capri, we returned home about at 2:00 am the next day, exhausted.

In July of 1981, my wife, three children and I visited the city of Sorrento, when I was on my Sabbatical leave visiting the University of Hamburg. Sorrento, like Amalfi and the area surrounding, are resort towns on the sea south of Naples. The whole area has been invaded over centuries by many different countries including Greece, Romans, Saracens, Normans, France, and Spain.

Near Sorrento there was a small Convent for nuns called Santo Agnello. It was a retirement home for nuns. My family and I visited this Convent by chance. It was sticking right out on top of a hill overlooking the sea below, two km from Sorrento. My wife and I thought that the view from there must be awesome. Frankly, Sorrento was full of tourist and we were looking to escape from them. We went there and introduced ourselves to their Madre Superiore (not the same one as in Avella) and explained that we were there for the view. The Madre Superiore realized as much.

All of sudden and out of nowhere Suora Felice appeared on the scene, but I did not recognize her. I stopped in the middle of my conversation and proceeded to approach the sister. As I got near to her she shouted in pure Neapolitan dialect: "capitaniel, vien a ca", "little captain, come here". It was not an order like years past expressed in a Florentine dialect, when I was in school. The tone was possessive and soft, as if to say: come here, little bugger, and give me a hug. She hugged me so hard that I was gasping for air, and my family was introduced to the nuns. She told me that she has followed my career for a long time and she was well aware what I have been doing. Nothing that I did surprised her. She wanted me to know two things: first, all the sister nuns knew the location or the house where I skipped the lines on the way to church at Saint John in Avella; second, we, including Madre Superiore, loved me very much. I was a wild goat, but our goat always. So, all was forgiven. The house that Suora Felice was alluding to, during the excursions to the church of Saint John, belonged to a shoe repairman, Pasquale. His illegitimate son was Bruno, the black kid who was a very good friend of mine. Pasquale's wife was raped by a Goumier soldier during their occupation of Avella.

Suora Felice took us on a personal guided tour of the properties where she was pensioned. The view from there at the tip of the mountain, jutting right into the sea, was truly splendid. It is too bad one cannot encapsulate such a view in an envelope and store it forever. Also, we were invited for dinner at the convent as special guests. The dinner was prepared by none other than the famous chef I knew way back in kindergarten, Mustacciola! Her name was Suora Michelina. On the way back to Avella we drove by the coastal highway to Naples and savored in the scenery.

On the way to Naples we stopped to visit my good old friend, Vito. He took over his father's business in real estate and bought many buildings in the town of Torre del Greco (Greek tower). Part of the town was still in ruins. The Germans mined the harbor at

Torre Annunziata and Torre del Greco and this was 40 years after the war! As the name implied, the watch tower at Torre Annunziata, overlooking the bay of Naples across from the Vomero district, was blown to smithereens by the Germans. To this day it has not been repaired. Vito played major league soccer for Naples, as I knew he would. He was a solid midfielder who, when we played together, would go "through a brick wall" to get the ball to me. I am sure it was that type of tenacity that got him to the major leagues in soccer. It was heartwarming to see him again and reminisce about soccer games we played together as children and our days spent as altar boys. Finally, the nightmare was about to end and a promising future loomed. The magic moment finally came and we received the paperwork from the American Consulate in Naples, clearing us for departure to America. Grandfather Carmine sent the money to pay for the trip. We bid farewell to family and friends. For me the hardest thing that I ever did was to say goodbye to Nonno and my friends Vito, Paolo and Bruno.

Nonno suffered through three deaths in his immediate family due to the War. In addition, his farm was taken away By the British, his business was taken away from him and his career as a musician came to an end. On my mother's side of the family we had four casualties (father, sister, grandmother and aunt) as a result of the war. Grazing land on the mountains was stolen from the family and mother's store was robbed of all the inventory. I am certain that a lot of other people in Avella went through similar experiences. Nonno and I went through hell and back on this earth during the war and came up smiling thanks to my grandfather's steady and even keel approach to life. He has had a tremendous influence on my life and it was very difficult for me to let go of him. We shared so much memory together during the nightmare years. As hard as it was for both of us, we knew that it was best for me to leave Avella.

Nonno sacrificed his career for his family. He must have been a good musician playing his trombone in orchestras. He was trained in the Army and, afterward, joined a traveling orchestra in Montefalcione, near Avellino. They performed at festivals, opera houses and theaters until retirement. I never knew about Nonno's background in music until one day at a religious festival in Avella. Saint Anthony church sponsored the performance of the opera "Don Pasquale" composed by Donizetti. The live performance was going to be staged in the main piazza of Avella, near City Hall. Mastro Nicola's father, Don Nicola, was to conduct the orchestra. The problem arose when the trombone player got sick (drunk). Quickly, Don Nicola motioned for me to come over to him and said: "Please have your Nonno come over and substitute for the other trombone player, and the opera starts in about an hour". He added that he could stall for half an hour, but no more. I ran to Nonno's house and relayed the message to him.

In all the years that I spent with him, I never saw such a content smile from him at that time. He was extremely moved, when he heard that Don Nicola made the request. He disappeared into his bedroom for a long time. Finally, he appeared in a tuxedo with his trombone in hand. He asked me what opera was being performed, but I didn't know. No matter, he said, and we rushed to the piazza. I believe now that this bravura was Nonno's last hurrah, and wanted to go out in style. He must have saved that tuxedo for a special occasion like this. He played the trombone for the opera without any music notes. After the performance, I pleaded with Nonno to allow me to carry the trombone for I was so proud of him.

As for my friends Vito and Paolo, we were like the three musketeers inseparable in our escapades to the farms, creek, foothills, Fusaro and the castle. The fourth musketeer, Bruno, joined our group later, by accident. Bruno was the illegitimate black kid in town. He was a pugnacious little bugger that kept following us on the way to the castle. We got tired of telling him to go back to his house for he was too small and, finally, we decided to take him along. He turned out to be a good companion and fearless. He was much smaller and younger than we. The problem was that when the water level was high in the creek, he had a difficult time navigating the treacherous water. We had to carry him on our backs.

We would climb the hill to the castle raiding every cactus tree on the way for cactus pears. When we were raiding fruit trees in farms, we had to slide through fences. Fortunately, Bruno could walk right through them. It was truly fun and the comradeship was unforgettable. I believe most farmers let us do whatever we wanted with fruit trees as long as we stayed away from the hazelnuts. Nonno warned me that farmers were liable to shoot at us, if we touched the hazelnuts. None of us needed to go out raiding farms. We just enjoyed roaming around and shoot the breeze and enjoyed each other's company. For example, Vito's and Paolo's parents were wealthy enough to buy the farm including the fruits with it, if they wanted to.

So, there was no need to raid anything. We roamed around like a herd of goats daring each other to do things. For us, summertime was easy living here in Avella like anyplace else in the Naples area.

At the port of Naples we boarded the American ship S.S. Constitution on January 21, 1953. At the port there was a large welcoming party from Avella and the Naples area. The contingent of people from Avella included all family members from Nonno's side, Uncle Joe's family, Mastro Nicola, Mastro Antonio and the "three musketeers" with their families. Unbelievably, Madre Superiore came to say goodbye. She came from Santo Agnello Convent for retiring nuns near Sorrento, but I was not aware that she retired at that time. She said to me: "Capitaniello, we loved you the minute that you came in our presence, but I more than others". She also said that she prayed for me and kept an eye on me throughout my stay in school. Perhaps, that explained why I survived scarlet fever at a time, when there was no medicine in town during the war. Somebody was looking over our shoulders.

Francesca was more surprised than anyone to see Madre Superiore, given their relationships in school years in Avella. They waved long after departure of the boat from port. The next day, Uncle Pierino bid goodbye at the port of Genoa. For him it was a short hop from Reggio Emilia where he was the Prefetto chief. He was able to reserve a private room at the port and we had time to enjoy an espresso and sfogliatella pastry for the last time in Italy. It made me feel better for I vomited the whole night in the ship from Naples.

However, one incident that occurred affected me as to my real identity. Once I got to feel better Francesca sat me down and wanted to have a serious talk with me. She said my name was not "capitaniello", but that I knew. She also said that my name was not Michele either as the whole town of Avella called me formally in school. My real name was Carmine, and she produced my birth Certificate right on the spot to prove it. It was and is an understatement to say that I was devastated. It was like somebody stole my childhood which I held so proudly. I asked why they called me Michele. She said,"those f…..g bitches of seamstress aunts of yours thought that after Papa died that I should have been called the same name as Papa and the name stuck in town". That was the cause of a lot of discord and resentment throughout my childhood in the family without my knowledge of it. Eventually, I liked the name Carmine and the new beginning in USA.

The boat ride on the ship Constitution from Genoa to the Strait of Gibraltar was uneventful. Once we reached the Azores Islands, ocean waves were enormous, almost reaching the deck. At times, I wondered if we were going to make it to NY. The sea calmed down, as we approached the East coast of the USA. When the ship arrived in New York harbor in the morning of January 29, people were scurrying to be on deck. Francesca and I were clueless as to what the excitement was about, but we followed the crowd. Suddenly, we caught sight of the Statue of Liberty, but for us it didn't register as anything special. We debarked soon after at Ellis Island, where custom officers examined the cheese packages and olive oil cans that Francesca brought along for the trip. The officers confiscated the cheese, but allowed the oil to move on with us. Before entering this beautiful country, we were tested for tuberculosis and required to register. It was not until afternoon that we were allowed to meet our welcoming party that included Franco, and his wife.

We were driven in a 1953 Cadillac by Uncle Franco (Uncle Joe's brother). It was an unbelievable ride. It was like floating on air compared to a ride in a Fiat 500 car, caccavella (cooking pot). Uncle Franco owned a construction company with more than fifty employees. His home was huge, but the first thing that impressed me was the television set. In Avella, we heard about the invention of television, but I had no idea how it operated. To me, it was like an apparition. What a beautiful toy. In Nonno's and Francesca's houses there was no comfortable furniture, just a chair, if one was lucky. Here in this NY house, comfortable chairs and sofas were spread all over the living room. Every room was equipped with a telephone! In Avella, I saw someone use the phone once. The contrast between an ordinary house in USA, in terms of modern conveniences, and Nonno's, for example, was enormous. Clearly, Avella had not caught up with the 20th century.

Although modern conveniences of an American home were impressive, it was more impressive to see freedom exercised to the fullest in the USA. People had no inhibition as doing anything their hearts desired at any time and at any place. On the spur of the moment, Sebastiano and the two teen ager boys got in the car and went out to cruise around New York City, Broadway, Times Square, Little Italy District, and Chinatown.

In another instance, Franco and his wife suddenly decided to go to a Broadway show, South Pacific, starring Mary Martin and Ezio Pinza, former opera singer. Franco loved the Yankees and Yogi Berra. So, one day he drove me, Sebastiano and his two sons to Yankee Stadium and visited the dugout, although it was in the middle of winter. I had no idea who the Yankees were or, for that matter, Yogi Berra, but I knew it was important to Franco. Nothing was going to stop him from trying to get into the stadium. Our impression was that people in the USA did not talk about what was not possible. That mind set was foreign to us, but much welcomed.

As for Francesca, she came upon a great discovery. Franco's wife introduced "Betty Crocker" cake mix to Francesca for the first time. It blew her mind. Now, she could bake a cake in a matter of one hour at most. Back in Italy, baking cake was a big deal and it took forever. The rest of her life in the USA she continued to bake cakes using the cake mix. There was not a cake that she didn't try to bake. To her, America was wrapped up in that "Betty Crocker" box. As for me, I was glued to the television set. In the afternoon, it featured mostly old movies of cowboys and Indians. In late afternoons, there was a show for kids called "Howdy Doody Time". In the evening Francesca or the adults took over the TV. Those four days in New York were very revealing about the American culture and mind set.

Finally, we hit the road on the way to Ambridge, Pa and were more prepared for the American lifestyle. We boarded an overnight train to Pittsburgh. I was excited about the trip for I thought that I would be able to see American Indians from the train. I was told by my friends that there were still Indians in America and I thought for sure there would be Indian camps on the way to Ambridge. What a shocker! We didn't see any Indians, but we saw two feet of snow at the train station in Pittsburgh. Our first reaction was: where in the ….. are we? The only snow that we ever saw was on Monte Avella. It was cold and we were lightly dressed. Grandfather Carmine was not at the station, but the caretaker's family was there to receive us. They explained that grandfather was sick and staying at their house. Their house was located on a hill overlooking the town of Ambridge. The caretaker family consisted of husband, wife and two adult sons and they all spoke Italian. The husband worked at the steel mill in Ambridge.

The major industry in Ambridge was the American Bridge Steel Company which employed half the town. The other half worked in small stores where the steel workers spent their money. Across the Ohio River was the town of Aliquippa, made famous by the football player Mike Ditka, where Jones and Laughlin Steel Company was located. This is where my grandfather worked his adult life. His duties were to clean the inside of large steel furnaces. He became ill with the dreaded "black lung" disease which in those days was not recognized as such. In the end, he was too sick to take care of himself and employed a caretaker.

The reunion with grandfather was very joyous. A journalist from the local newspaper was at the house to take a picture of us. Francesca and her father talked the whole afternoon. Much was planned from those talks, the results of which were that, for the winter and spring, Sebastiano and I would attend a remedial school in Aliquippa to learn English. In the beginning of summer, all of us moved to downtown Ambridge, where grandfather had a house.

Weather in the winter was dreary and bitter cold. The daily routine was that we boarded two buses to arrive at the remedial school. On weekends we looked forward to the Friday night pugilist fight on television. Names like Roland LaStarza, Joe Giardello, Archie Moore, Sugar Ray Robinson, etc. were regulars on TV. However, grandfather was not able to partake of the viewing of the fights because he was too sick. Francesca took over the role of caretaker, and slept in the same room as grandfather. The only good outcome was that, for the first time, I had clothes suited only for me. No more hand-me-down clothes. In particular, my winter coat covered me from head to toe and I wore ear muffs, as I was sensitive to the cold.

The remedial school ended in early June and the teacher, Miss D'Occhio, recommended me to attend the ninth grade at Ambridge High School. She handed the reference letter to me to bring to the Principal of the School. I was pleasantly surprised. In Avella, I was the oldest student in elementary school, and in the USA I was going to be the youngest student in the class. What a transformation! Suffice to say that grandfather suffered greatly and died a month after we moved.

The house was located on First-Street in Ambridge, abutting Main Street. The neighborhood was inhabited mostly by Greek immigrants. There was a townhouse settlement of about fifty apartments that was inhabited by African Americans. I now think that the settlement represented a form of segregation whereby all of the African Americans were quartered in one part of town. We weren't aware of this segregation mentality or the civil rights movement and lived harmoniously with our neighbors. Simply put, we were oblivious of any racial problems in America. In the back of our house we had a small garden subdivided into four plots of land. Francesca loved to plant an assortment of vegetables in three plots, but, on the fourth plot, she invited our neighbors to plant vegetables. They were so happy to be able to do little farming. She continued doing that until the day we sold the house to the City. The City of Ambridge bought our house and the African-American settlement in order to build a road over the properties. The road was never built. It was just a recognition of the fact that segregation was over in the USA, since the Civil Rights Act was passed in 1964.

On First-Street there was a café (owned by Tony Massimo), Drug Store, Mosque, Greek Cafe and gambling house, three bars and an empty lot where kids played stick ball. That is where I met my American friend, Enrico, Rigo. He was a football player for the High School team. Together, we were the odd couple of the neighborhood. He was over six feet tall and 230 pounds and I was a skinny runt over five feet. He introduced me to the American sports football, baseball and basketball. He also introduced me to shady games like rolling dices in secluded buildings. I was hired as a lookout person while they rolled dices. I came to learn the American slang, as well as expressions like seven come eleven, Nina from Pasadena, snake eyes, etc. At these games, Rigo warned me not to ask too many questions about where Pasadena was. Many years later I learned Tony was a Mafia boss (reported by The NY Times), but I never knew it then. Yes, it was a wild neighborhood, but I liked it very much. Everyday something new was happening on that street, and I spent a lot of time there playing stick ball.

I enjoyed the Friday night High School football games where class mates, cheerleaders, pep rallies, and happy people were attending the game. Western Pennsylvania was the hot bed of High School football. Big time Colleges with large football programs recruited heavily in Western Pennsylvania. Rigo was the first string fullback and kicker on the football team. He broke the High School record in Pennsylvania for field goal kicking. Eventually, he received a College scholarship in football not as a fullback, but as a kicker.

By fall, we were completely settled in the house. We had furniture, a TV set and even a telephone, but nothing like Uncle Franco's living quarters in New York. Our proudest possessions were the telephone and radio, because we knew from the war years how important and useful those electronic communication gadgets were. Television was just a toy for us that everybody had and it was more of a curiosity thing. We bought an espresso machine as a holdover habit from the past saying goodbye to chicory coffee once for and all times. We were surprised, more like shocked, at how small the radio was compared to the radio Uncle Joe bought after the war. We didn't know that with the discovery of semiconductor materials in the late forties, vacuum tubes were replaced with semiconductor devices in radios making them a lot smaller. Francesca was nervous about how to use or answer the phone. I asked Rigo to have his mother, Beatrice (named after Botticelli's Beatrice), call our phone. When Beatrice called, Francesca was a nervous wreck. Timidly, she answered. Thereafter, that phone seemed permanently attached to her ear.

We were happy with what we had, including our wardrobe. Schooling was terrible as I was flunking English and Algebra courses. I went to see the English teacher for help and asked her what it would take for me to get a passing grade. I could not make "heads or tails" of reading about Ivanhoe. She said that if I could memorize one page from "The Merchant of Venice", she may consider giving me a passing grade. At that time, I could barely write a sentence in English, let alone comprehend Shakespeare. The survival skills kicked in from the old days. I memorized two pages from the book and passed the course. She was impressed, but I was not. That was nothing compared being chased by Goumiers.

Getting a passing grade in Algebra took a monumental effort. Rigo and I attended the class and he warned me to drop the course because it was for scientists. I explained to the teacher that I can multiply and divide numbers, but what do I do with the variables x and y, add or subtract? The teacher thought that I was joking, but I was not. One day Rigo came to my homeroom in school and explained the mystery of x and y.

Once I solved that riddle, I was making up my own rules to solve algebraic problems. Besides, I was not able to read the rules or theorems as explained in the book. The teacher thought that it was great, but I was just exercising the spirit of survival learned from the past.

Just about when I was reaching a steady state with my schooling, I began to realize that roads in America were not "paved with gold". Money did not grow on trees and everybody worked hard for their money. I came to the stark realization that none of us had a job and the money from the rental properties was just enough to support us. The apartments were owned by grandfather. The future looked bleak. Whereas in Italy the probability of my attending a University was virtually zero, here in the USA, there was a clear opportunity to attend one. As Francesca aptly put it: it is a lot easier to push a pen than a wheel barrow. Realistically, it was the only option for me. Soccer was out, as there were no professional teams in USA. I made schooling the only option in life to pursue.

A friend of the family in Ambridge kept saying to me: "La montagna e' fiorita". This is a typical cryptic Sicilian innuendo. The literal translation means "The Mountain has flowered". The comment per plexed me for years until now. It is a riddle that defies literary translation. The implied meaning is that like flowers on a mountain, opportunities are forever part of the landscape in the USA, and are available to anyone regardless of color, creed, or money. Like flowers in full bloom in the spring, opportunities are to be seized or plucked at the right time. Thus, the United States is more than a country; it is an invention created by people for the purpose of re-generating opportunities for all. I believe now that is what was meant by the riddle.

EPILOGUE

Direct collateral damage claimed the lives of six members of our family. The loss of life was typical for towns in the Naples area. Also, direct collateral damage resulted in the destruction of railroad stations from Avella to Naples. Via Appia from Baiano to Nola was bombed many times over until not even a bicycle could be driven over it. Some towns along Via Appia were bombed back to the stone ages. This destruction was so unnecessary. The War in Italy never accomplished any military missions in ending the War earlier for either belligerent. If anything, it prolonged it. The beneficiaries were the generals who were promoted at the expense of the victims.

Hidden collateral damage was responsible for the breakdown of law and order and increase in criminality. The AMG replaced Fascist Mayors with criminals. This was like putting foxes in charge of chicken coops. Police were nowhere to be found in towns. Nonno and my mother's grocery stores were robbed of everything and that was a common occurrence in the Naples area. The increase in criminality in Southern Italy has had global ramifications. Before WW II the Camorra and Mafia were nearly eliminated in Italy by Mussolini. Assigning civil authority to the AMG, during and after the war, allowed replacing Fascist mayors and government officials at small towns like Avella by known Camorra and Mafia thugs. As such, the Camorra and Mafia were revived from the dead. After the War, they controlled the black market and initiated the heroin trafficking in the USA. The Camorra, for example, thrived beyond Naples and local areas. Today, the Camorra and Mafia are the scourge of societies globally. There is not one major illegal business throughout the world in which they are not involved. It has caused more collateral damage to societies in every continent than the War itself.

It is ironic that the decision makers who were responsible for all the devastation in Italy were either promoted during the war or launched new careers after the War. The war was viewed by some decision makers as an exercise in playing military games with people lives, and in enhancing their own careers. The allied campaign in Italy started out with full of hopes of liberating people from the yoke of Fascism and Nazism, but it ended up with the people suffering from anarchy, corruption, destruction and social demoralization.

After the retreat of the British Army from the beaches of Dunkirk, the British decision makers were reluctant to commit large numbers of British soldiers in direct confrontation anyplace in Europe, since their army was not at full strength. After the Allied invasion of Sicily, the Italian Army ceased to exist. The British convinced the Americans to commit more American troops to the Italian campaign. The purpose of the British Army was to stall and delay their troop commitments at major battle fronts. For example, British Field Marshal Montgomery was late in engaging the battles at Messina, Salerno, Cassino and Rome. Instead, colonial troops were deployed at Anzio and throughout Southern Italy. From the British point of view, it was acceptable for casualties to occur among civilians and colonial troops as long as British casualties were minimized throughout the campaign in Southern Italy. If colonial troops mistreated the locals as in Avella, who would know and who cared? Besides, atrocities committed by the Goumiers were not reported in newspapers.

The British legal system organized and regulated the military court system all over Europe and adjudicated culpability for atrocities committed during WW II. Basically, they had the final word on any judgement handed out by the military courts. British Royalties, General staff and Government officials were influential in commuting death sentences for the Ardeatina massacre. According to General Alexander of the British Army, Kesselring was a great German "soldat" (soldier) who deserved respect as foe. Thus, personal opinions superseded hard evidence. To me, Kesselring was an ordinary criminal found guilty by military court of law, period. The extra five civilians executed at the Ardeatine caves were murders by any code of justice, and not a clerical mistake. There was nothing respectful about the killing of innocent and defenseless civilians in Rome, and the scorched earth and destroy policy carried out by Kesselring. The German general staff and Gestapo officers claimed that they did it in the name of duty. That argument never carried much weight at Nuremberg. The war was lost for the Axis powers in 1944 and everybody knew that. It was just a matter of time.

Clearly, to these criminals, there was never a thought of sorrow for the massacre at the Ardeatine caves, only their careers mattered. None of the victims committed any violent crime. To the Gestapo, the victims represented a number to meet a quota at all costs. The Gestapo carried out their dirty duties knowing full well that they would never be penalized or affected for the crimes they committed in the name of duty.

The Nuremberg trials were predicated on the premise that only Nazis committed evil crimes against humanity. Let me state here unequivocally that the French Expedition Force also committed evil crimes against humanity in Southern Italy. The French Expedition Force under the leadership of General Juin was part of General Clark's Fifth Army. General Juin had no control whatsoever over the North African troops, the Goumiers. He was well aware of their behavior, and was just a criminal, just as much as some German generals convicted at the Nuremberg trials. French Officers actually condoned the behavior of the Gourmiers. The "raping" of Italy by the Goumiers constituted violation of Articles 46 and 47 of the 1907 Hague Convention which stated: "Private property cannot be confiscated (46) and pillage (including rape) is formally forbidden (47)". The participation of the French Expedition Force in Italy caused more damage than help to the Allied war efforts. The Goumiers created unimaginable atrocities on earth and especially in Southern Italy. General Juin should have been tried for War crimes by the Military Tribunal Court in Rome after the war.

The American General staff was not cognizant of the landscape and terrain difficulties during the rainy season in Southern Italy. They were duped by the British General staff into invading Italy, when, all along, General George C. Marshall, chief of the American General staff, wanted to invade France. As a compromise, General Patton suggested to invade Sardegna and Corsica in order to provide air coverage for an invasion north of Rome. I uncovered the fact that on September 9, 1943, remnants of a German division (15,000) left Sardegna. It implied that if General Patton's plan was to be adopted, it would have negated most, if not all, of the one million casualties and destruction of southern Italy. Patton's plan never merited any consideration by the General staff. General Clark substituted proper preparation, and military intelligence with more bullets, casualties, boats and planes to make his dream of conquering Rome from the South come true. He would have been an ideal subordinate to General Grant, if he had lived during the American civil war. General Grant believed in other people's blood and his glory.

The price of Clark's dream was too costly to the American soldiers and to the people in Southern Italy.

Well before the outcome of WWII, my mother claimed that Mussolini was a coward. History has proven her right most people thought that Francesca was bitter about the fact that in three years her husband, daughter, mother, aunt and uncle died as a result of the War. I was too little to understand any of that constant chatter, but I liked the controversies that she was stirring up. In a way, it was like watching a live show with my mother and neighbors shouting at each other about Mussolini.

Mussolini didn't have the courage to oppose Hitler, when Hitler partitioned Italy into two occupation zones. He didn't have the courage to oppose Hitler, when Hitler put to the father of his grandchildren to death. He didn't have the courage to oppose Hitler on racial laws in Italy. When the war was not going well, at the meeting with Hitler in Feltre, near Venice, on July 18, 1943, Mussolini was ordered by King Victor Emmanuel III, via instructions from the General staff (General Mario Roatta), to pull out of the alliance with Germany and declare neutrality. Mussolini did not have the courage to sue for neutrality. He allowed the hysterical man, Hitler, to do all the talking at the meeting. As a consequence, the King incarcerated Mussolini after the Feltre meeting. Most authors are mistaken to assume that it was the July 25th meeting of Fascist leaders that was responsible for his incarceration. The vote of confidence, or the referendum, on July 25th was just a pretext for the King to incarcerate Mussolini. At that meeting, Mussolini's son-in-law, Ciano, voted for no confidence. It was his lack of courage, not the "no confidence" vote that got him incarcerated by the King.

There were plans in the Nazi government to deport the Pope to Germany [34]. A detente between the Pope and Hitler (the devil) was struck in Rome; it allowed the Pope to stay in the Vatican as long as the "devil" had a free hand in dealing with Romans. The Pope invented a smokescreen by requesting Nazi protection from an imminent partisan and Communist raid on Vatican properties. Thus, it legitimized the brutal activities of the Nazis against the people of Rome. The raid never materialized. In fact, there is no historic evidence [79, and 98] of a plan to raid the Vatican by the Communists. Palmiro Togliatti [79], leader of the Italian Communist and partisan movement, never gave such an order. Besides, Stalin [98] would never have approved of such a raid. He could not afford to jeopardize the shipments of arms and food from the USA to Russia. Also, a raid would have alienated one billion Catholics. At that time, he needed as much help and as many friends as possible. During the war, Togliatti lived in Russia and Stalin was a mentor to him; there were no political secrets between them. Historic facts have consistently pointed out that Nazis were not protectors of properties or people, because protectors do not steal from people, randomly pick people off the streets at gun point, and do not deport innocent Roman Jews to their death. The controversy today in Italy about the Rasella/Ardeatina affairs was created by the obfuscation on the part of Pope Pius XII to hide his motive to remain in the Vatican during occupation. The smoke-screen created by the Pope is the genesis for the controversy today.

In 1946, Russia was no longer an ally and there was a Communist plan to take over the Italian government by revolution or at the ballot box. It is not clear to me now whether or not it would have led to confiscation or re-distribution of church properties. For example, the partisan activities in Avella led by Don Camillo never entertained the thought of taking over the farms owned by the church, although they were advocating in the streets a new order or revolution. The wives of Communist leaders in Avella were very religious people and they would not have allowed any harm to the church by their husbands. As an altar boy, I can attest to the wives' religious devotion to the church.

The Marshall plan was a great idea to help in the recovery of Europe from the devastation of the War. Industries, factories, railroads and infrastructures were rebuilt. Italy received food and about 1.5 billion dollars (equivalent to 600 billion dollars today) for three years. Most of the money went into re-building heavy industries in the north of Italy. These were the same companies that profited the most from the war in Italy, such as Fiat, Pirelli, Montecatini, AGIP, and Sinclair. The same can be said about German heavy industries involved in the war.

However, today the concentration of heavy industries is still in the North of Italy. The Marshal plan exacerbated the differential in the industrial base between northern and southern Italy. As such, there is great disparity between North and South in terms of job opportunities and economic well-being. Only about 10% of the food shipped to Italy was made available to the South of Italy. To make matters even more dire, thugs assigned by the AMG at City Halls distributed the food and medicine to their friends and to the highest bidders. Nevertheless, Naples and towns like Avella survived the War and the post-War periods.

The Naples area adapted and survived starvation during the occupation and the inequities of the Marshal plan. Occupation by German troops may have killed many people in the Naples area, but it did not kill the spirit of the area molded from so many occupations of the past 3000 years. It was this Neapolitan spirit that forcibly threw the Germans out of Naples. Naples was the only city in Italy to have achieved that during the War. Thus, in the long run, WW II had no effect whatsoever on this unique Neapolitan spirit. It has outlasted all invasions and it is simply stated as "Ci Arrangiamo", "We adapt (to survive)".

In Avella, the effects of the War were also equally devastating. The War brought starvation, sickness, years of political vacuum, corruption at all levels, and economic depression. There were many civilian tragedies not accounted for whenever casualties of war are listed in general. Whereas foreign Armies came and went in Avella, the American Army remained in Naples long after the war. The naval base in Naples has helped the local economy more than the Marshall plan. Since the war, there are two museums in Avella that are attracting tourists from all over the world for the first time. Approximately half the population of Avella left town after the war, only to come back as tourists. Avella has doubled its population and geographical area. Obviously, the people of Avella did not need the War to improve their lot. They needed to get a monkey off their back in the form of Fascism. Wars over the years may have changed life temporarily and rewarded decision makers with notoriety and trophies, but, in the long run, life and that immutable spirit of the people of Avella have remained the same since the days of the Samnites. People of Avella have simply gone on with their lives as if nothing ever happened during WW II.

People in the area have returned to their natural stupor of life enjoying simple things, such as a cup of sweet espresso. This state of mind is beautifully expressed in a Neapolitan proverb: "Chi avut, avut, avut e chi ha dat, dat, dat, scurdam'ci do passat. Nu simm e Napoli, paesan". The rough literal translation is: "To whomever received, received, received and to whomever gave, gave, gave, forget the past. We are from Naples, my friend". A meaningful interpretation is the following. "After all it is said and done, forget about the past. We Neapolitans have survived another day".

MY FAMILY, 1940-49

PATERNAL   MATERNAL

GRANDPARENTS

Sebastiano; Caterina   Carmine; Imalda

AUNTS, UNCLES AND PARENTS

Paternal	Maternal
Caterina	Francesca (mother)
Antonio	Giovanna
Michele (father)	
Anna	
Pellegrino	

SIBLINGS

Sebastiano
Caterina

MAPS

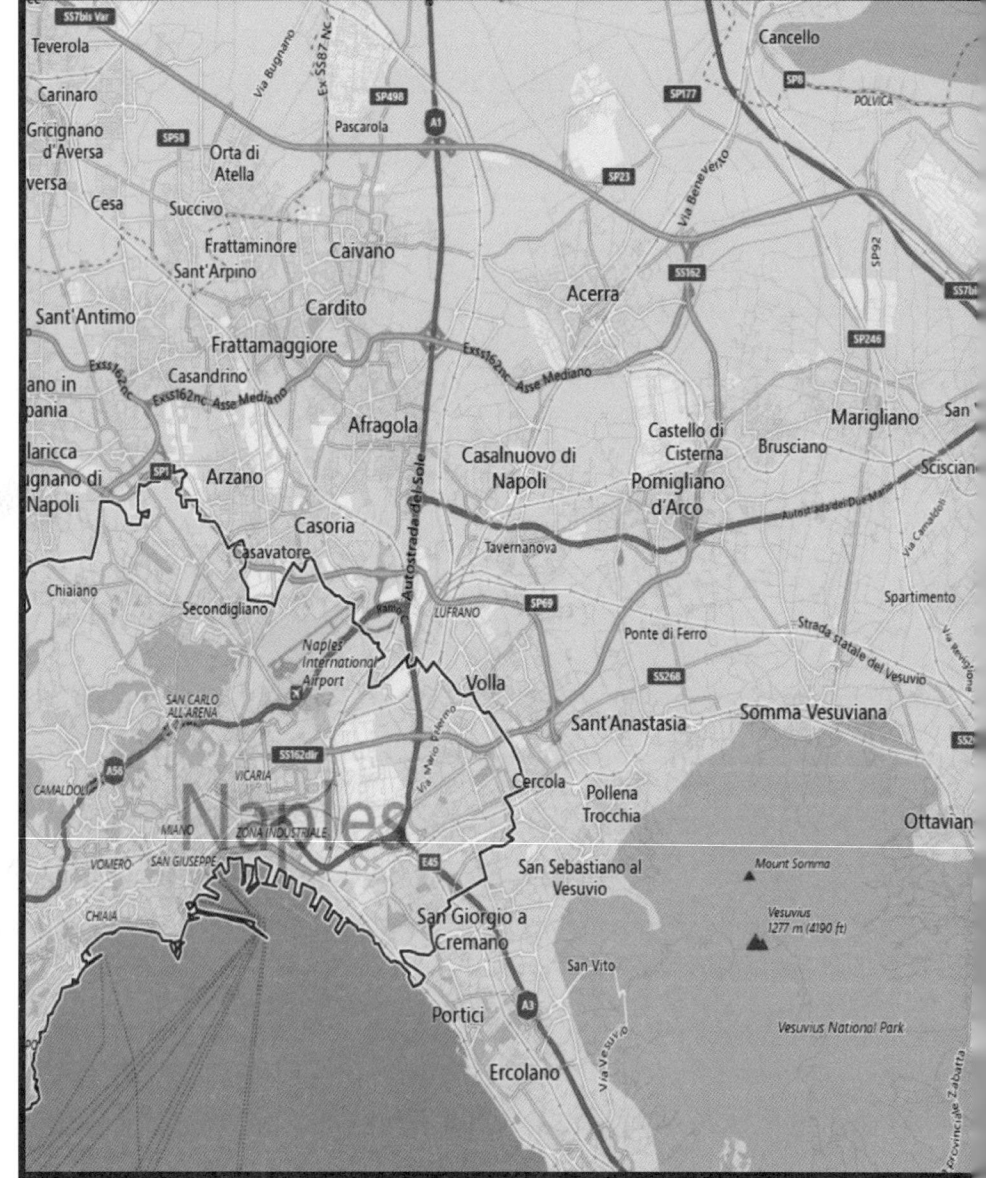

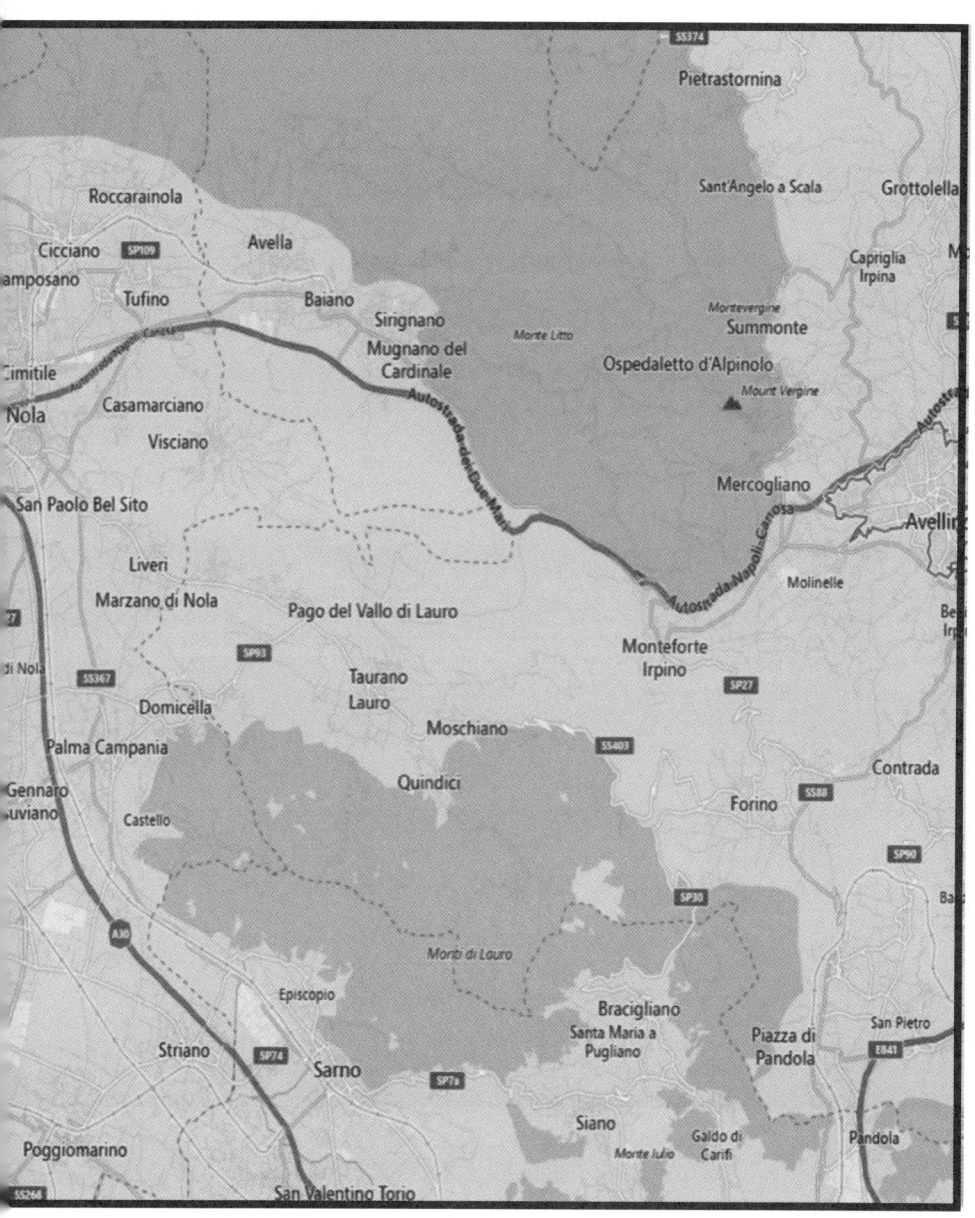

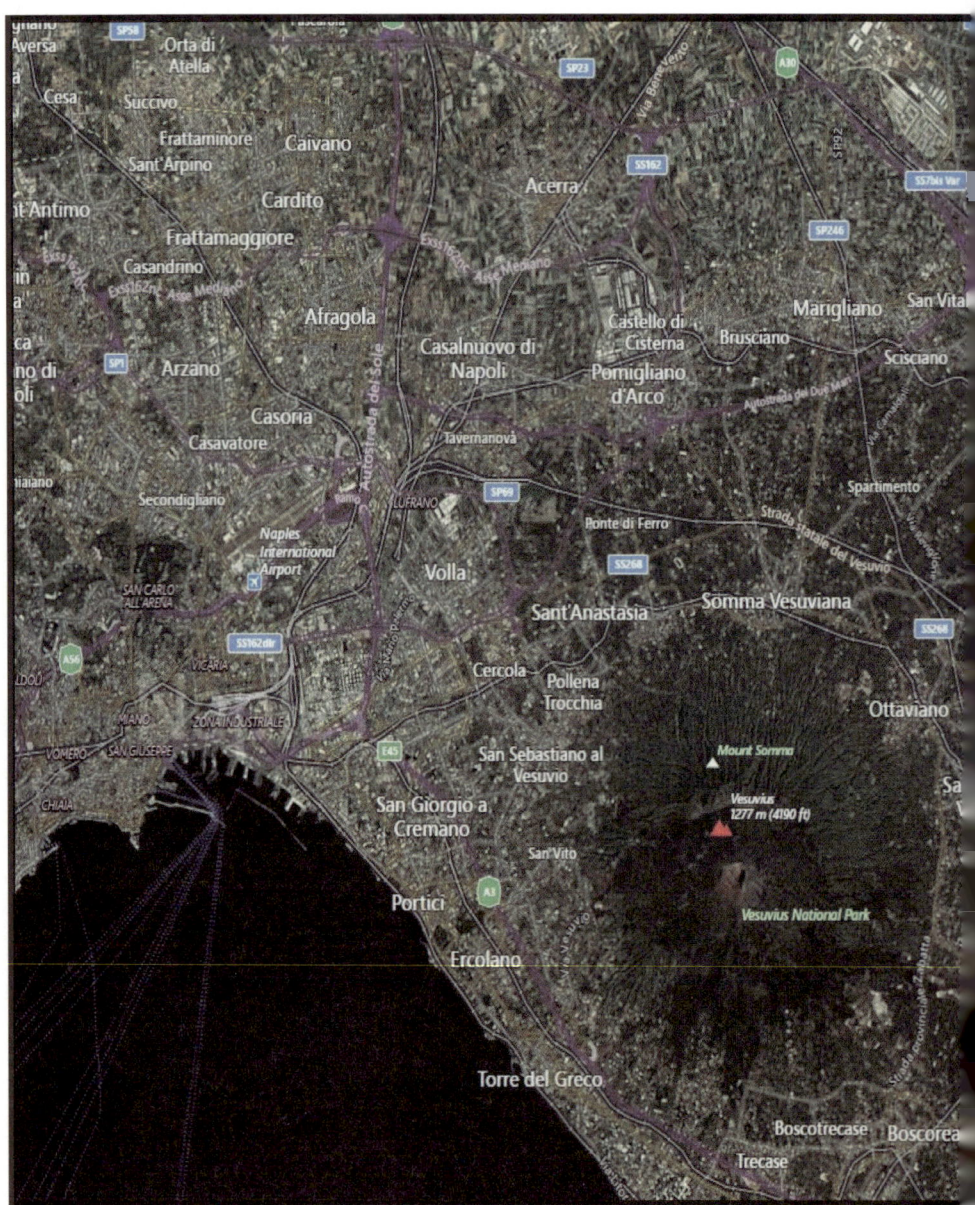